Promoting Gender Equality
in Political Participation

Africa: Past, Present and Prospects

Series Editors: Toyin Falola (The University of Texas at Austin) and Olajumoke Yacob-Haliso (Babcock University)

This series collates and curates studies of Africa in its multivalent local, regional and global contexts. It aims fundamentally to capture in one series historical, contemporary and multidisciplinary studies which analyse the dynamics of the African predicament from deeply theoretical perspectives while marshalling empirical data to describe, explain and predict trends in continuities and change in Africa and in African studies.

The books published in this series represent the multiplicity of voices, local and global in relation to African futures. It not only represents diversity, but also provides a platform for convergence of outstanding research that will enliven debates about the future of Africa, while also advancing theory and informing policy making. Preference is given to studies that deliberately link the past with the present and advances knowledge about various African nations by extending the range, breadth, depth, types and sources of data and information existing and emerging about these countries.

The platform created proceeds from the assumption that there is no singular 'African experience', nor is it possible to, in any way, homogenise the identities, histories, spaces and lives of African people.

Titles in the Series

Ghanaian Politics and Political Communication, edited by Samuel Gyasi Obeng and Emmanuel Debrah

Beyond History: African Agency in Development, Diplomacy and Conflict Resolution, edited by Elijah Nyaga Munyi, David Mwambari and Aleksi Ylönen

Reflections on Leadership and Institutions in Africa, edited by Kenneth Kalu and Toyin Falola

Imagining Vernacular Histories: Essays in Honour of Toyin Falola, edited by Mobolanla Ebunoluwa Sotunsa and Abikal Borah

Insights into Policies and Practices on the Right to Development, edited by Serges Djoyou Kamga and Carol C. Ngang

Guerrilla Radios in Southern Africa: Broadcasters, Technology, Propaganda Wars, and the Armed Struggle, edited by Sekibakiba Peter Lekgoathi

Identities, Histories and Values in Postcolonial Nigeria, edited by Adeshina Afolayan

A Tight Embrace: Narratives and Dynamics of Euro-African Relations, edited by Marco Zoppi

Promoting Gender Equality in Political Participation: New Perspectives on Nigeria, by Damilola Taiye Agbalajobi

Promoting Gender Equality in Political Participation

New Perspectives on Nigeria

Damilola Taiye Agbalajobi

ROWMAN & LITTLEFIELD
London • New York

Rowman & Littlefield
4501 Forbes Boulevard, Suite 200, Lanham, Maryland 20706, USA
With additional offices in Boulder, New York, Toronto (Canada), and Plymouth (UK)
www.rowman.com

British Library Cataloguing in Publication Data

A catalogue record for this book is available from the British Library
ISBN: HB 978-1-78661-520-6

Library of Congress Cataloguing-in-Publication Data

Names: Agbalajobi, Damilola Taiye, 1973- author.
Title: Promoting gender equality in political participation : new
    perspectives on Nigeria / Damilola Taiye Agbalajobi.
Description: Lanham : Rowman & Littlefield, 2021. | Series: Africa: past,
    present & prospects | Includes bibliographical references and index. |
    Summary: "This book analyses patterns of women's political participation
    and evaluates disparity between levels of women's participation in
    politics and representation in governance in Nigeria. It also examines
    the causes of women's underrepresentation in governance and
    decision-making as well as their implications for the country's
    socioeconomic development and describes strategies for increased women's
    representation in governance and decision-making in Nigeria. This study
    relies on political-culture and liberal-feminist theory and adopts a
    mixed-method research design involving quantitative and qualitative
    methods. It uses multistage sampling in selecting Nigeria's South-East,
    North-West and South-West geopolitical-zones and 1206 women of electoral
    age for the study survey conducted using structured questionnaire and
    in-depth interview"—Provided by publisher.
Identifiers: LCCN 2020053428 (print) | LCCN 2020053429 (ebook) | ISBN
    9781786615206 (cloth) | ISBN 9781538198810 (paper) | ISBN 9781786615213 (epub)
Subjects: LCSH: Women—Political activity—Nigeria. | Nigeria—Politics and
    government—2007-
Classification: LCC HQ1236.5.N6 A345 2021 (print) | LCC HQ1236.5.N6 (ebook) |
    DDC 323.3409669—dc23
LC record available at https://lccn.loc.gov/2020053428
LC ebook record available at https://lccn.loc.gov/2020053429

Contents

Preface

There has been a notable and rapid increase of interests and focus on gender issues by different and varied groups of practitioners in the academics, and in the policy management space. This notwithstanding, most of the works concerning Nigerian women and political participation are usually in journals and edited volumes. There is as such, an almost unacceptably alarming chasm in facts, figures and findings on the subject of gender equality in the political field of play. During my doctoral studies, I discovered a dearth of single go-to volumes that dealt with women underrepresentation in governance and participation in politics, even though libraries were awash with a plethora of journal articles and contributions. The writing of this book generated motivation from that gap in the literature and the need I experienced during my studies. Besides, this book allows presenting gender equality and political participation of women in Nigeria through a single volume based on empirical research.

Gender Equality and Political Participation in Nigeria as a book sets out to provide crucial and empirical evidence on the varied patterns of women's involvement in politics across a multicultural nation like Nigeria. Moreover, at a time like this when there are many Nigerians who are supportive of a more inclusive political process, this book will provide a veritable alternative perspective with regard to suggested strategies for engendering the process of governance in Nigeria. Issues discussed include, but are not limited to, gender, women and political power structures, the sociopolitical equation, dynamics of power and power sharing and the very politics of politics.

This monograph may therefore very well be seen as reserving a practical and multidimensional applicability for integrated epistemological adventure, especially with regard, first to political theory building, as the book is deliberately predicated on the use of a multidisciplinary approach that cuts across women and politics – providing an innovative lens for a more verisimilitude understanding of women's interests and needs; and it is particularly relevant for policy and global studies, within the context of immediate exigency and precise contemporariness. The book highlights different possibilities for the political inclusion of women within the three major Nigerian geopolitical zones. Furthermore, in terms of practice, most studies on women's participation in politics have focused on a micro-level analysis. The foci here however, are on macro-level analyses that involve comparing the level of women's participation in politics across the said three geopolitical zones to determine if there are variations – where variation exists –and the factors aiding or hampering the participation of women in politics. This way, the research broadens the debate on the empowerment of groups or communities, and avers the need to adopt a bottom-up approach (Robinson, 1996).

The way women are constricted in language by others and by themselves might enable us understand their involvement in the political process, especially within the geopolitical zones. The crucial roles of location, culture and ethnicity of women within the geopolitical zones as a possible means of understanding women's needs are ignored. Nevertheless, all these are essential ways through which people construct reality.

This work looks into women's participation in Nigeria's three major geopolitical zones to find the variation through comparisons; and the reasons underlying the differences regarding the number of women in the assemblies. This treatise should be useful to policymakers who are in a position to address challenges women face on issues of gender disparity and to help enact policies that will engender their inclusion in the process of governance. The book promises to inundate politicians, gender activists, political scientists and the tag-rag with essential facts, figures and findings on the subject. The findings might also form a basis for disseminating information on the role geopolitical locations play in the participation of women in the process of governance.

This book has been based on empirical research. It indicates what the populace thinks about the issues relating to gender equality and participation across different zones of Nigeria. It provides an opportunity for a one-stop access to the basics in issues relating to gender equity, women participation and representation in governance in Nigeria – and outside Nigeria – and will be of use to scholars in the field of women / gender studies; to policy and development analysts, political scientists, sociologists and anthropologists, historians, international relations connoisseurs and arbiters, graduate students in the social sciences and humanities and to civil society organisations and non-governmental organisations.

D.T. Agbalajobi
2020

Chapter 1

Introduction

Over the years, the deficient presence of women in politics has been a source of concern around the world, particularly in Nigeria. Thus, at the Fourth World Conference on Women: Action for Equality, Development and Peace convened by the United Nations in Beijing, China in 1995 it became imperative for the United Nations to propose enduring support for the inclusion of women in some critical areas of human endeavour. The inclusion or exclusion of women in Nigerian politics is crucial to the overall development of the nation, given the nation's numerical strength. Nigeria boasts the largest population in Africa – some 206 million people (Statista.com; Worldometers, 2020). Of this number, 49 per cent are female – some 100.94 million girls and women (National Population Commission, 2006; National Bureau of Statistics, 2016/2017; British Council Nigeria, 2012). It would, therefore, seem that any discussion about Nigeria's future should necessarily entail a consideration of the feminine world: girls and women – the roles they play and the barriers they face in making the future better, as far as politics and generally speaking, life, are concerned. The geographical and ideological disparities in Nigeria make her a unique country with global, yet dramatically peculiar challenges and opportunities, even as these relate to gender inequality.

Furthermore, most studies on women's participation in politics have focused on a macro-level analysis, but that may not make for adequately practical evaluation of the issues. The foci here are on macro-level analyses that involve comparing the level of women's participation in politics across Nigeria's three geopolitical zones. This is to enable us determine if there are variations (where variations exist) and the factors aiding or hampering the participation of women in politics. This way, the research broadens the debate on the empowerment of groups or communities and avers the need to adopt a bottom-up approach Robinson (1996).

1

CONCEPTUAL FRAMEWORK

Participation as a general concept is a central issue of our time. Politicians and policymakers make it significantly relevant in recent times as it encourages people to be part of events and processes that shape their lives (United Nations Development Programme [UNDP], 1993; White, 1996; Jochum et al., 2005; Cornwall, 2008). As clearly stated, women are a significant force behind people's participation in the life of society today. Women not only comprise the majority of those excluded from participation, but they also play a leading role in the emergence of groups, organisations and movements worldwide. Women are becoming increasingly active in their communities, governments and the international arena (Karl, 1995). There are different forms of participation, and the *UNDP Human Development Report* identifies four basic forms of participation, namely: household, economic, social and cultural and political. These forms of participation are interrelated and cannot be viewed in isolation. The *Human Development Report 1993* states that:

> Since participation can take place in the economic, social and political arenas, each person necessarily participates in many ways, at many levels. In economic life as a producer or a consumer, an entrepreneur or an employee. In social life as a member of a family, or of a community organisation or ethnic group. And in political life as a voter, or as a member of a political party or perhaps a pressure group. All these roles overlap and interact, forming patterns of participation that interconnect with – and often reinforce – each other. (5)

Participation is an essential element of human development that encompasses involvement in the events and processes that shape lives and society (Cornwall, 2008). Participation means people are intimately involved in the economic, social, cultural and political processes that affect their lives (UNDP, 1993). While it involves both sexes, women are the primary force behind the call for participation, considering their population and roles in all facets of life (Karl, 1995). Scholars such as Paterman (1970), Dahl (1971, 1998) and O'Toole, Marsh and Jones (2003) contend that participation is a prerequisite for proper democratic governance while Verba, Nie and Kim (1978) opine that individuals ought to have equal opportunities to influence the decision-making process. As aforementioned, the UNDP (1993) in a study entitled, 'Human Development Report' identifies four basic forms of participation including household, economic, social and cultural, as well as political participation, all of which are interrelated and cannot be viewed in isolation. However, political participation, among other forms of participation, is the focus of this book.

Political participation is 'a political engagement or public involvement in decision-making and a set of rights and duties that involve formally organised civic and political activities (such as voting or joining a political party)' (Riley et al. 2010, 347). Bourne (2010) avers that its forms include being a member of a political party, displaying an active role within a range of political interaction, contacting politicians to express concern or even attacking politicians during demonstrations. Smith (2004) – in Burrell (2004) and Panda (1995) – asserts that it is a cornerstone of the theory and practice of democracy. Also, Anifowose (2004) argues that participation is a sine qua non of democracy. It views democracy as individuals participating in decisions that involve their lives and such voluntary activities as holding public and party offices, being a candidate for an office, attending election campaigns, voting and exposing self to political stimuli.

According to the (Nigeria) National Electoral Commission (2004), political participation is understood as citizens' activities aimed at influencing government and the public policy process. Verba et al. (1978) define *political participation* as legal activities by private citizens that are more or less directly aimed at influencing the selection of governmental personnel, the actions they take or both. This is in line with Brady (1995), as cited in Teorell et al. (2007, 336), who defines it as 'an action by ordinary citizens directed towards influencing some political outcomes'. Dunn (2007) states that it refers to an act that seeks to influence rules, laws or policies. Political participation is also identified with donating money to, or raising funds for, an organisation; voting in an election, signing a petition, boycotting certain products or buying products for ethical, political or environmental reasons; contacting a public official or a politician, an organisation or the media; attending political meetings, rally or protest; and taking part in a strike or illegal protests. Brown (2014) categorises political participation into three: voting, traditional and non-traditional forms. Voting is identified as a unique act of democracies. The traditional form, regarded as 'formal' by Henn and Foard (2012), has the attributes of attending political meeting or rally, working for a candidate, contributing money to campaign and contacting government officials. Non-traditional forms, presented as unconventional, consist of participation in activities such as signing petitions, protests and boycotts (Bourne, 2010).

Political participation, to Munroe (2002) is defined by the degree of exercise of citizens' rights to engage in political activities, through which citizens communicate their concerns and preferences to government and pressurise them to respond. Hence, political participation is a form of activity which is instrumental or expressive, voluntary or mobilised, legal or illegal, conventional or unconventional, with or without the use of violence by the individual, man or woman, acting as a citizen, exercising political power for public or particularistic purposes, directed at state authorities or other entities that exercise political powers, or have an influence on, politics (Nilges, 2005). However, this raises the question: Why is this preponderantly the prerogative of men, instead of men and women? There is, therefore, the need to generate empirical evidence to explain this. This is one of the foci of this study.

Albritton and Bureekul (2005) identify two types of political participation: conventional or institutional; and unconventional or less institutional. For institutional or conventional forms, voting gaps appear to shrink while party politics and running for office remain dominated by men (Paxton et al., 2007). Differentials in gender patterns vary even further among the less institutional or more informal participation (Coffé and Bolzendahl, 2010) hence, scholars increasingly emphasise the importance of less institutional participation (Dalton, 2008; Burns, 2007; Pattie et al., 2003).

Political participation can also be viewed as a two-dimensional concept involving the level of electoral interaction and the level of influence on actions taken by governments. This distinction is similar to Teorell et al.'s (2007) two distinctions along two-dimensional modes of participation – the first, pertaining to the channel of expression; the second to the mechanism of influence. In this work, the level of electoral interaction is measured by the

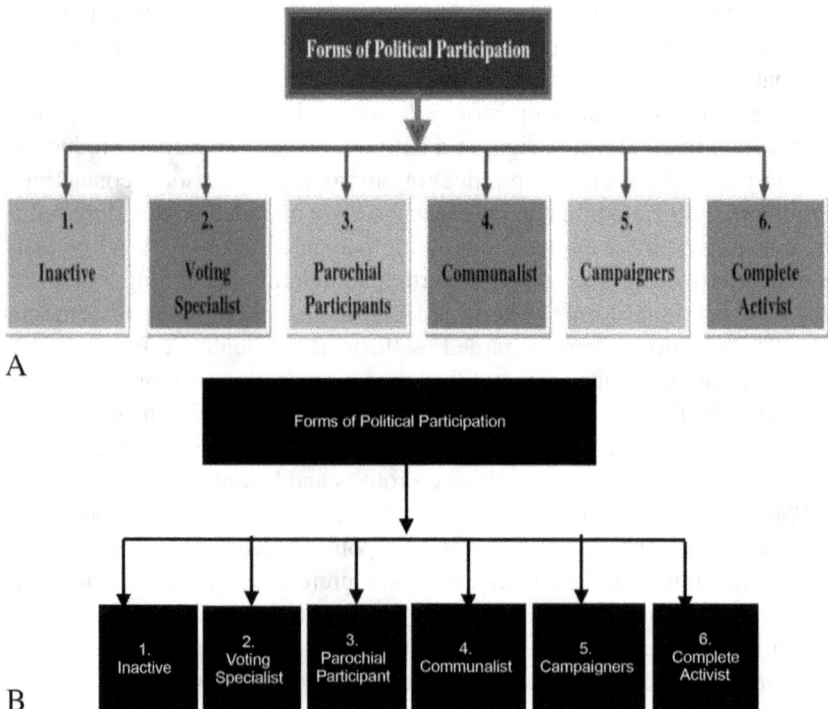

Figure 1.1　Illustrating Patterns of Political Participation.

level of political activism including membership of political groups and other interest groups and the level of voting in terms of being an active and consistent voter. On the other hand, the level and nature of influence on actions taken refer to the extent to which individuals have decision-making powers. This is measured by being elected into a position, being appointed into a government position at any level and having any kind of access or influence on political decision-making processes beyond voting.

As illustrated in figure 1.1, (Verba and Nie's model), political participation is adopted and conceived as involvement in political processes and all activities aimed at influencing government and policy procedures. Verba and Nie (1972) present a model of political participation which classifies individuals into six different groups: inactive, voting specialist, parochial participants, communalists, campaigners and complete activists. The inactive are women who do little or nothing; voting specialists vote regularly but do nothing else; parochial participants contact officials concerning specific issues; communalists intermittently engage in action on broad social issues but not intensely involved in politics; campaigners are intensely involved in campaigns; and complete activists participate in several acts of activism.

GAPS IN THE LITERATURE

There are great pieces of literature and emerging perspectives that reflect the various roles women play in politics; reasons women are less democratised, the issue of quota as a global phenomenon and analysis of women's substantive representation UNDP (2000). Hoare and Gell (2009) as well as Domingo et al. (2015) in looking at the position of women in leadership aver that there is a need to push for a high level of women's representation in parliament. Krook (2006, 2009, 2010, 2016), as well as Childs and Krook (2006), emphasise the need for quotas to enhance women's representation in parliament.

Most literature on this subject focuses on general factors affecting women's participation, and many of the literature (Taiwo and Ahmed, 2015; True et al., 2014; Ngara and Ayabam, 2013; Bulloch, Kroeck, Kundu, Newhouse and Lowe, 2012; Hogstrom, 2012; Bari, 2005; Ologbenla, 2003) view religion, education and cultural orientation as the major factors affecting women's participation in politics. Some of the studies on women's participation in politics in Nigeria used secondary data (Olufade, 2013; Erunk and Shuaibu, 2013; Akindele et al., 2011; Arowolo and Aluko, 2010; Okoosi-Simbine, 2007). Some were based on field survey (Aina, 2012; Ogbogu, 2012; Oni and Joshua, 2012) while others combined descriptive and qualitative approaches (Okpilike and Abamba, 2013; Aina, 2012).

Lamidi (2014) examines various determinants of women's decision-making power across the six geopolitical regions in Nigeria and identifies factors relating to women's household decision-making power in Nigeria but does not consider political or public decision-making, subsumed in women's political participation, nor was the study a geopolitical analysis. UN Women (2014), with specific reference to women, only examines the effects of sociocultural and religious influences on voting patterns in Nigeria and how it affects women as voters and candidates for election; it fails to adequately cover other forms of political participation and factors that might affect it. Awofeso and Odeyemi (2014) examine how cultural values have impeded the female folks from participating in politics in Nigeria without a geopolitical comparison, while Udokang and Awofeso (2013) undertake a theoretical study. The British Council (2012) *Gender Report* focused on northern Nigeria alone. Oni and Joshua (2012) combined an in-depth interview and structured questionnaire as instruments to collect data. However, their study population consisted of women in the South-West geopolitical zone, in particular Lagos and Ogun States, without making a comparison with other geopolitical zones in Nigeria. Oni and Agbude (2011) examine factors responsible for the low level of women's political participation in Ogun State, while Ogbogu (2012) captures the views of target groups across the six geopolitical zones in Nigeria on the role of women in politics; Taiwo and Ahmed (2015) used data from the National Bureau of Statistics (NBS) to examine the correlates and predictors of the spatiotemporal pattern of voter apathy in presidential elections in all states of Nigeria between 1999 and 2011. The study, which was limited to a singular elected political office neither relied on primary data that involved other acts of political participation. It also did not cover the 2015 general elections in Nigeria.

Having pointed out the strengths and limitations of existing literature, it is pertinent to examine the peculiar locational (geographical, socioeconomic and cultural) influences on women's participation in politics by analysing the patterns of women's participation in politics and adding to the existing knowledge in the area of women and politics. This is a significant concern for this work.

THEORETICAL FRAMEWORK

The approach adopted in this book is interdisciplinary, cutting across the broad spectrum of International Relations, History, Political Science, Women Studies, Sociology and Gender Studies. It adopts a mixed or eclectic theoretical framework which addresses the contending views on the exclusion of women in token, if not symbolic, political participation; the reasons for women's underrepresentation in governance and decision-making as well as the need to overcome challenges confronting women in their quest for fair inclusion and participation in politics.

THE POLITICAL CULTURE THEORY

Culture has been given different definitions by various scholars. Here, *culture* is referred to as the cumulative deposit of knowledge, experience, beliefs, values, attitudes, meanings, hierarchies, religion, the notion of time, roles, spatial relations, the concept of the universe and material objects as well as acquired by a group of people in the course of generations through individual and group striving.

According to Almond and Verba 1963 cited in Bove, 2002, The term 'political culture' first appeared in modern empirical Political Science in the late 1950s or early 1960s and is chiefly associated with the American Political Scientist, Gabriel Almond. In a 1956 essay, Almond states that 'every political system is embedded in a particular pattern of orientation to political actions' (Pye and Verba, 1965).

Political culture is defined as 'the specifically political orientations – attitudes toward the political system and its various parts and attitudes toward the role of the self in the system'. The political culture of a nation is 'the particular distribution of patterns of orientation toward political objects among the members of the nation' (Almond and Verba, 1963, 1–12). Bove (2002) notes that the three modes of political orientation are then identified as the cognitive, the affective and the evaluational – which refer to what Almond and Verba take to be the three major kinds of belief that influence the character and policy outcomes of political systems. Thus, *political culture* refers to something like the psycho-sociological limits or conditions within which individual political agents act. More generally expressed, it refers to the belief structure of a given polity, outside of which structure political action would be incoherent (Bove, 2002). Welch (2013) points out that the concept of political culture is derived from the Structuralist Anthropology of Claude Levi-Strauss. Its origins may be traced more generally to neo-Kantian thought about symbolic forms and structures of meaning such as that of Ernst Cassirer. Its deployment in twentieth-century Political Science has not taken the hermeneutical course that the notion of culture has taken in modern Anthropology, notably in the "interpretivist" approach of Clifford Geertz (Kroebar, 2018).

Bove (2002) avers that political culture was brought in as an ally of, and soon became a crucial term within, a behaviouralist Political Science whose primary mode is strict causal explanation, not interpretive description. As

Brint 1991(cited in Bove 2002, 3) remarks, 'Almond believed in the promise of the behavioural revolution to open up the field to the examination of cultural factors that had been previously left to the fringes of analysis or excluded entirely'. The introduction of culture into modern empirical Political Science did not replace or displace behaviouralist analysis of individual political decision but was thought to supplement and indeed complete such analysis (Welch, 2013).

Scholars such as Gabriel Almond, Lucian Pye, Sidney Verba, James Coleman, Beer, Ulam, Dalh, and Powell, were prominent among those who were concerned with the study of political culture in the 1950s and 1960s. The theory is anchored on the sociological aspect of the subject of political development and 'it has come to stand as a very important variable for a morphological study of the political system' (Agagu, 2007, 16). This standpoint has come to influence 'the system analyst's assertion that one political system is distinguished from another not only in terms of its culture but also in respect of the political structure in which it is embedded' (Johari, 1982, 222). The concept, as noted by Dawson and Prewitt (1969, 26) summarises a complex and varied portion of social reality.

This research aligns with Verba's (1969) and Erson and Lane's (2008) perspectives on political culture. This is because political culture, as seen by these authors, allows examining the diversity in values among different women within the different communities and theorise the political consequences of their action or inaction. Given the multicultural nature of the study population, culture as a political dimension presents itself as a necessary element for the recognition of politics and how it plays out. Erson and Lane (2008) see political culture as a vital tool in the analysis of how women in various communities engage in politics and also a useful tool in predicting political consequences from cultural phenomena.

Generally, political culture can be seen as a product of many interrelated factors such as historical, geographical and socioeconomic (Johari, 1982, 226). This explains why so many Third World countries, particularly African countries, are still struggling to enthrone democracy, whereas it has become a way of life in Western countries. For instance, Nigeria, within fifty-five years, is in its Fourth Republic; whereas the constitutions of Britain and the United States have survived for centuries.

Further, 'culture' has become a useful analytic tool used in Social Sciences. This occurs because the study of the cultural dimension of political institutions and processes has emerged as a significant research factor for social scientists and students. More specifically, the study of culture today helps social scientists to reveal the political aspect about the legitimisation of formal organisations, the social determinants of art and ideas, the reproduction of hierarchies, the acquisition of cultural capital and the normalisation of the self. Revealing the political purposes hidden behind all of them, social scientists will be able to show that an idea or institution is socially constructed as social scientists mainly focus on the constructivist, for example, they argue that everything in political reality is constructed (Jasper, 2005, 115). This theory is therefore significant to this study given the fact that it examines why gender differentials exist, where they exist and what accounts for these differentials. It is also important because it notes that the differentials are likely to be influenced by existing social context entrenched in the traditional, cultural, religious and institutional frameworks across the geopolitical zones in Nigeria. The theory of public culture allows examining the diversity in values among different communities and theorising the political consequences. It is, however, evident from this study that women's underrepresentation in decision-making and governance in Nigeria goes beyond the cultural analysis of their interaction, as women are still struggling to have more representation.

THE LIBERAL FEMINIST THEORY

Historically, women had not been given opportunities to play major roles in their communities. In Europe and America, women were denied the right to vote until Emmeline Pankhurst, who was a British political activist and leader of the British suffragette movement, rose to help them win the right to vote. Many variants of the feminist theories are applicable in the discussion of women's political participation and gender equality, such as the radical feminist, socialist and black feminist. The liberal feminist theory is essential to this study because it explicates the reality of the plight, status and aspiration of the Nigerian women concerning their participation in politics. Introduction of women's right perspective by liberal thinkers such as Mary Wollstonecraft (1806–1873), Harriet Taylor (1807–1858), John Stuart Mill (1806–1873) and Elizabeth Cady Stanton (1815–1902) marked the beginning of liberal feminism (Knuttila and Kubik, 2000; Tuana and Tong, 1995). An attempt to extend the liberal notions of freedom, individuality and autonomy to women is in a 1792 publication by Wollstonecraft titled, *A Vindication of the Rights of Women* where she argues against limitations on citizenship, freedom and autonomy of women to ensure they are treated as individuals, as men are.

Contemporary liberal feminists seek to reform the legal and political system for women to have access to opportunities and resources to produce a state of equality between both sexes (Burrell, 2004). They see women as autonomous individuals who will achieve great heights based on their merit and efforts (Ford, 2002). The liberals and the liberal feminists are of the view that freedom is a fundamental value, and that the state should ensure freedom for an individual. The liberal feminists' perceptive of freedom for women is categorised into personal and political autonomies; where personal autonomy is 'living a life of one's choosing' while political autonomy is 'being co-author of the conditions under which one lives'. (*Stanford Encyclopedia of Philosophy*, 2007)

Liberal feminists are of the view that the needs and interests of women are insufficiently reflected in the necessary conditions under which they live, thereby lacking legitimacy because women are inadequately represented in the process of governance or that social arrangement often fails to respect elements of women's flourishing (*Stanford Encyclopedia of Philosophy*, 2007). To them, these forms of autonomy deficit are due to the gender system (Okin, 1989) 'or the patriarchal nature of inherited traditions and institutions'. (*Stanford Encyclopaedia of Philosophy*, 2007) They hold that there must be enabling conditions which are not sufficiently present in women's lives for them to exercise personal autonomy. Enabling conditions that are currently not present in women's lives, according to the liberal feminists, include being free from violence and the threats violating their dignity, fracturing self and reducing self-respect (Brison, 1997); unfairly disempowering and limiting women (Cudd, 2006); limitations set by patriarchal/paternalistic and moralistic law (Cornell, 1998; Brake, 2004); option restriction due to economic deprivation and feminisation of poverty (Alstott, 2004; Pearce, 1978); stereotyping and sex disorientation in education and employment (Smith, 2004; Rhode, 1997); and cultural homogeneity, assigned identities and social roles by sex (Chambers, 2008; Alstott, 2004; Meyers, 2004). The factors as mentioned earlier all affect women's political participation and therefore make liberal feminism applicable in this work.

Liberal feminism emphasises the importance of political autonomy; that democratic legitimacy of the primary conditions under which citizens live depends on the inclusion of women in the processes of public deliberation and electoral politics, which inform political participation. Okin (1989) claims that this political autonomy deficit is due to the gendered system or the patriarchal nature of the society; leading to women being underrepresented in influential forums of public deliberation (*Stanford Encyclopedia of Philosophy*, 2007). The liberal feminists gave several reasons for the underrepresentation of women in politics (Barlow and Selin, 1987). Attempts to increase women's participation in politics are often deadlocked by a vicious circle of their exclusion. The liberal feminists provide ways out, such as providing justice in the distribution of societal benefits and burden to enable women participate in politics on equal terms with men (Okin, 1989). Other ways include expounding the need for cultural change from stereotyping and recommendations of legal mechanism such as targets, quotas, party slots or proportional representation in elected bodies (Peters, 2006; Phillips 2004, 1991; Rhode, 1994) and ensuring a guaranteed, equal representation of both sexes in parliament (Green, 2006).

The liberal feminists aim to incorporate women into the mainstream of contemporary society by bringing to the fore the extent to which women are underrepresented within traditional areas of national and international political activities, and sought ways by which they may overcome barriers to their political participation (Jaggar, 1983). The liberal feminists suggest changes in societal attitudes, division of labour in homes, as well as increased educational and career opportunities for a more significant number of women. They accept the public/private and political/non-political bifurcation and dichotomy and aver that once women are represented in corresponding numbers to their presence in the general population, equality will be achieved (Whitworth, 1994). Despite their well-articulated approach to issues of women's political participation, there are some criticisms to their views, such as the claim that promotion of gender fairness and women autonomy may end up consciously hindering autonomy, while others criticise their view on quotas, stating that it may be illiberal (Cudd, 2006; Peters, 2006).

Using the liberal feminist perspective as propounded by Mary Wollstonecraft (1759–1797), the theory emphasises 'equal individual rights and liberties for women and men and downplaying sexual differences' (*Stanford Encyclopedia of Philosophy*, 2007). This dimension reiterates the importance of structuring social, family and sexual roles in ways that promote women's autonomous self-fulfilment. According to Wilson (1989), many of the supposed differences between the sexes were either fabricated or exaggerated and therefore, could not be used as the basis for differential rights and roles. According to Wilson (1989), Wollstonecraft argued that both sexes could reason; hence both should be educated to enhance their rationality. Given this analogy, it, therefore, implies that women should be allowed to participate in politics, and all barriers militating against their equal representation should be removed. In addition, the economic condition of women is also considered. At the same time, the structure of the family – which forms this study – was observed as a significant determinant of the women's level of participation and representation in politics.

The political culture and the liberal feminist theories are integrated in this book to guide the line of questioning and explaining issues regarding the possibility of variation in the forms of participation of women in politics, given the different cultural settings. The two theories combined bring to the fore the challenges women face and what accounts for the disparity in their political participation and representation in governance.

METHODOLOGY

This work is based on the tradition of the positivists and the interpretivists. The positivists' orientation suggests that there is an absolute truth in the reality of the world, and as such, the world can be captured quantitatively. The interpretivists on the other hand, aver that there is also the need to understand people's views and opinions, accept their interpretation of the social world and make room for the researcher to interpret and explain the social reality of the world according to the people. Therefore, this study's conviction is that applying the positivists' and interpretivists' ontological and epistemological positions, will give another dimension looking at women's participation in politics and their struggle for political power in Nigeria.

Research Design

The study is mixed-method research design. It combines quantitative and qualitative methods. As explained by Johnson and Onwuegbuzie (2004), such a mixed method in research provides opportunities for maximising gains in social sciences research. The two methods combined include a cross-sectional survey and comparative case study approach through in-depth interviews (IDIs). The essence of the mixed method is that the combination of multi-methods in a single study adds depth and breadth to an investigation (Isiugo-Abanihe, 2002) and results in an accurate representation of reality (Williams, 2007). While the quantitative method allows for deductive thinking, qualitative method emphasises inductive thinking, exploration of complex issues, and the building of models and theory (Johnson and Onwuegbuzie, 2004) to improve quality, integrity and accuracy of cross-cultural research (Creswell, 2003; Tashakkori and Teddlie, 1998; Hines, 1993). Hence, the mixed method, a combination of the qualitative and quantitative, is used in the collection and analysis of data in this study, that is, descriptive statistics was used and complemented with qualitative research.

Study Location

Nigeria is Africa's most populous country currently with approximately 206 million people (Worldometers, 2020) and one of the most ethnically diverse states with over 200 ethnic groups and 374 languages (British Council, 2009). Nigeria is a federation of thirty-six states grouped into six geopolitical zones and a Federal Capital Territory (FCT) Abuja; this was adopted at the 1995 constitutional conference as proposed by former vice president Alex Ekwueme. There is also a typical division of Nigeria by the two-way system (North and South) and the three-way system (East, North and West). The three-way system is a product of ethnic and religious identities from old regional structures where identities were shaped by dominant ethnic groups – Hausa/Fulani in the North, Igbo in the East and Yoruba in the West. This study is based on the three-way division; hence, three geopolitical zones were selected, accordingly. The three zones selected for this research were: South-West, North-West and South-East. While the North-West presents similar characteristics to what obtains in most parts of northern Nigeria, the South-South is fused with similar political features into either the South-West or the South-East. These choices were also informed by the gender rating and participation in the 2011 general elections as statistics showed that female participation in the 2011 general elections in the North-West was the lowest (2.35%). Despite her high women population, the South-West had the largest with 15.55 per cent, while the South-East had 11.86 per cent (Gambo and Lenshie, 2013). In addition, the three zones were also selected because they all had historical dominance in precolonial, colonial and postcolonial eras; they each had a capital in the old regional structure; and they had a majority of the three dominant ethnic nationalities.

Population of the Study

The target population is all Nigerians who are females from the age of eighteen years upwards within the selected geopolitical zones; who are constitutionally qualified to participate in politics and enjoy the rights and duties of a citizen. (Total population of each location is given in table 3.1) A representative sample was drawn from each geopolitical zone to permit for external validity of the study.

Sampling Procedure and Sample Size

A multistage sampling procedure was adopted in selecting the study sample for the cross-sectional survey. Stage one of the study involved the purposive sampling technique used for selecting the three geopolitical zones – North-West, South-West and South-East. The second stage used simple random sampling technique to select a state from each of the three selected geopolitical zones. This was achieved by using the 'deep-hit' method such that the name of each state in a particular geopolitical zone was written on different paper, neatly folded, then placed in an opaque container. After that, a state was picked randomly from the container. This process was applied to the three geopolitical zones to derive the following three states viz, Kaduna, Anambra and Ondo. At the third stage, one local government area (LGA) each in the selected states' capital was purposively selected making three LGAs which are Kaduna north; Awka south and Akure south (figure 3.2, 3.3 and 3.4 see Appendix III).

At the fourth stage, the sample size was derived through a statistical formula of Research Advisors (2006) initiated by Krejcie and Morgan (1970), and it was based on the total female population in 2006 for the selected LGAs

Table 1.1 Population Projection and Sample Size for the Survey per Location

Selected Location						Projection to 2015 at 3.5%	
Zones	States	LGA	Males (2006)	Females (2006)	Total (2006)	per annum (Female)	Sample size
North-West	Kaduna	Kaduna- North	186,263	171,431	357,694	357,694	480
South-East	Anambra	Awka- South	97,815	91,234	189,049	124,242	479
South-West	Ondo	Akure- South	175,495	177,716	353,211	242,014	480

Source: National Population Commission (2006) and Authors Analysis (2015).

projected to 2015 estimates using appropriate formula (see Appendix IV). This is presented in table 1.1. (See table 1.1).

As indicated in table 1.1, having calculated the 2015 population figures by making a projection based on the 2006 population figures and using the sample size calculator and as on the sample size table, the required sample size for the South-East (Anambra State, Awka South LGA) was 479; North-West (Kaduna State, Kaduna North LGA) was 480; and South-West (Ondo State, Akure South LGA) was 480. For this sample size, 95 per cent level of confidence, 5 per cent margin of error with an additional 25 per cent purposively added for retrieval error were considered to ensure reliability in this study. The sample size was determined with the formula on Appendix III.

In addition, qualitative data were collected using Key-Informant Interviews (KIIs) or In-Depth Interviews (IDIs) with purposively selected stakeholders. A total of five individuals were targeted for IDIs in each of the three states selected for this study. The KII participants were selected at the states and local government area levels. These included political party leaders, development partners working in the area of women's participation in politics, (members of civil society organisations [CSOs]) and female politicians. Structured validated interview schedule was used to elicit relevant information from the respondents, and an interview guide was developed for this study for the different categories of people interviewed.

RESEARCH INSTRUMENT

Instruments in this study are structured questionnaire for quantitative data and in-depth interview guide for qualitative data.

Instrument for Data Collection

Questionnaire and in-depth interview techniques were used to elicit the primary data for this study. The questionnaire, the instrument for the quantitative data, comprised five sections. (Sections I–V) which dealt with sociodemographic characteristics; political participation patterns; factors affecting women's participation in politics; strategies that could enhance women's representation in governance; and options for additional comments (Appendix IV). Qualitative data were collected through IDI sessions with the five purposively selected stakeholders from the state and local government area levels in each selected study location with the aid of an interview guide developed for this study. The guide contained general and specific questions for the different categories of people interviewed (see Appendix VI).

Pre-test of the Instrument

Questionnaire and interview guide were pre-tested for reliability and validity among some respondents outside the study location. Questionnaire was self-administered on fifty respondents in Ife central LGA while some other respondents were also interviewed.

Validity of the Instrument

Face and content validity of the instrument was carried out with the aid of field assistants in the field from the departments of Political Science, Demography and Social Statistics, and Geography of Obafemi Awolowo University, Ile-Ife. Content rating of the instrument was achieved by judgement agreements of five experts in the identified institution concerning the appropriateness of the content of the instrument. This was ascertained with the coefficient of concordance (W) with a value of 0.75 and above, which indicated a strong agreement among the judges and considered the instrument relevant and valid.

RELIABILITY OF THE INSTRUMENT

A test-retest method was carried out to determine the reliability of the instrument. Reliability coefficient (r) of 0.70 achieved was considered adequate and determined the reliability of the instrument.

Collection of Data

The primary data in this study were gathered through quantitative and qualitative methods between January and May 2015. Various strategies were adopted at different locations in selecting the respondents due to the nature of the respondent's culture and background.

COLLECTION OF QUANTITATIVE DATA

Questionnaires were administered to elicit quantitative data per location. Figures administered, retrieved and used per location are presented in Table 1.2
    Table 1.2 shows that for Kaduna, out of the 480 administered questionnaires, 441 (92%) were retrieved from which 90 per cent (398) were filled

Table 1.2   Questionnaire Administration, Retrieval and Usage per Study Location

Selected Location				Questionnaire		
Zones	States	LGA	Sample Size	Administered	Retrieved	Properly Filled
NorthWest	Kaduna	Kaduna- North	480	480	441 (92%)	398 (90%)
SouthEast	Anambra	Awka- South	479	479	421 (88%)	395 (94%)
SouthWest	Ondo	Akure- South	480	480	437 (91%)	413 (95%)
TOTAL			1439	1439	1299 (90%)	1206 (93%)

Source: Author's Survey, 2015.

correctly and used for analysis. In Awka, out of the 479 administered questionnaires, 421 (88%) were retrieved from which 94 per cent (395) were filled correctly and used for analysis. For Akure, from the 480 administered questionnaires, 437 (91%) were retrieved from which 95 per cent (413) were filled correctly and used for analysis. Hence, out of a total of 1,439 administered questionnaires, 1,299 were retrieved from which only 1,206 were filled correctly and used for analysis.

The questionnaires were administered at different areas in each location. In Kaduna, questionnaires were administered at Kawo, Malali, Kabala Doki, Doka, Kabala Costain, Banawa, N. D. A Kawo, Kotoko Barracks, Unguwan Shanu and UNG/Garbah/Banki. In Akure, the areas of the administration included Federal Secretariat, Akure market, Adegbola junction, Akure south LG Secretariat, School of Nursing and Midwifery, Federal University of Technology, Akure (FUTA) and Ministry of Women Affairs. For Awka, the areas included Akwa-south LG secretariat, State Ministries (Women Affairs, Science and Technology and Education), UNIZIK Campus, Udoka Housing Estate, Works Road and Nibo and Nise community. Women were the respondents in all locations since they were targeted for the study.

COLLECTION OF QUALITATIVE DATA

The qualitative data involved in-depth interviews (IDIs) with selected women who were politicians, policymakers, NGO operators and community leaders. Five women from each specified category were purposively selected per study location for the IDIs. Interviews were conducted between March and May 2015.

Research assistants were employed during fieldwork. They were PhD students in Political Science department who are familiar with the concepts, and were equally trained on the use of the research instruments having done a pilot study to ensure that all errors identified during the pilot study were corrected. There were a total of ten research assistants used for the study in the study location. However, not all ten were used at the same time. For example, in Anambra, three research assistants were not available at the time of the fieldwork; the study therefore engaged the service of only those available given the location and also in Kaduna.

To get respondents, contact persons were first established, and the snow-balling technique was employed. In Awka and Akure, the IDIs conducted were face to face with most respondents, but some preferred phone interview while one opted for the use of email. In Kaduna, phone interview was adopted. During the IDI sessions, having done same through letter and contact persons, the researcher introduced herself, and the lead research assistant explained the purpose of the interview, the confidentiality of the responses was underlined while permission was sought for recording. Consequently, questions were asked using the interview guides (see Appendix V), and the responses were recorded although parts were also hand-written as back up.

PROCEDURE FOR DATA PRESENTATION AND ANALYSIS

Analysis, Variables and Scale of Quantitative Data

Completed copies of the questionnaire were entered with Epidata while Stata Version 12 software was used for the analysis. Descriptive statistics tools, including frequency counts, percentages, mean and charts, were employed.

The variables of interest in this study are the dependent and independent. The dependent variable is the level of political participation measured with ten items in section II of the questionnaire focusing on numbers of political activities in which women participated. If the number of activities was three then it was considered as low political participation level; women who participated in any four to six political activities were considered to be moderate in level of political participation; while women who participated in any seven political activities and above were considered to have high political participation level. The independent variables are selected items, including geopolitical zones, factors affecting women's participation in politics as well as the socioeconomic and demographic characteristics in sections I and III of the questionnaire (see Appendix IV). To identify the forms of political participation, the study relies on classification by Verba and Nie (1974), which classifies citizens into six categories based on the types of activities they undertake (see section 2.1.3). Hence, patterns and levels of women's political participation are made conforming to Verba and Nie's standard through the ten items in section II of the questionnaire.

Table 1.3 shows the different models, the standard definition, the variable to measure each form of participation and the scoring pattern (see table 1.3).

The 'inactive' was determined through answering 'negative' to all items; 'voting specialist' responded 'positive' to only items 5 and 6 and 'negative' to all others; 'parochial participants' responded 'positive' to only item 8 out of the 10; 'communalist' respond 'negative' to items 4, 7 and 10; 'Campaigners' are measured by responding 'positive' to all items except 8; and 'complete activist' measured by responding 'positive' to all items 1 to 10.

On the causes of women's underrepresentation in decision-making, statements relating to social, cultural, political violence, institutional design and religious factors were presented to the women. These statements were rated using four-point Likert scale of Strongly Agree to Strongly Disagree. For ease of analysis and simplicity, Strongly Agree and Agree were recoded as 1 while Disagree and Strongly Disagree were recoded as 0. These values were used to generate an index with 0 meaning No to all the items listed under each factor and1 meaning at least one item was identified under each factor. After that, each of the statements was ranked in order to identify the percentage of people who mentioned at least one item under each factor, and after that, each factor was broken down to identify the most prevalent issue confronting women's underrepresentation in decision-making and governance in Nigeria.

To examine the disparity between women's participation and representation in governance, secondary data were used. For participation, the number of registered voters who were women in Nigeria and the number who contested for various elective positions within the study period were identified (1999–2015). To measure representation, secondary data were used by listing the number of women at the state and federal levels in the following positions – governor, deputy governor, secretary to the state government, commissioners, chief judge, membership of state house of assembly, president, vice president, secretary to the government of the federation, ministers/ minsters of state, ambassadors / high commissioners, permanent secretaries, chief of staff to the president, chief justice of the federation, house of representative and senate.

On the strategies for continued participation of women in politics and increased representation of women in governance and decision-making, section V of the questionnaire identifies various factors which are categorised into seven, namely: training, networking and mentoring, policy-related strategy, orientation and enlightenment, value-change and socialisation, as well as financial support and women empowerment. A cumulative of each variable under each strategy was summed up, and the average was found and then converted into a percentage. This was then presented in a table as strategy for increasing women's representation in governance and decision-making.

Table 1.3   Variables and Scales for Measuring Political Participation

Forms of Participation	Standard Definition	Variable to Measure (Items 1-10 on Appendix VIII)	Scoring
Inactive	Those who avoid all forms of political participation	Items 1-10 must be answered in the negative	0/10
Voting Specialist	Those who restrict their political participation to voting in election	Respond positively to only items 5 & 6 and negative to others	2/10
Parochial Participants	Those who avoid elections and civic organisations but will contact officials regarding specific problems	Respond positively to only item 8	1/10
Communalist	Those who join organisations and participate in politics but not in partisan campaigns	Respond negatively to items 4, 7, & 10	7/10
Campaigners	Those who both vote in elections and get involved in campaigns	Respond positively to all items except item 8	9/10
Complete Activist	Those who take part in all forms of political activity	Respond positively to items 1 - 10	10/10

Source: *Study Guide, Advanced Placement Edition* – American Government (2008).

Test of Hypotheses: The stated hypotheses (H1 and H2) were tested with the chi-square statistical tool.

H1: There is a significant relationship between geopolitical locations of women's political participation level.

H0: There is no significant relationship between geopolitical locations of women's political participation level.

H2: Socioeconomic characteristics of women influence their participation in politics across the geopolitical zones in Nigeria.

H0: Socioeconomic characteristics of women do not influence their participation in politics across the geopolitical zones in Nigeria.

PROCEDURE FOR ANALYSIS OF QUALITATIVE DATA

Content analysis was used to analyse qualitative data in this study. Directed content analysis occurs when the analysis is guided by a more structured process (Hickey and Kipping, 1996); beginning with identifying key concepts or variables as initial coding categories guided using operational definitions and theories (Potter and Levine-Donnerstein, 1999); this is followed by in-depth round coding where additional themes are captured from the selected text (Hsieh and Shannon, 2005). In this study, the transcripts (from the audio recording) were compiled and organised into central themes based on the research questions and objectives. All statements, phrases and words that captured each theme and sub-themes were identified, and similar sub-themes were grouped to emerge as major themes.

LIMITATIONS OF THE METHODOLOGY

Only three geopolitical zones were covered in this study. The other three were not covered because of logistics, locations, size of the population and cost and lack of access to data. Despite the limitations, the study still achieved its research objectives while restricting its generalisation to the three geopolitical zones. Future research should undertake confirmatory data analysis of the other three geopolitical zones in Nigeria. Hypotheses can also be tested using inferential statistics to confirm the study.

DATA PRESENTATION, ANALYSIS AND DISCUSSION OF FINDINGS

This section presents the key findings of the study. It includes a description of the social and demographic contexts of the respondents and a description of the patterns of political participation of women across the selected geopolitical zones using descriptive statistics and typological theory. The section also presents data on factors that affect women's political participation beyond voting. This section ends with a presentation and discussion of how variations in geopolitical zones explain differences in levels of women's participation in politics in Nigeria.

PRESENTATION OF SOCIODEMOGRAPHIC CHARACTERISTICS OF RESPONDENTS

Data on the respondents' sociodemographic characteristics such as age, marital status, religion, education, income, employment status and occupation were presented, interpreted and discussed. This was done to fit the women's sociodemographic characteristics with their responses to the issues explored in the study. Also, such information on the sample gives a clear picture of the composition of the respondents for this study. Table 1.4 presents the description of women survey respondents (see table 1.4).

Table 1.4　Distribution of the Sociodemographic Characteristics of the Respondents

Socioeconomic Characteristics		Anambra	Kaduna	Ondo	Total
Group	Options	Freq. (%)	Freq. (%)	Freq. (%)	Freq. (%)
	<=20 years	23 (5.8)	98 (24.6)	63 (15.3)	184 (45.7)
	21–30 years	102 (25.8)	169 (42.5)	95 (23.0)	366 (91.3)
	31–40 years	77 (19.5)	69 (17.3)	70 (16.9)	216 (53.7)
	41–50 years	65 (16.5)	22 (5.5)	34 (8.2)	121 (30.2)
	Above 50 years	128 (32.4)	40 (10.1)	151 (36.6)	319 (79.1)
Marital status	Married	179 (45.3)	95 (23.9)	225 (54.5)	499 (123.7)
	Widowed	16 (4.1)	20 (5.0)	7 (1.7)	43 (10.8)
	Divorced	4 (1.0)	7 (1.7)	3 (0.7)	14 (3.4)
	Separated	4 (1.0)	15 (3.8)	4 (1.0)	23 (5.8)
	Never Married	192 (48.6)	261 (65.6)	174 (42.1)	627 (156.3)
Religion	Christianity	378 (96.4)	151 (37.9)	370 (89.6)	899 (223.9)
	Islam	9 (2.3)	245 (61.6)	42 (10.2)	296 (74.1)
	Traditional	5 (1.3)	2 (0.5)	1 (0.2)	8 (2.0)
Education	Primary	9 (2.3)	11 (2.7)	7 (1.7)	27 (6.7)
	Secondary	31 (7.9)	64 (16.1)	22 (5.3)	117 (29.3)
	Technical	51 (12.9)	17 (4.3)	41 (9.9)	109 (27.1)
	Tertiary	243 (61.5)	285 (71.6)	293 (71.0)	821 (204.1)
	Postgraduate	61 (15.4)	21 (5.3)	50 (12.1)	821 (32.8)
Income (N)	Below 20,000	46 (11.7)	306 (76.9)	159 (38.5)	511 (127.1)
	20,001–40,000	39 (9.9)	35 (8.8)	40 (9.7)	114 (28.4)
	40,001–60,000	30 (7.5)	11 (2.7)	23 (5.6)	64 (15.8)
	60,001–80,000	33 (8.4)	7 (1.8)	12 (2.9)	52 (13.1)
	80,000+	247 (62.5)	39 (9.8)	179 (43.3)	465 (115.6)
Employment Status	Working	258 (65.3)	83 (20.9)	243 (58.8)	584 (145.0)
	Not-Working	137 (34.7)	315 (79.1)	170 (41.2)	622 (79.0)
Occupation	Trading	28 (10.8)	21 (25.0)	47 (19.3)	96 (55.1)
	Farming	11 (4.2)	20 (23.8)	5 (2.1)	36 (30.1)
	Artisan	1 (0.3)	2 (2.4)	12 (4.9)	15 (7.6)
	Professional	32 (12.4)	13 (15.5)	57 (23.5)	102 (51.4)
	Civil service	134 (52.1)	21 (25.0)	100 (41.1)	255 (118.2)
	Private Employee	51 (19.8)	7 (8.3)	22 (9.1)	80 (37.2)

Source: Field Survey (2015).

Table 1.4 presents a summary of the demographic characteristics of the respondents. The age distribution of the respondents indicates that women in the three geopolitical locations were mainly young adults (twenty-one to thirty years) and older (above fifty years) women. The age group could be tagged as political-active age, being the age group that dominates Nigerian politics and will provide useful information as regards women's political participation. The other age groups (below twenty and thirty-one to fifty years) were students and nursing women. As regards the respondents' marital status, it can be deduced from all the geopolitical zones that the respondents were either married or divorced or widowed, while others are never married. This is expected because majority of them were young adults. This status is likely to allow them to participate freely in partisan politics if they wished.

In addition, table 1.4 shows that the women across the geopolitical zones were religious. There is variation in religion and faith across the geopolitical zones, and this is likely to influence their perception of women's participation in politics. In term of education of respondents, the results from table 1.4 further reveal that in all the three geopolitical zones, women were at least educated up to primary school level. This will, however, give the majority of them opportunity to participate in politics in this country because one of the requirements for any political offices is education, at least, up to secondary school level. At the same time, the distribution reveals that they were mostly degree holders. Table 1.4 indicates that most of the respondents had a given income. This is supported by the fact that the majority were engaged in one employment or the other. The women are engaged in various forms of occupation with the minority being into farming and trading while some were artisans; others were civil servants, professional and private employees.

Chapter 2

Political Participation

Global Trends in Gender Disparity

Over the last twenty years, the world has witnessed a dramatic rise in the number of women serving in elected and appointed political positions. Having more women in politics has been viewed in mostly favourable terms, as leading attention to a broader range of policy issues, including those beneficial to women. It also inspires more significant interests and engagement in politics among women as a group – particularly younger women. Again, it erodes the historical associations previously attached to menfolk in politics and, generates a broader transformation in gender roles. The significant shifts towards greater gender equality in elected offices being experienced in the world is driven by global and grassroots political activities that associate gender matters with dividends of democracy (Krook, 2009; Krook and True, 2012). This balance of power between men and women is an indicator of political development in any human society. Nations that give more opportunities to women in the political space are more likely to provide more chance for democracy to thrive for the common good of humanity.

There is a growing awareness of a backlash and resistance against female leaders, ranging from efforts to subvert the impact of gender quotas to institutional rules and practices hostile to women's participation – and to physical attacks, intimidation and harassment directed at female politicians. It further mirrors attempts to restrict women's policy contributions which deter women's political participation, while reinforcing prevailing gender norms. Such resistance poses a serious threat to democracy and, in turn, questions the progress that has been made globally in terms of incorporating women as political actors.

Interest in the topic of women's participation has stemmed mainly from the observation of a long-standing disparity in the levels and patterns of such participation at different periods of the political cycle. Specifically, by observation over time, the number of women participating in political activities at the local levels as well as those who vote at elections always outweighs those represented in governance and decision-making (Carothers, 2016). This book is concerned with the explanation for this variance and the implications of gender disparity in politics and on women in society at large.

The Afrobarometer survey (2014) by Chingwete, Richmond and Alpin (2014) reveals that women remain at a marked disadvantage compared to men in their economic and social life. This is evident in the wide educational gaps, discrimination at the workplace, courts and among traditional leaders in their communities. Also, according to the same source, women exercise their political rights – participating in campaigns and talking to political leaders – less frequently than men. This disparity impedes economic productivity and results in unequal access to, and unfair distribution of, collective resources which ultimately impair development. Although women play a variety of roles in politics as voters, party members, candidates and officeholders as well as members of civil society organisations (CSOs), there are few exceptions to the laws restricting women's right to stand for election in several Middle Eastern bloc, including Saudi Arabia (Alsharif, 2011) and the United Arab Emirates (Habboush, 2011).

In emerging democracies, women's voting right was only accomplished about 50 years ago, whereas women have had their legal franchise for almost 100 years in established democracies (Kiley, 2014). Differences in rates and patterns of political participation have been observed among groups and explanations offered for this gap range from structural and legal to social or cultural norms (Markham, 2013). These differences are problematic because they point to the inequalities in democracy (Brown, 2014).

Analyses and issues of gender disparity as well as women's participation in politics spread across the globe (Peterson and Runyan, 1999; Akinboye, 2004; Lewu, 2005; Quadri and Agbalajobi, 2013; Quadri, 2013). Political participation is at the heart of democracy because the legitimacy of a democratic government is hinged on it. Democracy presupposes equal opportunities for participation in politics and the decision-making process (Sodaro, 2001). Equal political participation, therefore, is the sine qua non to democracy (Anifowose, 2004). In this view, a society cannot be genuinely democratised without the full and active participation of women. Gender equality and women empowerment are not only forms of human rights, but they are also imperative for achieving inclusive, equitable and sustainable development. These requirements are globally accepted as a prerequisite for achieving development and democratic governance. This entails giving men and women equal voices in decision-making, policy implementation and attaining sustainable development goals (Ezeilo, (2008) cited in Oni and Joshua, 2012, 4). With less than 20 per cent of the world's parliamentary seats occupied by women, it brings to the fore, the need for political parties to do more to ensure support for women's political empowerment (UN Women Nigeria, 2014).

Despite widespread democratisation and the struggle by feminist movements for the integration of gender balance in national politics the world over, low participation of women in politics is still a universal phenomenon, while gender equality and women empowerment remain unresolved universal challenges (Mohammed, 2014; Rai, 2005; Lewu, 2005; Akinboye, 2004; Waylen, 1996). Mohammed (2014) states that even though the global average of women in parliament, women ministers and women heads of state and government have recently increased to 21.8 per cent, this level of progress is insufficient as it masks the deep gender inequalities between and within countries. Consequently, this has resulted in increasing studies (Hillman, 2017; Clayton et al., 2016; Paxton and Hughes, 2016; Clayton, 2015) on the position of women in the political arena in various countries. Studies indicate that women's participation in politics remains an exciting issue of concern at global, regional, national and local levels (Randall, 1987). Studies and debates have focused on such issues as women's political participation, and the effect of such involvements on their social standing and feminism in general. Randall (1987) avouches that much of these debates and studies generally lie within the boundaries of political science, focusing on women's political participation.

WOMEN'S PARTICIPATION REVIEWED

Over the years, there has been increasing research (Olufade, 2013; Peterson and Runyan, 2010; Matland and Montgomery, 2003; Luka, 2011; Dahlerup, 2006; Kinnear, 1997; Beckman and D'Amico, 1994) on the position of women in the political arena in various countries across the world. Political researchers and feminists alike have aired their views in this regard (Birt, 2000). Available studies on this issue indicate that women's participation in politics remains an exciting issue and concern at global, regional, national and even local levels (Randall, 1987). Findings in existing literature, however, show a significantly low level of participation on the part of women and lack of their inclusion in governance. The general argument is, although women constitute half of the world's population, they are mostly ignored when it comes to decisions that concern them and their presence in the political setting is not a fair representation of the their percentage in Nigeria and in the world (Aina, 2012; Randall, 1987). Interestingly, 'The UN Women' (2017) specifically gave a statistical estimate that as of June 2016, only 22.8 per cent of all national parliamentarians were women. According to them, it is a slow increase from 11.3 per cent in 1995. 'The UN Women' also affirms that, globally, there are thirty-eight states in which women account for less than 10 per cent of parliamentarians in the single or lower house as of June 2016. However, 'The UN Women' (2017) observed that there are four countries: Haiti, Micronesia, Qatar and Vanuatu – which were yet to elect any female legislators. In other words, women representation according to studies so far is still below the 30 per cent minimum representation proposition in the affirmative action plan on women by the Convention on the Elimination of All Forms of Discrimination against Women (CEDAW).This is except for the two countries – Rwanda and Bolivia (Inter-Parliamentary Union, 2017) that have achieved gender parity in their national parliaments. With all intent and purpose, this is highly unfair to women-folk as it constitutes an infraction on their fundamental rights. Various studies have covered the entire history of women's struggle on the political scene.

Existing literature shows a significantly low level of women's participation in politics, while also vividly demonstrating their exclusion – or limited participation – in governance. The argument is, despite constituting half of the world's population, women's presence in the political setting is not a fair representation of their percentage in Nigeria and around the world. Hence women are mostly ignored when it comes to decision-making (Aina, 2012; Randall, 1987). Inter-Parliamentary Union (2017) based on information provided by National Parliaments by 1 January 2017, reveals that the World Average Percentage of women in both Houses combined is 23.3 per cent. Africa has 23.6 per cent in both Houses. It is important to note that Rwanda is ahead of the United States in gender equality (Paquette, 2015) with 64 per cent of this African nation's politicians being women compared to 19 per cent of the United States.

Various studies have covered the history of women's struggle on the political scene (Pogoson, 2012, 2013; Okoosi-Simbine, 2012; Osinulu and Mba, 1996). Sapiro (1983) argues that women were not entirely restricted in politics before the advent of colonialism, which arrived with women visibility, from the era of a modern political campaign. This view is supported by many scholars who analysed the visible involvement of women in struggles or movements, especially in the colonial era (Mba1982, 1990; Mama, 1995). Ogundipe (1985) avers that though the role of women in politics in Africa today is negligible, avenues existed traditionally for their political participation. It was such that female traditional rulers before, and in, colonial Nigeria were recognised for not only their political powers but also for their diplomatic manoeuvres; as with South African women who also played huge roles in the ANC during the apartheid regime (Geisler, 2004).

Markham (2013) observes that global conversations on women's political participation have been taking place for almost forty years. That started with the adoption of the Convention on the Elimination of All Forms of

Discrimination against Women (CEDAW) which opened for signature, ratification and accession in December 1965 and entered into force on 4 January 1969. It continued with the Beijing Declaration and Platform for Action of September 1995 and the UN's Millennium Development Goals (MDGs) – a landmark commitment entered into by world leaders in the year 2000 (and up to the 2030 Agenda for Sustainable Development) aimed at transforming our world – a resolution adopted on 25 September 2015. He further argues that through the conferences, declarations and action plans, there was a consensus that women should be able to play equal roles with men in politics.

Globally, there is a shortage of literature that addresses gaps explicitly in women's political participation concerning data, but there exist studies that examine gender gaps in politics. Previous research on gender gaps in political participation among Western industrialised nations has offered at least two sets of explanations. First, researchers found that the gap is significant due to systematic individual-level differences between men and women in terms of socioeconomic resources. They found that women are less likely to engage in politics because of their lower access to such resources (Schlozman et al., 1999, 1994). Also, women are more likely to be burdened with house and care work, placing further demands on their time and resources, leaving them less available for political participation (Burns, 2007). Thus, factors such as employment, education, marital status and parental status are found to accentuate the gender gap in political participation (Burns, 2007; Harrison and Munn, 2007). While there has been some progress on women's political participation globally, the numbers of women heads of states or governments have remained relatively low as presented in UN Women (2017) showing women in the highest positions in states across the globe. Other research findings suggest there is an independent influence of attitudes on participation, regardless of socioeconomic resources. Political engagement requires motivation and interest (Inglehart and Norris, 2003). A piece of research carried out in the United States suggests that women's low levels of political information, interest and efficacy are essential explanations for a gender gap, independent of other characteristics (Verba et al., 1997).

Women's lack of political interest and information may be rooted in the social processes of gender socialisation, in the interplay between children and adults (Burns, 2007; Lovenduski, 2005; Rapoport, 1981; Verba et al., 1997). Women are socialised towards a gender role that is passive, private, rule-abiding and compassionate, while men are oriented towards leadership, public roles, autonomy and self-reliance (Brownmiller, 1984; Fox and Lawless, 2004; West and Zimmerman, 1987). This socialisation concept and process may contribute to women's lower levels of political engagement (Atkeson and Rapoport, 2003; Rapoport, 1981) with differences in political attitudes and participation beginning early in life (Fridkin and

Kenney, 2007; Hooghe and Stolle, 2004) and continuing throughout life (Alwin et al., 1991). Thus, controlling for political attitudes has also been found to substantially mediate gender differences in political participation (Verba et al., 1997).

Whether the explanations for gender gaps in participation from Western democracies can be extended to Sub-Saharan African nations remains unclear. Participation may follow different patterns in fragile, new democracies compared to established democracies (Bratton, 1999). Research explaining gender gaps in political participation across African nations is minimal, and the Western-based measures of individual socioeconomic and attitudinal explanations of the gender gap may have to be reconsidered. More generally, Dalton et al. (2009, 72) conclude that 'democratic institutions facilitate the translation of individual resources into political action'. This conclusion suggests that socioeconomic characteristics will have a more substantial effect on engagement in political activities in affluent democratic societies than in more deprived, less democratic societies. Bratton's (1999) study of Zambia shows that the standard socioeconomic status and political attitude variables have little explanatory power on political participation.

Looking at the experiences of women in Sub-Saharan Africa exemplifies why standard accounts may not hold. For example, women's participation in the economy is not as strongly linked to control or autonomy as it might be in Western nations (Geisler, 2004). More specifically, Western colonial culture emphasised the ideal of the 'real housewife', with women as the primary providers of unpaid family labour and men as public, political figures (Geisler, 2004). However, in reality, Sub-Saharan African women were pressured to remain active in the formal (and informal) economy – typically without supportive rights. This situation has contributed to a type of de facto economic marginalisation that may be independent of employment status. It is further exacerbated by the fact that unemployment hits African women harder than men (McEwan, 2000).

In terms of marital roles, colonialism sometimes inadvertently made marriage more financially advantageous to women by changing divorce laws to reflect Western values (Geisler, 2004). However, women may still struggle under customary marriage arrangements that offer them few rights but a lower status (McEwan, 2000). In some ways, these mirror the Western stories about women's lower access to resources as these findings show that African women have unequal access to education. There is evidence of a positive relationship between education and support for democracy (Evans and Rose, 2007; Lindberg, 2004), but in other ways, it highlights the ways women's and men's negotiation of work and family roles may be quite different. Thus, it is unclear whether standard controls substantially mediate gender gaps among the nations investigated.

The map of women in politics does provide both the country ranking and statistics on ministerial appointments, parliamentary representation and other women in political leadership positions.

'The Women in Politics 2017 Map, created by the Inter-Parliamentary Union (IPU) and UN Women, depicts global rankings of women in the executive and legislative branches of government as of 1 January 2017.' At both regional and national levels, the map reveals unequal access and does not seem to support the possible attainment of the Sustainable Development Goals (SDGs). With limited growth in women's representation, the advancement of gender equality and the success of the SDGs are jeopardised. 'The 2017 edition of the map shows a slight drop in the number of countries with a woman Head of State or Head of Government from 2015 figures (from 19 to 17)' (UN Women, 2017). The data show an increase in women appointments or elections as either Head of State or Head of Government (from 8 to 17) (UN Women, 2017).

According to Stange and Oyster (2011) since 1950, apart from appointees of monarchs, only about eighty women have served as heads of government. Until recently, the majority of women who were able to become influential presidents did so through familial ties (UN Women, 2017).

In Asia, almost all women leaders come from political dynasties (Markham, 2013, 5). In Latin America, women typically come to power in the place of an assassinated husband or through other family connections (Markham, 2013, 5). Although it remains a challenge, the trend seems to be slowly changing. In 2016, Theresa May became the United Kingdom's second female prime minister. Estonia, Taiwan and the Marshall Island all elected their first female prime ministers in 2016. Since 2006, nine women have come to power in Latin America, Africa and Europe, mostly without family connections. Latin America has had the highest number of female presidents, Michelle Bachelet of Chile, Cristina Fernández de Kirchner of Argentina, Laura Chinchilla Miranda of Costa Rica and Dilma Rousseff of Brazil. As at 2015, Africa had two female presidents, Ellen Johnson Sirleaf of Liberia and Joyce Banda of Mali, neither of whom came from political families – nor did President Dalia Grybauskaité of Lithuania or Atifete Jahjaga of Kosovo. Out of the 152 states identified, 11 had women heads of state giving a percentage of 7.2 and 11 had women heads of government out of 193, which is 5.7 per cent. Two countries have the heads of states as the heads of government. HS means Head of State, while HG means Head of Government and those HS/HG means the Head of State is the same as the Head of Government. The countries are Bangladesh (HG), Chile (HS/HG), Croatia (HS), Estonia (HS), Germany (HG), Liberia (HS/HG), Lithuania (HS), Malta (HS), Marshall Islands (HS/HG), Mauritius (HS), Namibia (HG), Nepal (HS), Norway (HG), Poland (HG), Republic of Korea (HS/HG), Switzerland (HS/HG) and United Kingdom (HG) (UN Women, 2017).

Another measure of women's executive leadership is the number of cabinet or ministry positions. The map gives details of the ranking of women in ministerial positions according to the percentage reflecting appointments up to 1 January 2017. Bulgaria, France and Nicaragua are ranked highest at 52.9 per cent. Sweden follows this with 52.2 per cent, then Canada with 51.7 per cent and then Slovenia with 50.0 per cent (UN Women, 2017). There is a decrease in number from what we had in 2015. In 2015, Finland ranked highest with 62.5 per cent, followed by countries such as Cabo Verde, Sweden, France and Liechtenstein –ranging from 50 to 59.9 per cent (UN Women, 2015). Nigeria is ranked 124 with 12.0 per cent, having three women ministers out of twenty-five given the ranking on the women in politics map of 2017. The following countries are the least in the ranking with no woman occupying ministerial positions: Vanuatu, Tonga, Saudi Arabia, San Marino, Palau, Pakistan, Kiribati, Hungary, Guinea-Bissau, Comoros, Brunei Darussalam, Belize, Azerbaijan (UN Women, 2017). The women in politics map of 2017 reveals that there are 53 women speakers of parliament out of 278 (19.1%). The countries with women speakers are Antigua and Barbuda, Argentina, Austria (2 chambers), Bahamas, Bangladesh, Barbados, Belgium, Belize, Bolivia (Plurinational State of), Bosnia and Herzegovina, Botswana, Bulgaria, Denmark, Dominica, Dominican Republic, Ecuador, Equatorial Guinea, Fiji, Finland, Gabon, Germany, Iceland, India, Italy, Lao People's Democratic Republic, Latvia, Lesotho, Mauritius, Mozambique, Namibia, Nepal, Netherlands (2 chambers), Peru, Russian Federation, Rwanda, Saint Lucia, Serbia, Singapore, South Africa (2 chambers), Spain, Suriname, Swaziland, Syrian Arab Republic, Trinidad and Tobago (2 chambers), Turkmenistan, Uganda, United Arab Emirates, Vietnam and Zimbabwe (UN Women, 2017). Out of the 595 parliaments, 158 have women deputy speakers who are 26.6 per cent. And of the 230 chambers in 172 countries for which information is available, as of 1s January 2017, 102 have at least one woman deputy speaker (UN Women, 2017).

Even in countries with a high number of women in national office, women generally do not have high levels of participation at the local level, and particularly not in mayoral positions. Regional averages for the proportion of women in parliament reveal that the world average of women in a single house or lower house is 23.4 per cent. In contrast, that of the upper house or senate is 22.9 per cent. In Sub-Saharan Africa, women in a single house or lower house are 23.8 per cent, while for the upper house or senate are 22.1 per cent.

The account of women in parliament ranking – based on available information as at 1 January 2017 – reveals that Rwanda is ranked first with 61.3 per cent women in the lower house and 38.5 per cent women in the upper house or senate (UN Women, 2017). Bolivia follows with 53.1 per cent in the lower house and 47.2 per cent in the upper house or senate. Nigeria is ranked 180, with 5.6 per cent women in the lower house and 6.5 per cent in the upper house or senate (UN Women, 2017). There is a decline from what was in existence in 2015 with 6.7 and 6.4 per cent in the lower and upper house or senate, respectively (UN Women, 2015). This decline could be as a result of the political terrain that was in existence during the 2015 general elections.

INTERNATIONAL EFFORTS FOR THE INCLUSION OF WOMEN IN POLITICS

Parity in political participation has become a central goal of national and international organisations around the globe (Cole, 2011; Krook, 2015). Several efforts made by international organisations to enhance the participation of women in politics, given the recognition of women's political rights, reflect this goal (Anderlini, 2007; Tripp et al., 2009). Moreover, the fact that women effectively constitute half of the world's population and half of each nation's population (Karam, 1998), justifies this as a worthwhile ambition or desirable agendum. This right to participate in politics is enshrined in many international laws and treaties, which include conventions, protocols and international agreements. The international instruments that have addressed women's equal political participation, like Article 21 of the Universal Declaration of Human Rights (United Nations, 1948), expresses that everyone has the right to take part in his or her country's governance. Also, Article 7 of the Convention on the Elimination of All Forms of Discrimination against Women, under the UN resolution 34/180, declares that there should be no form of discrimination against women in terms of equal political participation. This article calls on all state parties to take all measures necessary to protect women against inequity. Additionally, the UN Security Council Resolution 1325 calls on all actors involved in negotiating peace agreements or writing constitutions to ensure that women's equitable participation is adequately addressed. There are other methods of ensuring political equality in the International Covenant on Civil and Political Rights (Articles 2 and 7), the third Millennium Development Goal as well as the Beijing Declaration and Platform for Action (1995); however, none of these has helped women succeed in attaining the target of 30 per cent of seats in parliament.

Hamadeh-Banerjee and Oquist (2000) argue that the movement for gender equality in the late twentieth century is closely linked to the human rights movements. They, however, state that the concept of women's participation in governance on an equal footing with men dates back to at least the fourth century. In their view, women were openly active in the political system up until the period of rebirth of democracy in the new United States and later in Great Britain, which led to the disenfranchisement of women.

Further, Hamadeh-Banerjee and Oquist (2000) state that the worldwide movement for women's equality took new impetus from the birth of the United Nations to the promulgation of the 1948 Universal Declaration of Human Rights which enshrined 'the equal rights of men and women', including the right to participate in government (Krook, 2015) (see Universal Declaration of Human Rights, Act 2). However, it remains worthy of note that it was not until the preparations for the First World Conference on Women, which took place in Mexico City in 1975 that the international community took systematic stock of the inequalities that kept rendering women second-class citizens in every country. Krook (2015, 1) notes that it was at this world conference on women, that delegates called on governments to 'establish goals, strategies and timelines' to increase 'the number of women in elective and appointive public offices and functions at all levels' (see also World Plan of Action).

In 1979, women's right took a codified form in international human rights instruments, while the CEDAW (often described as an International Bill of right for women) has been in force only since 1982 (Peterson and Runyan 1999, 11; Akiyode-Afolabi and Arogundade, 2003; Akinboye 2004, 13; Oyekanmi 2004, 44; Kukah 2003, 163; Rai 2005, 3; Omotola 2007, 33). Migirou (1998) states that CEDAW has received particular attention because it brings together, in a single comprehensive human right treaty, the provisions of previous UN instruments concerning discrimination based on sex and extends them further to create a tool dedicated to the elimination of all forms of discrimination against women. The Declaration on the Elimination of Discrimination against Women expressed the concern that extensive discrimination against women continued to exist despite instruments such as the Charter of the United States, the Universal Declaration of Human Rights and the International Convention on Human Rights (Isa, 2003). In summary, the CEDAW adopted in 1979 by the UN General Assembly and ratified by nearly every member state, reiterated that women have the right 'to hold public office and perform all public functions at all levels of government' (See Convention on the Elimination of All Forms of Discrimination against Women, Article 7).

Sapiro (1983) argues that women were not entirely restricted in the area of politics even before colonialism. She talks about the visibility of women from the innovative beginnings of modern political campaign. The literature supports this view by analysing the visible involvement of women in struggles or movements, especially in the era of foreign rule or pre-democracy. Ogundipe (1985) argues that though the roles of women in politics in Africa today are negligible, avenues existed traditionally for their political participation. For example, female traditional rulers in precolonial or colonial Nigeria were not only recognised for their political powers but also for their vicious diplomatic manoeuvres. In South Africa, women played a massive role in the African National Congress (ANC) during the obnoxiously opprobrious apartheid regime (Geisler, 2004).

Today, in many parts of the world, the level of women's participation in politics and public offices varies. Although the general view is that women are still stifled in their attempt to seek elective and appointive offices (Witaker, 1999), it is also important to acknowledge that in some cases, a lot has been achieved in recent times compared to what was in the ascendancy. There are variations in the average percentages of women parliamentarians in each region of the world. As of June 2017, these were (single, lower and upper houses combined): Nordic countries, 41.7 per cent; Americas, 28.1 per cent; Europe including Nordic countries, 26.5 per cent; Europe (excluding Nordic countries) 25.3 per cent; Sub-Saharan Africa, 23.6 per cent; Asia, 19.4 per cent; the Arab States, 17.4 per cent; and the Pacific, 17.4 per cent (UN Women, 2017). According to Gisela (2004), in 1999–2000, France embarked on a radical reform to address the issues of gender parity in politics; the parliament passed a constitutional revision and a set of legislations in order to achieve this goal.

Although Africa as a continent has produced and adopted many worthy policies and declarations (some of which look radical and visionary), there is little cause to celebrate just yet as the objectives are yet to be realised (Mama, 2008). On the upside, South Africa is an exception to this rule (Geisler, 2004). Analysis shows that apart from a high representation of women in general – which even surpasses the 30 per cent minimum benchmark – this representation includes various substantial positions. Thus, it showcases a strong inclination towards true gender parity in politics (Geisler, 2004). Women have also been given opportunities in places such as Uganda, Mozambique, Rwanda, Tanzania and Seychelles to have an average of 30 per cent. In Lesotho, 58 per cent of local government positions are filled by women. Exceptional cases are Liberia and Malawi (South African Development Community (SADC, 2012)).

Based on these manifestations and more, feminists have concluded that women have been ignored and are still largely ignored in political matters (Aina, 2012). Nigeria, as a signatory state to CEDAW in fulfilment of its obligations under Article 18, submitted its fourth and fifth Periodic Country Reports covering 1994 to 2002, outlining progress recorded in the implementation of the convention. CEDAW is yet to be domesticated in Nigeria – more than twenty-seven years after its ratification.

In democratic settings like Nigeria, political parties are regarded as critical channels through which access to government and active participation in the decision-making process is achievable, particularly by women. It has been implied that for women to participate better in the political arena, they have to be active members of political parties (Goetz and Hassim, 2003). By implication, parties can either create opportunities or barriers for women (Aina, 2012). Various studies looked into techniques for selection or elimination of candidates: the structure of the parties, the driving force behind the party, their role and the level of discipline, as well as the level of transparency in activities and dissemination of information (Akinyode-Afolabi and Arogundade, 2003). Although Matland and Studler (1996) suggest that proportional representation in party politics and electoral system is the key to improving the position of women in governance, Darcey, Welch and Clarke (1994) contradict this. They find that within the US context, women are not as discriminated against. In this regard, the political party structure is very much accommodating for women; yet, a level of underrepresentation to an extent still exists. Badmus (2006) does not rule out the negative role of political parties. However, he insists that the primary factor influencing the position of women is their lack of organisation and solidarity (Geisler, 2004). This leaves a puzzle for the real reason for underrepresentation and in a way, casts doubt on the view that proportional representation in the electoral system automatically leads to better representation of women.

In order to bring about a turnaround for women, there is an increasing number of international organisations and national women's movements as well as policies in place to fight for a better representation of women in politics. This is evident in the reports of the UN resolution on the End of Decade for Women (1976–1985), the Nairobi Conference of 1985 and the Beijing Conference of 1995 among others. Consequently, various countries have adopted, or adapted to the recommendations of these conferences in ways of policy documents, for example, the National Policy on Women of 2001 in Nigeria and the National Gender Policy of 2006. Despite these efforts, the level of women's participation in politics today across the country is still insignificant.

THE CONVENTION ON THE ELIMINATION OF DISCRIMINATION AGAINST WOMEN (CEDAW)

According to the UN (1999); UN Women (2001), the International Bill of Human Rights – combined with related human rights treaties – lays down a comprehensive set of rights to which all persons, including women, are entitled. However, UN (1999) and UN Women (2001) argue that the status of women as human beings has not sufficiently guaranteed them the enjoyment of their internationally agreed rights. This has led to the Commission on the Status of Women (CSW) to define and elaborate on the general guar-antees of non-discrimination in these instruments from a gender perspective. This has resulted in several vital declarations and conventions that protect and promote the human rights of women by the CSW. Between 1949 and 1959, the UN Commission on the Status of Women elaborated the following Conventions: Conventions on the Political Rights of Women (as adopted by the General Assembly – GA – in 1952); the Convention on the Nationality of Married Women (adopted in 1957); the Convention on Consent to mar-riage, Minimum Age for Marriage and Registration of Marriages (adopted in 1962); and the Recommendation on Consent to Marriage, Minimum Age for Marriage and Registration of Marriages (adopted in 1965).

As noted by the UN Women (2001), each of these treaties protected and promoted the rights of women in areas in which the commission considered such rights to be particularly vulnerable. It was believed that except in those areas, women's rights were best protected and promoted by the general human rights treaties. Although these instruments reflected the growing sophistication of the UN system with regard to the protection and promotion of women's human rights, the approach they reflected was fragmentary, as they failed to deal with the discrimination against women in a comprehensive way. There was concern, however, that the general human rights regime was not working as well as it should, to protect and promote the rights of women. The UN (2001) General Assembly, on 5 December 1963, adopted its resolu-tion 1921 (XVIII), in which it requested the Economic and Social Council to invite the CSW to prepare a draft standard that would combine in a single international standards articulating the equal rights of men and women. This process was supported throughout by women activists within and outside the UN system. Drafting the declaration (by a committee selected from within the CSW) began in 1965, with the Declaration on the Elimination of Discrimination against Women ultimately adopted by the GA on 7 November 1967 (UN, 2001). In the view of the UN (2001), the declaration could amount only to a statement of moral and political intent without the contractual force of a treaty; yet, its drafting was a complicated process. It included:

Article 5, concerning sex roles and stereotyping
Article 6, separation of the exploitation of women
Article 7, relating to non-discrimination of women to participate in political and public life
Article 8, ensuring women can participate on equal terms with men in inter-national governance.

In many parts of the world, the 1960s saw the emergence of a new con-sciousness of the patterns of discrimination against women and a rise in the number of organisations committed to combating the effect of such discrimination (UN, 2001). This brought into the fore the adverse impact of some development policies on women. In 1972, the CSW considered the possibility of preparing a binding treaty that would give normative force to the provisions of the declaration and decided to request the secretary general to call upon UN member states to transmit their views on such a proposal (UN, 2001). At its twenty-fifth session in 1974, the CSW decided to prepare single, comprehensive and internationally binding instruments to eliminate discrimination against women. At the special ceremony that took place at the Copenhagen Conference on 17 July 1980, sixty-four states signed at the convention and two submitted their instruments of ratification (UN, 2001). On 3 September 1981, thirty days after the twentieth member state had ratified it, the convention entered into force – faster than any previous human rights convention had done, thus bringing to a climax, United Nations' efforts to codify comprehensively international legal standards for women (UN, 2001).

The UN (2001) states in a landmark decision for women that the General Assembly, acting without a vote, adopted on 6 October 1999 a 21-article Optional Protocol to the CEDAW and called on all states sympathetic to the convention to become party to the new instrument as soon as possible. By ratifying the Optional Protocol, the UN (2001) notes that a state recognises the competence of the CEDAW to receive and consider complaints from individuals or groups within its jurisdiction. The Optional Protocol became enforceable on 22 December 2000, following the ratification of the tenth state party to the convention. The entry into force of the Optional Protocol puts it on an equal footing with International Covenant on Civil and Political Rights; the Convention on the Elimination of All Forms of Racial Discrimination; and the Convention against Torture and other Forms of Cruel, Inhuman or Degrading Treatment or Punishment, which all have communication procedures (UN, 2001). Isa (2003, 294) states that 'the Optional Protocol to the Convention on the Elimination of All Forms of Discrimination against Women has significantly enriched the protection mechanism of women's rights at the international level'.

AFRICAN UNION MECHANISM TO ENSURE WOMEN'S POLITICAL PARTICIPATION

The African Union (AU) in recognition of the importance of women's participation in politics, and to make democracy effective, has adopted to this end, some mechanisms to foster women's political participation. According to Martin (2013), women's equal participation leads to governments being more representative and accountable. However, this research notes that inadequate participation by women in the decision-making process is a reality. In similar a tone, Martin (2013) argues that, though in many countries legislation has changed, customs have not and because of this, women's struggle for political power continues.

The growing recognition of the leadership role of women in all spheres of development, including their participation in decision-making at the international, regional and national levels, according to Martin (2013), is reflected in the creation of platforms of action related to gender. It is in this context that the AU has developed a gender policy and other instruments that focus on addressing gender inequalities and adopted a new resolution in 2011 that calls on countries to take concrete steps to increase women's political participation and leadership. According to the MDGs 2012 *Report*, the proportion of seats held by women in single or lower houses of national parliaments in North Africa rose from 3 per cent in 2000 to 11 per cent in 2012. In Sub-Saharan Africa, the proportion of seats rose from 13 per cent in 2000 to 20 per cent in 2012. Rwanda, one of the Sub-Saharan states, has the highest number of women in parliament (56 per cent after the 2008 elections) in Africa, and the world. This sustained progress is mostly due to the existence of quota (Martin, 2013). He further states that, though quotas are important, they need to be accompanied by other factors such as societal support for women's representation and structural change in the political system towards more public participation and accountability. Further, Martin (2013) observes that the AU's approach to the advancement of women's right and gender equality has been informed by the UN frameworks and instruments.

The AU is composed of fifty member states and seven regional economic communities (RECs) representing Africa's sub-regions, as well as crucial programmes and instruments such as New Partnership for Africa's Development (NEPAD) and the African Peer Review Mechanism (APRM), all of which Martin (2013) states, reflect the commitment of Africa's leaders to gender equality. At the national level, the AU is involved in legislative reviews and amendment processes.

At regional levels, the AU has encouraged its member states to adopt, ratify, implement and domesticate treaties, conventions and decisions; it has established a consensus on gender equality issues among member states and plays a vital role in supporting research on gender issues and collecting regional data as well as statistics. At a sub-regional level, the AU has guided the RECs in complementing and harmonising global and regional frameworks by integrating and translating various resolutions and commitments into their policies and plans of action. Of the six pillars of AU gender mainstreaming, four specifically address the issues of gender disparity. The Reporting framework – The Solemn Declaration on Gender Equality in Africa (SDGEA), was adopted by the AU heads of state and government in their July 2004 summit, and it is divided into six thematic areas of action: Health, peace and security, governance, human rights, education and women empowerment. The policy framework – the AU Gender Policy and Action Plan, was approved in 2009 and adopted in 2010, The Gender Policy provides the basis for the elimination of barriers to gender equality. It fosters the reorientation of existing institutions by making use of gender-disaggregated data and performance indicators.

The implementation framework – the African Women's Decade – was a declaration of the Women's Decade (2010–2020) which provides a road map for the realisation of the objectives for the Decade and it is intended to strengthen the directorate. This is done through the funding of initiatives and plan for the Decade as well as the Women and Gender Development Directorate (WGDD). It will also establish a coherent dialogue on gender. The last is the financing mechanism – the Fund for African Women – which was created as a single mechanism to ensure policy implementation as well as effective mainstreaming of gender in policies, institutions and programmes at regional, national and local levels. Although all these instruments have enabled the member states and the RECs to advance their legal, administrative and institutional frameworks to make progress on women's rights and gender equality, many lack political backing and resources, inhibiting the tools and the implementation of strategies. Martin (2013) reiterates that most instruments adopted by the AU since 2003 make provision for gender equality and women's participation. In addition to the provision of these instruments and provisions for gender equality, the AU has launched the Common African Position (CAP) on the Post-2015 Development Agenda. The CAP identifies the importance of actions to:

> enhance occupational mobility and eliminate gender-based wage inequality; ensure access to and ownership of land and other productive assets, credit and extension services, training; eradicating all forms of violence against women and children, and harmful practices such as female genital mutilation (FGM) and early marriage; and eliminating gender-based discrimination in political, economic and public decision-making processes. (Mohammed, 2014, 12)

At the global level, the post-2015 development planning process, Mohammed (2014) explains, provides a unique opportunity for Africa to plan for the massive investments required for broad-based inclusive, sustainable development. It offers the impetus as Mohammed (2014) reaffirms, for Africa to take the driver's seat in designing the next global development agenda, and changes the development discourse to a new frontier by shifting the focus to economic transformation and social justice, ending extreme poverty and putting the planet on a course for sustainable development.

This shift, Mohammed (2014) believes, allows casting a strong foundation for the visions of Africa's Agenda, 2063. According to Mohammed (2014), defining the next development agenda though daunting, is inspiring and a historic task for the United Nations and its member states. He is also of the opinion that, the United Nations has a solemn responsibility to the international community to go beyond existing geopolitical and ideological divides and come together to shape a bold and ambitious agenda. This, Mohammed (2014) believes, will provide a terrific opportunity to empower women, everywhere, especially in Africa.

NATIONAL GENDER MACHINERY FOR PROMOTING GENDER EQUALITY

The United Nations has sponsored activities aimed at promoting equality between men and women such as the proclamation of 1975 at the International Women's year (Pietila and Vicker, 1993), and other International Conferences on Women (Karl, 1995). All of these conferences, Isa (2003) contends, have been significant steps leading to the recognition and achievements of women's rights. The endeavour to enhance women's participation by the international community has not been limited to state actors and agencies of the United Nations (Cole, 2011). The Beijing Platform for Action emphasised that women's equal participation was not only a demand for justice or democracy but can be seen as a necessary condition for their interest to be taken into account. Without the perspective of women at all levels of decision-making, the goals of equality, development and peace cannot be achieved. The national machinery has probably been the most affected, while the women's world conference has impacted government institutions significantly. The Mexico Conference gave birth to Women's Desk popularly known as Women's Bureau, which between Copenhagen and Nairobi (Women in Development WID Era) remained dormant and only transformed into Departments and Ministries with decision-making policy mandates in the 1990s. Gender and Development (GAD) and the Beijing Conference are the climax. To achieve full equality between men and women, the government continues to commit themselves to setting up institutional structures to promote women's advancement and enjoyment of their human rights. These structures are referred to as national machinery for the advancement of women.

The framework at the national level can be discussed at four levels:

Government Level

Many governments now have key ministries dedicated to advancing gender equality and women empowerment. There is a ministry for women's affair and social development in Nigeria. There are also gender focal points in ministries at national and local levels. The role of the ministry of women's affairs is that of coordinating and facilitating the implementation of government policy and programmes on women. The gender focal points implement gender programmes in their respective departmental programmes.

Legislative Level

In almost all countries, the National Assembly has multiparty parliamentary women caucuses that work together to ensure that parliaments embrace gender equality. This group of women is also engaged in monitoring government's implementation of national and international commitments made on gender issues.

Statutory Bodies Level

There are statutory bodies established by Acts of Parliament to ensure gender equality within national jurisdiction, often referred to as the National Gender Commission. The commission has responsibility to raise awareness on gender issues through public education, and it is aimed at strengthening gender equality and women empowerment in the country. The Gender Commission also monitors implementation of government policy and commitment to gender equality. It also plays an advisory role to the government on gender issues.

Civil Society Level

The civil society plays a pivotal role in awareness creation on gender equality and women empowerment. It also acts as a watchdog over the government's actions in implementing gender equality.

Chapter 3

A History of Women in Political Activism and Governance in Nigeria

Precolonial societies did not conform to modernisation theorists' understanding of 'traditional' societies. Many studies of precolonial African societies have described societies which were dynamic and developing (Rodney, 1972). This is despite the problems in analysing precolonial and colonial periods (because knowledge is so dependent on mediation by colonial texts and sources). The dynamics of change varied in intensity from one society to another (Mba, 1982). While gender relations in precolonial African society were not characterised by equality, they often entailed greater independence than 'modern' societies, with men and women having different but, in many ways, complementary roles. Women often had a degree of autonomy and control over their lives with high levels of solidarity along the lines of gender, as much social stratification was based on gender (Staudt, 1989, cited in Waylen, 1996). Much of this autonomy stemmed from the access to, and control over, economic resources which many women exercised in different forms, although this was on unequal terms with men.

The economic status (enjoyed by women) which came through their role in production often brought with its certain political rights, particularly in those societies which permitted them to accumulate wealth (Johnson, 1986, cited in Waylen, 1996). Women usually had political control over some areas of activity, be it farming, marketing, trading or household and family affairs; had political institutions (usually councils) to decide how to rule in their affairs or to influence the affairs of men and are not subject to general control by men as much as they were autonomous in their areas of responsibility. This was often expressed through various women's groups and networks organised around kinship, age, culture and production. While never acting on equal terms with men, women often had well-defined political roles and structures which allowed them a certain degree of power and control within the society. Women could rarely become chiefs in their rights, for example, Mba (1982) noted that Yoruba women occupied the highest public office in the past but not in the nineteenth century. They were allowed formal direct participation in the political process through the institution of Iyalode and the Erelu Ogboni and as palace priestesses in Oyo as well as Ogboni in Abeokuta and Ijebuland. They were involved in judicial processes affecting the whole society; effectively controlled their affairs and were also involved in executive responsibilities covering the whole society.

Van Allen (1972) has analysed the female networks of political organisation and solidarity among the Igbo. The women had their structures of power which dealt with issues that concerned them, including the regulation of markets. These structures were headed by a female official, the Omu, who had her council of elders paralleling that of the male official, the Obi. Meetings named 'Mikiri' were held where women could resolve issues arising from their roles particularly as traders, but also as farmers, wives and mothers. Women could also resort to taking sanctions on other women and men to resolve individual or collective grievances.

Table 3.1   Statistics of Women Traditional Rulers in Precolonial Days

S/N	Name	Town/ Village	Current LGA	Present State	Type of Rule	Date
1.	Luwo Gbadiaya	Ife	Ife Central LG	Osun	Ooni of Ife	pre-colonial days
2.	Iyayun	Oyo	Oyo LG	Oyo	Alaafin	pre-colonial days
3.	Orompoto	Oyo	Oyo LG	Oyo	Alaafin	pre-colonial days
4.	Jomijomi	Oyo	Oyo LG	Oyo	Alaafin	pre-colonial days
5.	Jepojepo	Oyo	Oyo LG	Oyo	Alaafin	pre-colonial days
6.	Queen Amina	Zauzau		Zaria	Emir	pre-colonial days
7.	Daura	Daura	Daura Emirate	Katsina	Queen	pre-colonial days
8.	Kofono	Daura	Daura Emirate	Katsina	Queen	pre-colonial days
9.	Eye-moi	Akure	Akure	Ondo	Regent-Monarch	pre-colonial days 1705–1735 AD
10.	Ayo-Ero	Akure	Akure	Ondo	Regent-Monarch	pre-colonial days 1850–51 AD
11.	Gulfano	Daura	Daura Emirate	Katsina	Queen	pre-colonial days
12.	Yawano	Daura	Daura Emirate	Katsina	Queen	pre-colonial days
13.	Yakania	Daura	Daura Emirate	Katsina	Queen	pre-colonial days
14.	Walsam	Daura	Daura Emirate	Katsina	Queen	pre-colonial days
15.	Cadar	Daura	Daura Emirate	Katsina	Queen	pre-colonial days
16.	Agagri	Daura	Daura Emirate	Katsina	Queen	pre-colonial days
17.	Queen Kanbasa	Bony	Bony LG	Rivers	Queen	pre-colonial days

Source: Ngara and Ayabam (2013).

In the northern part of Nigeria, especially before Islamisation of the society, women took an active part in politics as some of them were war leaders such as Queens Amina and Nzingha according to Diop (cited in Omitola and Goke, 1998). While it is impossible to generalise about all precolonial societies, it is possible to argue that, while gender relations were not generally characterised by equality and an absence of male dominance, women often had a degree of autonomy over their lives. The precolonial African woman occupied a complementary position, rather than remaining subordinate to the man. In Nigeria, awareness about the role of women in government gained momentum in the latter half of the 1980s (George-Genyi, 2010). This awareness was further enhanced in 1995 because of the participation of Nigerian women in the international conference on women in Beijing, China (IDEA, 2000). Despite these efforts, it is appropriate to state that the role of women in governance has not been sufficiently emphasised. The position of women in precolonial Nigeria differed across the vast number of ethnic groups in Nigeria.

According to Rojas (1990), 'A woman's position varied according to the kingship structure of the group and the role of women within the economic structure of the society'. Common factors among women of different ethnic groups, however, included the domestically oriented jobs and the range of economic activities that predominate in patriarchal kinship structures in Nigerian societies.

The kinship group expected women who married outside their lineage to give birth to sons to ensure the future of the group (Obadiya, 2009). Furthermore, the position of the young girl improved as she grew older, bore children and earned approval from her older women. This allowed her to spend less time in the home and more time engaging in activities outside the household such as farming and craft-making which allowed her to provide the material resources needed in order to care for her family.

> Like the family and economic structure, the religion of many Nigerian tribal societies confined the position of women as complementary to that of men. However, the fact remains that the societies of precolonial Nigeria believed men were superior to women and to some extent in control of women.

According to Caroline Dennis, 1974 cited in Rojas (1994, 1):

> 'The religion of many Nigerian societies recognised the social importance of women by emphasising the place of female gods of fertility and social peace, but women were also associated with witchcraft which appeared to symbolise the potential social danger of women exercising power uncontrolled by men.'

Women in Nigeria were also part of the socioeconomic and political developments of the many ethnic groups that make up the nation

(Okoronkwo-chukwu, 2013). Many dynasties were founded and nurtured by women who determined the fate of kingdoms as well as men. Amina of Zazzau, whose mother Queen Bakwa Turunku was the founder of the ancient city of Zazzau (modern-day Zaria in Northern Nigeria), inherited her bravery from the latter (Okoronkwo-chukwu, 2013). The story of Queen Amina reminds one of the British Empire and her well-beloved 'Virgin Queen', Elizabeth I. These women were passionate about the enlargement of the territorial borders of their empires and were ready to pay any price to be able to achieve their set goals.

Women held a complementary, rather than a subordinate position to men in indigenous precolonial Nigeria, which based power on seniority rather than gender (Rojas, 1990). Niara Sudarkasa has noted the absence of gender in the pronoun of many Africa languages and the interchangeability of first names among female and male as well as the different traditional culture. This, she argues, has its symbolic implications on the African perspectives by deemphasising gender in relation to seniority and other insignia status (Dennis, 1987, 1). However, despite the lack of emphasis placed on gender by Nigeria's indigenous societies, the state and its bureaucracy tried to dictate the lifestyles of women, endorsing the domesticity of women and the unwaged services they provided for the family. The beginning of colonial rule brought to Africa the European notion that women belonged in the home to nurture the family. At the same time, society expected women to work to complement the efforts of men. The state, therefore, began to change the roles of women through restrictive legislation, limiting their roles in society. Mba (1982) is of the view that colonialism was unfavourable to the development of the women since the administrators treated women and their affairs as though they had been invisible. The restrictions that the colonial government placed on women changed the position of women in indigenous societies. In Nigeria, the colonial state passed legislation restricting women; indirectly preventing them from performing their duties towards their families (Rojas, 1990).

HISTORICAL EVIDENCE IN THE COLONIAL ERA

Conventional Politics had a very narrow and restricted meaning in the colonial context. Colonies were administered bureaucratically, and as they were not run on a liberal democratic model, competitive electoral politics did not function (Waylen, 1996). Except at the lower levels, the colonised – particularly colonised women – were excluded from the running of the colonies. Colonialism brought essential changes, profoundly altering political, social and economic systems. These changes were gendered in crucial ways, and men and women were affected very differently (Tanko and Best, 1990;

Waylen, 1996). The social and economic changes brought about through the colonial imperative of capital accumulation, therefore, had a contradictory impact on women. Many women found that their position worsened, for example, because their control over economic resources such as land was reduced, or their overall workload was increased perhaps because of the absence of male relatives (Waylen, 1996).

With the advent of colonial rule, women lost much of the power they had in the precolonial period, and their indigenous political authority became invisible. Indeed, Staudt (1989, 81) argues that many women initially rejected or withdrew from the state and the redefined political order during the early period of colonial rule. In the later phases of colonialism, women came together to promote their interest and also acted to protect themselves against the encroachments of colonial rule. Parpart (1988, 213) argues that there is clear evidence that the 'most dramatic female opposition to colonial authority was carried out by women where the status differentials of men and women were small enough that it was not unthinkable for women to challenge male authority', and allied to this, women with an independent economic base were often the most successful at challenging colonialism.

Three well-documented instances in the colonial period, where Nigerian women resisted the threat of the imposition of taxes and changes to their control of land and farming practices, are here noted. The 'Women's War' in southern Nigeria is perhaps the best-known example of women's anti-colonial action, which demonstrated the use of traditional forms of protests. The meaning and significance of this event grew to become known to the British as the 'Aba Riots' (Van Allen, 1976).

In 1929, following a decade when British authorities introduced indirect rule and increased controls over cash crop production, the Igbo women believed that they were about to be taxed, despite assurances to the contrary, as households and property were counted and re-counted – and, consider that officials had lied about taxation in the past! Rumours spread quickly through the women's communication networks, and 'Mikiri' meetings took place in market squares. These worries combined with resentment at the arbitrary acts of warrant chiefs who abused their power, for example, by helping themselves to women's produce and by not taking account of women's rights to refuse a particular suitor in marriage. This disquiet culminated in women taking customary action in the form of the women's war. Large numbers of women, wearing loincloths and carrying palm-wrapped sticks, gathered outside the district offices in Owerri and Calabar provinces, 'sat on' the warrant chiefs and burnt their buildings. At the same time, women in many areas attempted to get rid of the native administration. At the height of the disturbances, thousands of women were involved. The British authorities failed to realise that the women were using recognised channels for expressing discontent and reacted harshly to what they considered to be riots of 'frenzied mobs' and over fifty women were killed by troops (Van Allen, 1972, 1976).

Johnson 1986, (cited in Soetan, 1998) documented the ways by which the colonial state through its policies discriminated against women. These included 'refusing women the right to vote until 1954, not appointing them to any important governmental bodies and neglecting their education and employment'. For example, girl children were under-enrolled in educational institutions in Nigeria even as close to independence as of 1951. This became easily seen in the low enrolment figures of girls in secondary schools in Nigeria, which totalled 1,599. This comprised 125 in the North, 477 in the East and 997 in the West (Johnson, 1986, cited in Soetan, 1998).

Similarly, the growth of the cash crop economy further marginalised women's subsistence agricultural production. Women also lacked access to credit and capital required for large-scale trading activities, so, most remained petty traders. Lagos market women under the auspices of the Lagos Market Women's Association (LMWA) under the leadership of Madam Alimotu Pelewura resisted the taxation of women and attempts by the colonial government to enforce price controls in Lagos markets. They organised mass riots to protest the tax proposals. The women delivered a petition containing the thumbprints of several hundreds of them to the colonial administrator in 1940. Pelewura was reported to have turned down an offer to put her on the payroll of the colonial government in order to break the women's solidarity. Thus, the women forcefully resisted the colonial government's price controls of foodstuff.

Other examples of women's anti-colonial activity include their protest of colonial tax policies in Abeokuta under Mrs Funmilayo Ransome-Kuti-led Abeokuta Women's Union in 1947. It was reported that more than 10,000 women kept vigil outside the Alake's palace to protest the taxation of women and the lack of representation of women in government. The women succeeded in getting their demands, including securing or masterminding the abdication of the Alake from the throne (Kolawole et al., 2012).

Women's solidarity organisations also participated actively in the struggle for independence. The LMWA is reported to have contributed to the Worker's Relief Fund to assist workers in the General Strike of 1945, which was called to press the demands for self-government on the colonial government. Elite women such as Lady Oyinkan Abayomi organised female wings of political parties which worked for the enfranchisement of women and their greater participation in government. The Abeokuta Women's Union led by Mrs Funmilayo Ransome-Kuti was also integrated into the male-dominated National Council of Nigeria and Cameroun (NCNC) and Action Group (AG) where they participated in the nationalist struggle.

The extent of the changes inspired many Nigerian women to hold a series of protests throughout the colonial period against particular colonial policies and against colonialism itself. From 1918 till the end of the colonial rule, there were protests against different ordinances: the Native Revenue in South-Western Nigeria, Market Ordinance in Calabar – perhaps the most widespread and significant of these protests were the so-called Aba Women's Riot of 1929 and the Egba Women's Tax Riot of 1946.

Between 1928 and 1930, Aba women rose in a mass protest against the oppressive rule of the colonial government. The women feared that the head-count being carried out by the British was a prelude to women being taxed. The women were unhappy about the over-taxation of their husband and sons, which they felt was pauperising them and causing economic hardship for the entire community (Van Allen, 1972). 'They also resented the British imposition on the community of warrants chiefs, many of whom carried out what the women considered to be abusive and extortionist actions such as obtaining wives without paying full bridewealth, and seizure of property' (Turner and Oshare, 1994).

The Egba women's revolt was a protest to eliminate the flat-rate tax for women; the quest to remove King Ademola as Alake; the abolition of the Sole Native Authority (SNA) system; and the representation/participation of women in a reformed system of administration (Mba, 1982). Unlike the Igbo women in 1929, the Abeokuta women never carried any illegal implements of any sorts which could be construed for weapons. The women used other means including mass demonstration and varieties of traditional tactics with the effective use of new pressure groups. By January 1949, these objectives had been achieved (Mba, 1982).

The Aba Women's Riot of 1929 and the Egba Women's Revolt of 1946 consequently heralded the first female politicians and activists of modern Nigeria like Mrs Funmilayo Ransome-Kuti (the only female delegate to the United Kingdom to ask for self-government rule, civil right and equal rights for Nigeria's twenty million population at the time); this group of eminent women activists also included Lady Margaret Ekpo, Mrs Janet Mokelu, Hajia Sawaba Gambo, Lady Olayinka Abayomi, Madam Tinubu, Mrs Wuraola Esan and several others.

HISTORICAL EVIDENCE IN THE POSTCOLONIAL ERA

Colonialism created a new set of prolonged elite that spearheaded the nationalist government for independence in Nigeria. Because more men acquired colonial education than women, they enjoyed a head start in socio-economic progress, combined with the existent patriarchal system in place.

Corresponding with the low status of women, the nationalist movement excluded women in their institutional framework for the struggle for independence. By the time the British colonialists were departing Nigeria, only men assumed positions of leadership and also controlled the apparatuses of the state.

During the post-independence period in Nigeria, there was little to suggest that the position of women had changed for the better. In the First Republic, the state affair was largely monopolised by men. There were only three female legislators and no woman in a ministerial appointment. Women involvement in the Second Republic remained significantly low as well. There was only 1 female out of the 57 members of Senate and 3 of 455 Federal House of Representatives; and only 2 female ministers (Attoe, n.d).

With the active history of anti-colonial activity and their involvement in the nationalist struggle, women in post-independent Nigeria should have gained political leverage for themselves. The outcome showed that men excluded women from political participation. Women were massively under-represented in the federal civil service. Also, while women in the south had been enfranchised, women in the North were not so lucky in the immediate postcolonial era, and this was so even though major political parties in the North had 'women wings'. Indeed, these women's wings were peripheral to the party structure and decisions were made without inputs from the women's wing (Shettima, 1995).

In the South, no woman was elected to the federal cabinet, and none won a seat in the House of Representatives. One woman was appointed to the Senate and a second woman was appointed in 1964. In 1961, three women were elected to the Eastern House of Assembly, but there were no female ministers at the regional level. No woman occupied a prominent position in the political parties even in the South. However, several women were elected to the local government councils in the South (Mba, 1990). It is interesting to note that despite the disenfranchised female population in the North, the men insisted on being given seats in the first House of Assembly based on the male-to-female population (Mba, 1990; Mama, 1995). In discussing women's political participation, the militarised political character of the Nigerian State cannot be downplayed.

From independence till date, Nigeria has had more years under the military rule than under civilian regimes. Mba (1990) and Mama (1995) provide rich insights into the political participation of women in Nigeria's post-independent period. The Second Republic (1979–1983), just like the First Republic, produced only one female senator in the person of Late Franca Afegbuwa. A few Nigerian women won elections into the House of Representatives at the national level. Some of these women were Mrs J. C. Eze of the Nigerian People's Party (NPP) who represented Uzo Uwani constituency in former

Anambra State; Mrs V. U. Nnaji, also of the NPP who represented Isu constituency in Imo State; and Mrs Abiola Babatope of the Unity Party of Nigeria (UPN) who represented Mushin Central II of Lagos State (Soetan, 1998). In the 1990 elections into local governments that heralded the Third Republic, very few women emerged as councillors and only one woman, Chief (Mrs) Titilayo Ajanaku emerged as the chairperson of Abeokuta Local Government Council in Ogun State. During the gubernatorial elections, no female governor emerged in any of the states. Only two female deputy governors emerged, namely Alhaja Sinatu Ojikutu of Lagos State and Mrs Cecilia Ekpenyong of Cross River State (Kolawole et al., 2012). In the senatorial election held in 1992, Mrs Kofo Bucknor-Akerele was the only woman who won a seat in the Senate, and this followed the pattern of the First and Second Republics. Very few women won election into the House of Representatives. One of them was Chief (Mrs) Florence Ita Giwa who won the senatorial election in the Calabar Constituency, Cross River State under the banner of the National Republican Convention (NRC).

In the Interim National Government of Chief Ernest Shonekan, two female ministers were appointed to the cabinet. General Abacha had some female ministers at various times in his cabinet, including Chief (Mrs) Onikepo Akande and Ambassador Judith Attah. During the military regime of General Abdulsalami Abubakar (9 June 1998 to 29 May 1999), there were two women in the Federal Executive Council: Chief (Mrs) Onikepo Akande (Minister for Commerce) and Dr. Laraba Gambo Abdullahi (Minister of Women Affairs). In the Fourth Republic – which started on 29 May 1999 – the Nigerian political terrain witnessed an increase in the number of women political appointees. However, women did not perform well at the elections. In the elections held before 29 May 1999, few women emerged as chairpersons of local government councils. Several women won elections as councillors, but still there was no female governor in any state of the federation. Only Lagos State produced a female deputy governor in the person of Senator Bucknor-Akerele.

In the National Assembly, there were only three women in the Senate, namely: Chief (Mrs) Florence Ita Giwa, representing Cross River State South Senatorial District; Mrs Stella Omu from Delta State and Hajiya Khairat Abdul-Razaq (now Hajiya Gwadabe) representing the Federal Capital Territory (FCT). There were only twelve women in the House of Representatives, namely, Barrister Iquo Minimah, Mrs Patience Ogodo, Lola Abiola-Edewor, Patricia O. Etteh, Dorcas Odujinrin, J. F. Adeyemi, Binta Garba Koji, Gbemi Saraki, Florence Aya, Linda Ikpeazu, Temi Harrinnan and Mercy Almona Isei.

In the State Houses of Assembly, very few women emerged as members. While in some states, one or two women emerged in the houses, most other states had virtually no female in their legislatures. States such as Cross

River, Akwa Ibom, Rivers, Lagos and many others did not have female members in their states legislatures (Kolawole et al., 2012). Women were however appointed as Commissioners and therefore, they became members of the executive councils in all the states. In contrast, some states had one female; others had two females in the executive councils. President Olusegun Obasanjo appointed several women into the Federal Executive Council (FEC). They were Dr. (Mrs) Kema Chikwe (Minister of Transport), Mrs Dupe Adelaja (Minister-of-State (Defence), Dr. (Mrs) Bekky Ketebuigwe (Minister-of-State – Ministry of Solid Minerals), Dr. (Mrs) Amina Ndalolo (Minister-of-State, Federal Ministry of Health), Mrs Pauline Tallen (Minister of State – Federal Ministry of Science and Technology) and Hajia Aishatu Ismaila (Minister of Women Affairs). Chief (Mrs) Titilayo Ajanaku was the Special Adviser to the President on Women Affairs (Kolawole et al., 2012). In all, only four out of the twenty-nine senior ministers (13.7%) and three out of the eighteen junior ministers (16.6%) were female political appointees under President Obasanjo on assumption of office in May 1999 (Awofeso and Odeyemi, 2014).

NIGERIAN WOMEN IN POLITICAL STRUGGLES – THE 12 JUNE 1993 ELECTIONS DEBACLE X-RAYED

In this section, in relation to, and as an example of, women's relevance in contemporary Nigerian political struggle, an attempt is made to highlight the role of Nigerian women in the 12 June political debacle. There are five themes here. The first generally introduces the debacle, while the second section looks at the role women have played in the political process in contemporary times. The third theme provides an analysis on the background to the 12 June struggle, while women's involvement in the 12 June struggle forms the fourth section – as a credible exemplification of the strength of Nigerian women in political agitations. The fifth theme examines the struggle of women for political relevance in the Nigerian power space, since then.

BACKGROUND TO THE 12 JUNE CRISIS

Nigeria is Africa's most populous country, with a population of about 204 million (Worldometer, 2020). Nigeria is a combination of more than 250 ethnic groups. The three prominent of these groups are the Hausa-Fulani, comprising the majority of the population in the northern region; the Yoruba, which forms the majority in the Southwest and the Igbo, the largest ethnic group in the Southeast. The Hausa-Fulani people are predominantly Muslims.

This group dominated the top echelon of Nigerian political leadership during both the military and the brief spell with civilian administrations before 1993. The Yoruba and Igbo, who dominate the southern regions, are mostly Christians. Ethnic and regional conflicts have been a constant factor in Nigerian politics since independence. The most devastating experience was the thirty-month civil war, which broke out in 1967 and ended in 1970, with over a million lives lost. As at 1993 during the 12 June crisis, Nigeria had enjoyed civilian rule for only ten of its thirty-three years of independence. The outcome of 12 June 1993 election was therefore very unique and symbolic. For the first time, a Muslim Southerner won a majority of the vote in all regions of the federation. The development was a break with the traditions of ethno-religious politics. This raised the hope that an ethnically differentiated nation was moving away from the centripetal forces threatening its existence as a corporate entity.

Since coming to power in a palace coup – through the combined effects of a barrage of military decrees, brutal behaviour of security forces, a disregard for the rule of law and repeated attacks on civil institutions, General Babangida brought the country to the edge of ruin (Babatope, 1995, 29). The government created and significantly controlled the apparatus of two parties named the National Republican Convention (NRC) and the Social Democratic Party (SDP). Bashir Tofa of the NRC and Moshood Abiola of the SDP were the two primary contenders for the Presidency, and both were believed to be friends with the military leadership at that time.

Arthur Nzeribe, who had lost out in the race to contest as a presidential candidate, formed the Association of Better Nigeria and used that platform to encourage General Ibrahim Babangida to stay on in power (Ojo, 2004, 69). The ABN instituted a case in an Abuja court, urging the cancellation of the elections just two days before the election (TSM, 11 July 1993, as cited in Ojo, 2004). *The Guardian*, 28 September 1993, reported that (as cited in Ojo, 2004), 'Justice Bassey Ikpeme ordered the government not to conduct the elections until the charges had been investigated'. However, the election continued as the NEC relied on another court order. On the Election Day, more than 30 per cent of registered voters went to the polls (Ojo, 2004). Unlike previous elections in Nigeria, the election was unique because of the overwhelming interests from the global community. A total of 3,000 election observers across the globe participated in monitoring the conduct of the election. Among this, there were 135 international observers, according to Newswatch, 21 June 1993 (cited in Ojo, 2004). With minor exceptions, the majority of these observers reported that the voting went fairly and smoothly (*The Guardian*, 13 and 14 June 1993, cited in Ojo, 2004). It was adjudged a free and fair election. The National Electoral Commission (NEC) published results from fifteen states, on billboards outside their headquarters in Abuja, on 14 June, showing that Abiola was ahead in all regions of the country, including Tofa's home state of Kano (Babatope, 1995). The remaining results from the other sixteen states were halted on the ground that Justice Dahir Saleh (Chief Judge of the Federal Capital Territory) had received a message from the Presidency that the announcement should stop pending the determination of ABN's case, as claimed by *The News*, 28 June 1993 (cited in Ojo, 2004). Announcing the stoppage of the remaining election results, NEC Chairman, Professor Humphery Nwosu, stated: 'In the light of the current development, the commission had, in deference to the court injunction and other actions pending in court, decided to stay action on all matters of the presidential election until further notice', says Newswatch, 28 June 1993 (cited in Ojo, 2004).

Citing the restraining order issued by Justice M. D. Saleh, the Chief Judge of the High Court, Federal Capital Territory Abuja, which prohibited NEC from publishing the results, Radio Nigeria proceeded, on 16 June 1993, to announce the suspension of further announcements of the election results (Newswatch, 28 June 1993, cited in Ojo, 2004). Justice Saleh ruled that he would consider ordering the elections annulled, pending further investigations of the charges by ABN, who alleged corruption (Newswatch, 28 June 1993, cited in Ojo, 2004).

With the stalemate, the leader of ABN, Chief Arthur Nzeribe, called for the cancellation of the election on the ground that 'the so-called election was a fraud, a flop, illegal, unconstitutional and undemocratic' (*The Guardian*, 28 June 1993, cited in Ojo, 2004). The director of the ABN, Mr Abimbola Davies, who apparently had a rethink, proved this claim wrong. To him, the Association (ABN) 'has no other mandate than to plan and work out how the incumbent military President General Babangida would remain in power for at least two more years'. (*TEMPO*, 27 September 1993, cited in Ojo, 2004)

The annulment of the results of the 12 June election was a shock to many in and out of Nigeria. A litany of additional court cases were brought before the High Courts in Benin City, Lagos, Ibadan, Jos and Awka, Anambra State, which contradicted the Abuja court's decision and resulted in orders for NEC to release the election results (*Sunday Sketch*, 27 June 1993, as cited in Ojo, 2004). On 18 June in defiance of Decree 13 which prohibits the publication of unauthenticated election results, the Campaign for Democracy (CD) provided the remaining results of the election which showed that Abiola had won a majority of the vote in nineteen of the thirty states, with a total of 58.4 per cent of the vote to Tofa's 41.6 per cent (Newswatch, 28 June 1993, as cited in Ojo, 2004). Calls for recognition of the results came from individuals and organisations, including unions, women groups, politicians and prominent Nigerians. Professor Wole Soyinka said that 'any further delay in making the people's verdict official [is] . . . a deliberate cultivation of chaos' (Associated

Press, 19 June 1993). On 21 June, NEC filed an appeal against the Abuja court's order, and a hearing was scheduled for 23 June. The same day, Justice Saleh ruled that the elections were illegal because NEC decided to ignore the 10 June court order not to conduct the elections until allegations of bribery were investigated. As noted above, the government had previously reassured the nation that the court lacked jurisdiction in the matter.

On 23 June, the government announced what the nation had feared: NEC was suspended and the election was annulled. In addition, Decrees 13 of 1993 and 52 of 1992 which formed the pillars of the transition programmes were hurriedly repealed by the Federal Military Government (FMG), making it impossible to seek redress in the court of law. Justifying the annulment of the election, General Babangida disclosed that 'there were authenticated reports of election malpractice against party agents, officials of the NEC . . . there were proofs of manipulations, offer and acceptance of money and other forms of inducements' (*TSM*, 11 July 1993, cited in Ojo, 2004).

The same day, Nduka Irabor, press secretary to the vice president, said that the government would not hesitate to declare an emergency in any state where disturbances occurred. The government stated that such a drastic step was necessary in order to remove the confusion created by the conflicting rulings from the various courts. According to Babangida's statement, the election was annulled 'to save our judiciary from being ridiculed and politicised locally and internationally' (*Sunday Sketch*, 27 June 1993, cited in Ojo, 2004). Beyond the apparent contradiction posed by the swearing-in of an Election Tribunal to handle election-related controversies, the statement was belied by the regime's eight-year history of contempt for the rule of law and the independence of the judiciary. Many of the numerous and often retroactive military decrees promulgated by the government had contained clauses that excluded judicial inquiry. Military officials regularly and with impunity flouted court orders. Special Tribunals lacking due process guarantees had been established to try many cases of particular importance to the government, including those concerned with public disturbances, corruption and drug-related offences.

The southwestern part of Nigeria took the annulment of the election seriously, and civil violence erupted in pockets of places as a result, and this was reminiscent of what had happened in the first and second republics where electoral fraud led to civil unrest (Ojo, 2004). According to Ojo (2004), Southern resentment over Abiola's rebuff also threatened to create fissures within the military, raising the spectre of broader civil conflicts and state collapse. In his official reaction to the annulment, Chief M. K. O. Abiola was quoted as saying:

I might embark on the programme of civil disobedience in the country. If those who make the law disobey the law, why [should], I obey it? There is a limit to the authenticity one could expect from a military ruler who is anxious to hang on to power. (TSM, 11 July 1993, cited in Ojo, 2004)

The above statements made by Chief Abiola threw the country into an unprecedented crisis. The Campaign for Democracy (CD) spearheaded the mass protests by calling for a five-day non-violent protest. The protest later turned violent as many protesters lost their lives because of counter-opposition by the police. At least 100 protesters were killed (Lewis, 1994, 327). The violence prompted a mounting exodus from the major cities, as southern ethnic groups (most notably the Ibos), fearing a recurrence of the communal purges which had preceded the 1967 Civil War, fled to their home regions (Ojo, 2004, 71). Nwabueze (1989), lucidly and graphically described the crisis thus:

The annulment of the June 12 presidential election plunged the country into what indisputably is the greatest political crisis in its 33-years life as an independent nation. Never before, except during the murderous confrontation of 1966–1970, had the survival of Nigeria as one political entity been in more serious danger. The impasse created was certainly unequalled by anything the country had experienced before.

THE ROLE OF THE NIGERIA WOMEN
IN THE 12 JUNE STRUGGLE

There were spontaneous reactions from the civil society to push for the re-democratisation of Nigeria – first with the return of the mandate to M. K. O Abiola. During this period, there was insecurity of lives and property of perceived/imagined political opponents. Julius Ihonvbere and Timothy Shaw observe that 'women have perhaps been the most exploited and marginalised group in Nigerian society. In both precolonial and post-colonial Nigeria, women have remained oppressed and ignored in both political and economic terms' (Ihonvbere and Shaw, 1998, 149). Therefore, many of the women's organisations in Nigeria are cultural organisations whose functions are restricted and limited due to traditions and constraints imposed by men. This, therefore, accounts for lack of adequate literature to a large extent on the role women played in the 12 June struggle.

Ebenezer Babatope (1995) in his book 'The Abacha Regime and the June 12 crisis' stated that the people mobilised themselves to face the challenges of military leadership that had reneged on its promise to hand over power to democratically elected leaders. All working-class organisations in Nigeria, including market women and peasant farmers, were unanimous in their demand for democratic justice (Babatope, 1995, xiii).

Beginning with pioneer organisations like Women in Nigeria (WIN) in the early 1980s, the scope of the NGOs targeting women's interest have grown to include political involvement and mobilisation, health and economic security, legal rights, education and other concerns (Kew, 2004). WIN grew out of a seminar held in 1982 after a somewhat acrimonious debate on the nature of women's oppression among other social scientists working in Ahmadu Bello University in Zaria; but the seminar grew, through word of mouth alone, to draw participants from all over Nigeria's then nineteen states. In the 12 June struggle, WIN was closely associated with the human rights groups; was a member of both the Campaign for Democracy in 1992–1993 and National Democratic Coalition (NADECO) in 1994, and had been highly critical of military rule. Subsequently, WIN and its leadership faced constant harassment from security forces, and many WIN members were also members of the human rights groups in their states.

During the transition programme of General Abacha, especially when the heat of agitation was too much for the regime, the leader of the oil workers, Frank Kokori, was arrested for spearheading a national strike. Likewise, Chief Abiola, the assumed winner of the annulled presidential election, was arrested for his self-declaration as president-elect along with a host of others too. All the venom poured on the people did not deter them from their goal, which was to ensure the exit of the military with a specific objective of reversal of the annulment of the 1993 presidential election.

As part of the contribution of Nigerian women to the 12 June struggle, the late Alhaja Kudirat Abiola was one of the numerous wives of the SDP presidential flag bearer who was forced into the pro-democracy movement as a result of the annulment. She confronted the military government variously and inspired other groups to emerge for the same purpose of claiming the mandate of the 12 June election. While the oil workers' strike affected the nation adversely, Kudirat Abiola was at the forefront of the struggle and encouraged the strikes. Kudirat had frictions with the courts over her stance before her eventual release on bail.

She went on along with Alfred Rewane and others to fund pro-democracy activities that unsettled the military (*The Nation*, 12 June 2013). On 4 June 1996, a few days to the third anniversary of the 12 June election, Kudirat was shot dead by assassins in Oregun, Lagos State.

General Abdulsalam Abubakar took over the reins of power on 8 June 1998, after the mysterious death of his predecessor. He formed a new electoral commission known as Independent National Electoral Commission (INEC), which handled elections and the registration of new political parties. In the process of the transition programme in the country, Chief M. K. O. Abiola died in government custody on 7 July 1998. This ignited civil unrest that led to state paralysis, especially in the southwest from where he hailed.

Women, men, both old and young took to the street because it was generally believed that the acclaimed winner of 12 June 1993 presidential election was killed (*The News*, 20 July 1998).

With the unrelenting efforts of the Women Groups, Campaign for Democracy, NADECO and others, seeking a transition to democratic rule, the Abubakar administration demonstrated sincerity of purpose and elections were peacefully conducted. Elections for the local councils, state legislature and governorship post the National Assembly and presidential seats were conducted on 5 December 1998, 9 January 1999, 20 February and 27 February 1999, respectively. Finally, General Abdulsalam Abubakar's transition reached the climax with the declaration of General Olusegun Obasanjo (Retired) as the president-elect in late February 1999. He was duly sworn in on 29 May 1999. Though women played significant roles here, this cannot be compared to the role Nigeria women played during the colonial era, such as the Aba Women's Riot of 1929 and the Egba Women's Riot of 1946. Women during this period were more resilient and determined in the quest to fight against any form of injustice, discrimination and bad governance.

Nigeria witnessed a substantially free and fair election on 12 June 1993. However, there was no official release of the total results of the election. Nevertheless, unofficial results gathered through the various polling stations by the civil society groups across the country indicated broad national support for the presidential candidate of the Social Democratic Party (SDP), Moshood Abiola (Babatope, 1995, 33). Before the 1993 election, Nigeria had experienced several years of military rule, and the people were looking forward to having a democratically elected government. With this hope for a change, there was a high turnout for the election compared to past electoral processes in Nigeria. Women activism in politics also increased in terms of active participation in the political process.

The decision of the military head of state, then – General Ibrahim Babangida – to annul the results of the election deflated the expectation of the people. The annulment, according to the military leader, was expedient because of the need to save the nation rather than satisfying a particular group. He alleged that political activities that preceded the conduct of the election were inimical to peace and stability in the country (Babatope, 1995). This decision marked the beginning of the struggle to actualise the outcome of the election. The role of one of the wives of the presumed winner of the election, Alhaja Kudiratu Abiola, in this struggle introduced women's involvement in political activism in a different dimension. There exist international legal instruments that recognise the rights of women to participate in politics like their male counterparts. However, women participation in politics and the process of governance is still deficient in Nigeria. There are no justifications for denying women the rights of active participation in politics. Nevertheless, the problem of prescriptive gender roles often keeps a high number of interested and dedicated women out of politics.

The patriarchal nature of the society aggravates male dominance, subjugates women and makes them appendages to men. Therefore, women are hindered from actualising their potentials by making it difficult for them to perform effectively in the various roles expected of them in society as decision-makers in the process of governance. In addition to this, the socio-economic conditions under which most women live and work continue to deteriorate due to a decline in the economy. Women suffer a lot of inferiority complex, which confers on them the status of second-class citizens, and excessive dependence on men for support in the absence of access to educational opportunities and even more.

Despite all the perceived and visible hindrances, Nigerian women participated fully in the 12 June struggle. No struggle for democracy has ever been waged by men alone (International Institute for Democracy and Electoral Assistance, 2000), and Nigeria is not an exception. Women were called upon in almost every struggle to swell the ranks of the movements and forces for freedom, change and democracy (International IDEA, 2000). The Nigerian experience is rich with a history of women's involvement at all levels of the struggles for freedom, change and democracy. The extent and nature of women's involvement in these struggles have been determined by the needs arising out of a particular situation, the nature and length of the struggle itself. It is therefore important to note that women have not been spared the losses, pain and sacrifices that arise out of the conflict situations.

NIGERIAN WOMEN IN POLITICS SINCE THE 12 JUNE 1993 STRUGGLES

Despite the brutal violent experience of women in years prior, and the utmost dismal performance of many more women in the political space in the recent past, in the 2011 general elections, an increased number of women defied the odds, aspired and contested for party primaries. Many lost and only a few emerged as candidates. However, even fewer of them emerged as winners. The number and percentage of women who were successful at the polls in the 2011 elections were less than the figures in 2007, 2003 and 1999.

The 2011 election results suggest a regression from the apparent progress that followed the return to democracy in 1999. Only 9 per cent of the candidates for the National Assembly elections in April 2011 were women. Only 13 of the 340 candidates who contested on behalf of various political parties for the office of the governor were women. A mere 909 of the 10,037 candidates for available seats were women (9.06%). After only 25 women were elected to the 360-member House of Representatives, Nigeria is now ranked 118 out of 192 countries in terms of gender parity. The low 9 per cent representation of women in Nigeria's House of Representatives is significantly below the global average (15%) and far behind South Africa's and Rwanda's representation (43% and 56%, respectively). Nigeria's sixty-three registered political parties have failed to deliver gender parity in political representation at the national level (British Council, 2012)

Before the change of government after the 29 May 2015 swearing-in of the Buhari administration, there were only twelve (28.57%) female ministers out of which only eight were supervising ministers. Out of 154 top slots, including governors and deputy governors, women only accounted for 21 (13.64%) (Ndujihe, 2011) – a far cry from the internationally stipulated 30 per cent affirmative action. There was no female governor but just three deputy governors. Overall, according to the 2012 report from the British Council, only 9 per cent of candidates at the 2011 Nigerian general elections were women.

In the 2015 National Assembly election held on 28 March 2015, results show that only 8 of the 109-member chamber of the National Assembly were women. Three of the eight women senators were of the APC. They were: Oluremi Tinubu from Lagos Central Senatorial District; Alhaja Monsurat Sunmonu from Oyo Central, while the third was Binta Masi Garba from Adamawa North. The five others are from PDP. Two each from Anambra and Ekiti and the other is from Cross River State. From Anambra were: House of Representative member Uche Ekkwunife and former Aviation Minister Stella Oduah. The two elected senators from Ekiti were Abiodun Olujimi from Ekiti South, who was Governor Ayodele Fayose's deputy between 2003 and 16 October 2006, when they were impeached by twenty-four of the 26-member House of Assembly; and Fatima Raji-Rasaki from Ekiti Central, a House of Representative member between 2003 and 2007. Fatimah was the wife of the former Military Administrator of Oyo and Lagos States, Brig-Gen. Raji-Rasaki (Retired). The fifth PDP Senator-elect was Rose Okoh from Cross River North Senatorial District.

Chapter 4

Nigeria's Gender Policy

Affirmative Action, Women's Political Participation and Underrepresentation in Governance

As a member of the United Nations, Nigeria signed and ratified several UN treaties and instruments which emphasise the need to eliminate gender discriminations and ensure human dignity for all (Federal Ministry of Women's Affairs and Social Development, 2006). Nevertheless, there persists discrimination in national and state statutes, and customary and religious laws. It is well known that in Nigeria, traditions, customs, sexual stereotyping of social roles and cultural prejudice continue to militate against the enjoyment of rights and full participation of women on an equal basis with men in national development (Federal Ministry of Women's Affairs and Social Development, 2006).

Efforts to make men and women contribute to national development led to the adoption of a National Policy on Women in the year 2000. This policy was adopted to promote the contribution of women to development. However, according to Igbuzor (2008):

> After six years, it became clear that women focused strategies alone could only slow down the pace of achieving gender equality in the facets of development. An overarching strategy for gender equality in the development process is likely to be that which take women and men as partners in development, and more importantly, that which challenges the structure which continues to produce gender-based inequalities in the society, and balances power relations between women and men for growth and development both at the micro and macro levels.

This strategy led to the adoption of the National Gender Policy in 2006. There is no doubt that it is a veritable instrument for promoting gender equality and sustainable development. According to Igbuzor (2008), the National Gender Policy is unique for the following reasons.

First, it aligns with relevant international and national instruments such as the Beijing Platform for Action, New Partnership for African Development (NEPAD), AU Solemn Declaration for Gender Equality, African Protocol on People's Rights and the Rights of Women, the Convention on the Elimination of All Forms of Discrimination against Women (CEDAW), International Conference on Population Development Plan of Action, National Economic Empowerment and Development Strategy (NEEDS), MDGs and a wide range of sectors.

Second, the policy recognised the need for a different approach which will not only ensure women's empowerment but a sustainable development for the country through gender equality policy initiatives which would help balance power relations between men and women. Furthermore, the approach should transform the institutions which continue to perpetuate gender injustice, poverty and underdevelopment.

Third, the methodology of drawing up the policy involved some levels of consultation of stakeholders during the stages of problem formulation, data gathering, analysis as well as validation and policy formulation.

Fourth, the policy recognises that an efficient management system is necessary for the operationalisation of the policy. The policy points out what skills are required in policy analysis; programme planning; gender mainstreaming; strategic planning; communication; advocacy; networking; gender analysis; social analysis; report writing, and so forth.

Finally, the National Gender Policy Situational Analysis and Framework, (Volume One) contains a detailed description of the policy thrust, outcome, goals, objectives and priorities of the National Gender Policy as well as the roles of several stakeholders including the Federal Executive Council, ministry of women affairs and social development, other line ministries and parastatals, National Centre for Women Development, National Bureau of Statistics, National Planning Commission, National Orientation Agency, Federal Character Commission, Independent Electoral Commission, Human Rights Commission, Legal Aid Council, Education commissions (National Universities Commission (NUC), Nigerian Educational Research and Development Council (NERDC), National Agency for the Prohibition of Trafficking in Persons (NAPTIP), Universal Basic Education (UBE) and Mass Literacy Agency (Igbuzor, 2008; Federal Ministry of Women Affairs, 2006). Besides, there are roles for special committees of the Federal Ministry of Women Affairs in implementing the National Gender Policy such as the National Council on Women Affairs, National Consultative and Coordinating Committee on Gender Equity and National Technical Team of Gender Experts. Indeed, at the local government level, there is local government

Gender Equality and Women Empowerment (GEWE) unit and Community-Based Committees on Gender Equity (Igbuzor, 2008; Federal Ministry of Women's Affairs, 2006).

There is no doubt that the adoption of the National Gender Policy is a watershed to promote gender equality and sustainable development (Igbuzor, 2008). However, the challenge is in translating the policy into action in terms of concrete programmes and projects. The National Gender Policy, which supersedes and replaces the erstwhile National Policy on Women, would help to eliminate all such barriers (Igbuzor, 2008; Federal Ministry of Women's Affairs, 2006). The policy aligns with relevant regional and international protocols and instruments such as the Beijing Platform for Action (BPfA), New Partnership for African Development (NEPAD), AU Solemn Declaration on Gender Equality, African Protocol on People's Rights and the Rights of Women (APPRRW), the Convention on the Elimination of All Forms of Discrimination against Women (CEDAW), International Conference on Population Development Plan of Action (ICPD PoA), NEEDS/ Strategies for Ecology Education, Diversity and Sustainability (SEEDS), the Millennium Development Goals (MDGs) and a wide range of sectors. The policy seeks 'to equip stakeholders with strategic skills for engineering the levels of social change required for achieving the desired empowerment of all citizens' (Igbuzor, 2008).

Ultimately, the goal of the National Gender Policy is to 'build a just society devoid of discrimination, harness the full potentials of all social groups regardless of sex or circumstance; promote the enjoyment of fundamental human rights and protect the health, social, economic and political wellbeing of all citizens in order to achieve equitable rapid economic growth; evolve an evidence-based planning and governance system where human, social, financial and technological resources are efficiently and effectively deployed for sustainable development'. (Federal Ministry of Women's Affairs and Social Development, 2006)

Despite all these provisions made by the government and its subscribing to international commitments to encourage women's participation in politics, Nigerian women are still far behind the men. The current absence of legal backing for the National Gender Policy has hindered the full realisation of the benefits of the gender policy (Centre for Gender, Women and Children in Sustainable Development, 2014). Also, Aina (2015) cited in Opera (2015) believes that the effect of these policies has been infinitesimal. To her, the strong point is that as long as the position of the women is not equitable with that of the men, we will always see a disparity in development in the society (Aina, 2015, cited in Opera, 2015). On the National Gender Policy, Aina (2015) cited in Opera (2015), is of the view that most of these policies are only on paper and not in practice.

GAPS IN LEGAL/POLICY FRAMEWORK FOR GENDER
EQUALITY IN POLITICAL PARTICIPATION

Nigeria is a signatory to many international conventions and international efforts which are aimed at improving the participation and inclusion of women in politics but has not implemented many of these conventions and agreements. Its political arena is still male-dominated. There were almost 100 parties in Nigeria as at 2015 but currently as at 2020, there are only eighteen registered political parties in Nigeria (INEC, 2019), with none having clear structures that promise gender equality.

Sociocultural factors, tradition, patriarchy and religion affect the roles of men and women in terms of power attainment and participation in activities. The multi ethno-religious cum cultural character of the federation, coupled with its tripartite systems of law and administration of justice compounds the matters even more. Customary laws are somewhat discriminatory, but most women victims of gender-based violence nurse their wounds secretly.

There are apparent gender gaps in the Nigerian laws and policies, for example, the macro-economic framework is gender-blind or at best, gender-neutral. (Appendix I highlights the historical timeline of international events and treaties aimed at promoting gender equality.)

According to Edwards (2015), the Fourth World Conference on Women (FWCW) held in Beijing in 1995 and its resultant Platform for Action placed women empowerment and gender equality at the front burner of political considerations and has helped to focus more on violence against women, underrepresentation of women in governance and related issues. This led eventually to the creation of UN Women in July 2010 as an entity to meet the needs of women (Edwards, 2015).

Despite some gains and improvements in recent times, in gender equality matters, only 11 per cent of the world's political leaders are women (Edwards, 2015). The way forward according to Edwards (2015), is finding hope in the proposed Sustainable Development Goals (SDGs) 'with its inclusion of commitments on unpaid care, sexual and reproductive rights, tackling violence and equal participation of women in all aspects of public life, amongst other issues'.

THE CONCEPT OF AFFIRMATIVE ACTION

Affirmative action has attracted different views from different writers. To Weiss (1997), affirmative action seeks to overcome discrimination, increase diversity and reduce poverty among groups that have historically been victimised by discrimination. In the same vein, Francis (1998) avers that affirmative action is morally justified as s corrective for discriminatory employment practice. Francis (1998) made three kinds of argument for affirmative action – compensatory, corrective and redistributive – and for him, the emphasis is on corrective and redistributive in relation to higher education. In line with this, Lee (1999) defines *affirmative action* as 'the proactive policy of making special efforts in employment decisions, college entrance, and other areas of public behaviour as a way of compensating for past discrimination'. In the same vein, Ikpeze (2002) avers that *affirmative action* is otherwise known or referred to as positive policies or often defined as temporary policy measures (usually by the Executive arm of government) designed to favour a disadvantaged group or reverse discrimination. According to Ikpeze (2002), it is aimed at remedying past discriminations thereby preventing a continuum of inequity and/or injustice based on gender thereby generating discrimination against women in perpetuity.

Dessler (2005) asserts that affirmative action involves steps that are taken to eliminate the present effects of past discrimination. This is in line with Women in Law and Development in Africa (WiLDAF, 2010) that sees affirmative action as a deliberate move to reform or eliminate past and present discrimination using a set of public policies and initiative designed to help based on colour, creed, geographical location, race, origin and gender among others.

Alexander (2006) cited in Kaimenyi, Kinya and Samwel(2013) believes that affirmative action is transformational. To sum it up, Tsikata (2009) opines that, affirmative action is a set of measures adopted by governments and public and private institutions to address systemic discrimination.

AFFIRMATIVE ACTION FOR GENDER EQUALITY

Amadi and Amadi (2015) aver that, despite the rhetoric, liberal democracy's real achievement in the promotion of gender transformation in Africa has been relatively meagre. They note that despite global summits and conventions, Africa has not evolved the much-anticipated gender equality, which has been faced with numerous obstacles. Amadi and Amadi (2015) argue that the 35 per cent affirmative action on women participation in governance, decision-making and politics proposed at the FWCW held in Beijing in 1995, has not been effectual within Nigeria but has instead mainly been superficial in influencing policy decisions.

Kaimenyi, Kinya and Samwel (2013) in their study investigated affirmative action concerning representation in the Kenyan National Assembly. They observe that the two-thirds gender rule is not limited to only this institution but cuts across all other public institutions which may have different dimensions of its implementations. Tsikata (2009), on the other hand, made a case for affirmative action to achieve gender equality in the political representation of women in Ghana. Tsikata (2009) argued that the role of public policy is critical to the success of affirmative action. Public policy can mediate the debates on affirmative action and lay down the line a country will follow.

Ikpeze reiterates that affirmative action encourages and strives to maintain equality in the distribution of economic resources in all ramifications. According to him, it is designed to achieve in the easiest and best way, as well as in the shortest time, rights denied over some time. However, he notes that the resistance to women-based affirmative action has remained the enabling tool for perpetuating discrimination against women, notwithstanding the spirit and provisions of the constitution of the federal republic of Nigeria of 1999.

Sowell (2004), however, notes that throughout history, women have been discriminated against in various ways. This subordination of women is what Nzomo (1987) traces to the evolution of the class society where men were in control of the means of production. She observes further that those who control the economic domain invariably exercise similar control over the political arena. Schmidt (2006) reiterating both Sowell (2004) and Nzomo (1987) believes however that discrimination and subordination of women is universal and that there is no society where they are treated as equal with men.

ARGUMENTS FOR AND AGAINST AFFIRMATIVE ACTION

Proponents of affirmative action argue that it is subtle, systematic and gradual machinery for achieving both equity and liberation without force and a technique for jump-starting the process of integrating minorities into the fabric of the society (Ikpeze, 2002). Affirmative Action involves equity for every human being, meaning that it creates opportunities for women and other previously disadvantaged groups to showcase their talents, skills and leadership qualities thereby compensating for their historical discrimination (McLean, 2002; Taylor, 2002; Whiteneck, 2003). Without affirmative action, they would have remained untapped. Moreover, affirmative action provides role models (Patrick, 2004) since successful women encourage and motivate other women to be confident in knowing that excellence can be achieved.

Affirmative action promotes diversity and encourages public welfare for the common good by increasing opportunities for previously disadvantaged groups, which in turn decreases the potential for conflict as the members of the society find themselves at the same level politically, economically and socially. Furthermore, proponents have held that affirmative action creates organisational harmony (Rossett and Bickham, 1994), is socially just and morally desirable (Carnevale and Stone, 1994) and improves productivity (Gordon, 1992). In sum, through resilient affirmative action processes, women are now vocal in governance and decision-making processes in many countries (Torto, 2013).

Critics of affirmative action believe that it rewards people based on their genetically determined trait (in this case, they were born women). Affirmative action programmes that favour women undermine the democratic concept of equality of opportunity. They argue that women should be given a chance to compete for opportunities equally with men, without any favour. At the same time, Harris (2009) adds that affirmative action undermines the principle of compensatory justice. Compensatory justice requires that compensation be provided to the specific individuals who were wronged or harmed. It is unjust for a whole society to compensate a class of people for harm done to specific individuals among them.

Critics further claim that affirmative action lowers the self-worth and self-esteem of women. This is because one does not know whether they have sailed through because of their abilities and expertise or because of the preferential treatment accorded. Moreover, treating people differently conflicts with corporate philosophies of equality and unitary goals. At the same time, it increases social hostility since men who see themselves as lacking an opportunity because it has been given to a woman become hostile and resentful to women in general (Gottfredson, 1992).

Opponents also see preferential treatment as reinforcing the perception that women cannot make it on their own without assistance. Moreover, it lowers the standards of performance and delivery because people who have less qualification are given the positions in contention. They allege that had the positions been occupied by the other qualified individuals, the performance would have been better. Others view affirmative action as just but a component of inclusivity and propose that a diverse workforce requires a shift from affirmative action to a market-oriented debate (Dessler, 2005). As Sowell (2004) argued, affirmative action ultimately harms women by reinforcing the idea in them and in society at large that they are societal victims. In this light, even when women reach a goal without the support of societal policies, their achievements are diminished and discredited.

Following the opportunities provided by the Nigerian Legislative Council to provide some political space for the participation of indigenes, the Nigerian National Democratic Party was launched in 1923 that marked the beginning of political parties development in Nigeria. Franchise was, however, limited to the two cities of Lagos and Calabar (Liebowitz and Ibrahim, 2013). Nigeria operated a multiparty system during the First and Second

Republics. The aborted Third Republic in Nigeria witnessed the operation of a two-party system, until the return to democracy when the country reverted to a multiparty system in 1999.

Despite being a multiparty democracy, the electoral process for accessing public office remains problematic (Nwankwo and Domingo, 2010). Though Nigeria is a multiparty democracy, the dominant party governs. From 1999 until 2015, the ruling People's Democratic Party obtaining over 70 per cent of the votes in 2007 dominated (Nwankwo and Domingo, 2010). The coming on board of the All Progressives Congress (APC) to the political system in Nigeria is considered a welcome relief to the perpetual domination of the PDP government for the past sixteen years. The APC came about as a result of an alliance between the All Nigeria Peoples Party (ANPP), Action Congress of Nigeria (ACN), Congress for Progressive Change (CPC) and a faction of All Progressives Grand Alliance (APGA).

Most of the Nigerian political parties have a reasonably firm foundation in terms of their party constitutions (Nwankwo and Domingo, 2010). These constitutions provide for the establishment of a clear and coherent party structure and for the conduct of internal democracy within the party (Nwankwo and Domingo, 2010). All of the parliamentary party constitutions also prohibit discrimination based on gender (Ezeilo, 2012). Some parties go further to include commitments like 'ensuring gender balance in governance' (Labour Party) and mainstreaming women's concerns in all policies and programmes (PDP). However, it is less clear the extent to which the parties have rules and policies governing both elections and the day-to-day functioning of party offices and activities (Nwankwo and Domingo, 2010).

For this study, the PDP and APC are the two parties selected given the leading role the PDP has played in Nigeria politics since the return to democracy in 1999 and the alliance formed by ACN, ANPP, CPC and a faction of APGA, which brought about the APC in July 2013 (the party that won the 2015 presidential election in Nigeria). According to NOIPolls (2014), both the APC and the PDP have similar membership in terms of numbers, which came to 47 per cent each.

AFFIRMATIVE ACTION ON GENDER EQUALITY: GLIMPSES FROM NIGERIA'S POLITICAL PARTIES

Election poll results released by NOIPolls Limited show that although about 23 per cent of adult Nigerians have party affiliations, 8 per cent of these are not card-carrying members. In contrast, about 69 per cent of adult Nigerians are not registered members of any party but are interested in political matters. The lack of interest in joining partisan politics could be due to many factors relating to unfavourable perceptions of political issues from different quarters (NOIPolls, 2014).

In Nigeria, two groups of party supporters that remain particularly marginalised from membership and leadership are women and the youth. Parties have few women within their leadership structures and run a few female candidates. According to research conducted by Ezeilo (2012), women comprise less than 15 per cent of political party leadership structures and less than 6 per cent of all political party candidates. There are few, if any, explicit provisions for encouraging women leaders and candidates, or making special provisions to promote gender equality within party manifestos and other party policy documents. According to the 2008 Afrobarometer survey, at the membership level, only 44 per cent of women feel close to a political party, compared to 59 per cent of men. Several reasons stand out in terms of explaining the marginalisation of women within parties in Nigeria, including the domination of parties by rich 'godfathers' (who are almost exclusively men), the lack of leadership by the state in promoting gender equality in parties, the lack of gender sensitivity among party leadership, the lack of a critical mass of organised women within party leadership circles, the cost of participating in political leadership and specific values and norms that discourage women's participation in political leadership.

Although parties demonstrated some awareness of the need to increase opportunities for women, young people and persons with disabilities (PwDs), their proposals for redressing discrimination include quotas for women that fall well below that national standard of 35 per cent representation for women as enshrined in the 2007 National Gender Policy, such as the 15 per cent proposed by the PDP or the 45 per cent proposed by APC Women Leader. Most party leadership does not identify affirmative action for women, youth and PwDs in parties as a priority. The parties also do not make a particular effort to ensure that women, youth and PwDs are included in party decision-making processes.

THE PEOPLE'S DEMOCRATIC PARTY

The PDP used to be Nigeria's largest party by electoral strength. It won the 2011 presidential elections with a 27 per cent margin and also a significant majority of gubernatorial, senatorial and representative seats. The PDP demonstrated particular strength in the South-East and South-South, while its presidential candidate won in almost all states outside the North. The PDP had maintained a dominant position in Nigeria since 1999 and remained the catch-all party for a wide range of political elites until the 2015 general elections.

The People's Democratic Party is not perceived as a party with a particularly strong ideological identity. However, it has been described as a 'centrist' party that 'operates more as a catch-all organisation that houses a range of political positions'. (Nwankwo and Domingo, 2010, 5) The party espouses 'conservative positions on social issues' while promulgating 'economic liberalism' and 'welfare protection' (Domingo and Nwankwo, 2010, 5). The PDP's strength over time is based less on its ideology than on its incumbency and the access to resources and power that accompany its incumbent status.

The PDP still faces considerable challenges in the area of inclusiveness, despite real commitments on gender issues in its constitution – including affirmative action for women in the workforce, mainstreaming women's concerns into all policies and programmes, legislating against traditional practices harmful to women and strengthening women societies to make them more effective in the empowerment of women (Ezeilo, 2012). Despite these commitments, the party only provides initially for a minimum of 15 per cent of women in party leadership positions, which is well below the standard of the National Gender Policy at 35 per cent. The PDP, however, blazed the trail with a provision in its 2011 constitution as amended in section 1(6)(7) that 'in nomination for party office, not less than 35 percent shall be reserved for women'. The question is, has this been the reality?

THE ALL PROGRESSIVES CONGRESS

The APC was formed in February 2013 as a result of an alliance by Nigeria's three biggest opposition parties: All Nigeria Peoples Party (ANPP), Action Congress of Nigeria (ACN), Congress for Progressive Change (CPC) and a faction of a fourth, the All Progressives Grand Alliance (APGA). The party received approval from the Independent National Electoral Commission (INEC) on 31 July 2013, to become a political party. The three parties that merged fully had their operating licenses withdrawn. These four parties merged to take on the People's Democratic Party in the 2015 general elections, and the party became the ruling party by defeating the PDP which had been in power for sixteen years. The APC thus controls the majority in both Houses of the National Assembly.

The APC-led administration as part of their campaign strategy made various promises to Nigerians as contained in the APC manifesto of 2015. Most of the promises made touch on gender equality, guarantee the rights of women, a promise to develop innovative ways to encourage women and youth participation in politics, governance and the implementation of the National Gender Policy including the 35 per cent appointment positions for women. These were some of the promises made hinged on the 35 per cent affirmative action plan. Nevertheless, according to the APC-led govern-ment, the constitution says, leadership should be given to competent and capacity-driven affirmative action. Doing otherwise slows down the process of national development.

There is a yawning, eye-popping and wide-ranging disparity between women's participation in politics and women's representation in governance – in the very Nigerian context. It has been established that women's representa-tion in governance and decision-making was low, compared to the level of women's participation in politics. It shows that women's participation in poli-tics has not engendered women's representation in governance and decision-making in Nigeria. Paxton, Kunovich and Hughes (2007) and Paxton, Hughes and Barnes (2020) are also of the view that women's political participation and representation vary dramatically within and between countries. This posi-tion has also been emphasised by Krook (2010) and Barnes and Burchard (2012). Kassa (2015) also asserts that women remain underrepresented in decision-making positions.

NOTE: *Tables 4.1, 4.2, 4.3 and 4.4 and figures 4.1, 4.2, 4.3 and 4.4, show the levels of disparity that exist between women's participation in politics and women's representation in governance in Nigeria.*

From table 4.1, there is a decline in voter registration in 2015. This also could account for the reduction in the number of women registered voters. Since 1999, the country witnessed the lowest voter turnout during the 2015 elections. This was pegged at 43.65 per cent compared to the 54 per cent in 2011 or the 57 per cent in 2007 and lastly the 69 per cent and 52 per cent in the 2003 and 1999 elections, respectively. What this means is that the lowest rate of voter turnout in the last election is a continuous spillover of the yet-to-be-mitigated overtime increase in voter apathy in Nigeria.

In 1999, when Nigeria returned to democratic rule, 45.4 per cent of reg-istered voters were women. Between 1999 and 2007, there seemed to be a consistency in the number of Nigerian women who registered as voters dur-ing this period. The major challenge here is that there are no disaggregated data of those who voted during the elections within the selected periods. From

Table 4.1 Women's Political Participation 1999–2015 (Voter Registration)

S/N	Years	Number of Registered Voters(in Millions)	Number Registered Women (in Millions)	Percentage
1.	1999	57,938,945	26,294,350	45.4
2.	2003	60,823,022	27,671,793	45.5
3.	2007	61,567,036	28,014,478	45.5
4.	2011	73,528,040	34,769,327	47.3
5.	2015	69,288,177	32,873,723	47.4

Source: African Elections Database/INEC–Abuja (2016).

Table 4.2 Women's Political Participation 2007–2015 (Candidates and Women Elected)

	2007		2011		2015	
Offices	*Candidates*	*Elected*	*Candidates*	*Elected*	*Candidates*	*Elected*
Presidential	1 (25)	0	1 (20)	0	1 (14)	0
Vice President	5 (25)	0	3 (20)	0	1 (14)	0
Governor	14 (474)	0	13 (353)	0 (36)	23 (380)	0
Deputy Gov	21 (474)	6 (36)	58 (347)	1 (36)	64 (380)	4 (29)
Senate	59 (797)	9 (109)	90 (890)	7 (109)	128 (746)	8 (109)
House of Rep.	150 (2,342)	26 (360)	220 (2,408)	26 (360)	270 (1,772)	17 (360)

Source: Nigeria National Elections by International Republican Institute (2015).

2011 to 2015, there was an increase in the number of women who registered as voters for the 2011 and 2015 elections. There were increments of 2.2 per cent and 0.1 per cent in 2011 and 2015 elections, respectively. This is shown in figure 4.3. Figure 4.3 shows the upward turn from the number of women who registered in 2007 and 2011 elections, where 47.3 per cent of the registered voters were women.

Not only did women register to vote in the elections, but they also contested for various offices from 1999 to 2015. Table 4.4 provides details of the number of women against the total number of people who contested for the various offices listed in the table. For 2007, 2011 and 2015, only one female candidate contested for the position of president of Nigeria out of the twenty-five who contested in 2007, twenty in 2011 and fourteen in 2015. For gubernatorial elections in 2007, we had 14 women who contested out of 474. Similarly, in 2011, 13 women contested out of 353, while in 2015, 23 women contested out of 380.

Table 4.2 shows that all elected state governors have been men, except in Anambra State in the 2007–2011 era when a female deputy governor was briefly installed as governor. She later reverted to her position as the deputy governor. Since Nigerians started to participate in public leadership and politics, there has not been an elected female governor in any state of Nigeria.

Due to administration tenure overlap, the number of individuals indicated in table 4.4 during any particular era was not necessarily equal to the number of states. This was because some state government administrations did not coincide precisely with the four-year cycle, as a result of nullified and rescheduled elections.

Table 4.2 also shows that we have had few states producing female deputy governors, like Lagos State, which produced the only female deputy governor in 1999. In 2003, this increased to three as Anambra, Ekiti and Ogun States also produced female deputy governors. In 2015, the number of female deputy governors increased by four. In addition, a total of 990 members of State

Table 4.3 Women Representation at State-Level Offices (Elected and Appointed by Gender)

Years	Governor			Deputy Governor			SSG			Commissioners			State House			Average
	M	F	%F	M	F	%F	M	F	%F	M	F	%F	M	F	%F	%F
1999	36	0	0	39	1	2.6	40	3	7.5	565	136	24.1	961	29	3.0	13.1
2003	39	0	0	38	3	7.9	43	3	7.0	609	84	13.8	942	48	5.1	8.7
2007	38	1	2.6	34	4	11.8	40	2	5.0	710	105	14.8	944	48	5.1	10.0
2011	38	0	0	38	2	5.3	44	1	2.3	757	117	15.5	925	65	7.0	11.0
2015	36	0	0	31	5	16.1	35	2	5.7	462	82	17.7	890	51	9.1	12.6

Source: The Winihin Jemide Series –Research and Ranking Report (2016).

Table 4.4 Women Representation at Federal-Level Offices (Elected and Appointed by Gender)

Status	1999 M	1999 F	1999 %F	2003 M	2003 F	2003 %F	2007 M	2007 F	2007 %F	2011 M	2011 F	2011 %F	2015 M	2015 F	2015 %F
President	1	0	0	1	0	0	2	0	0	1	0	0	1	0	0
Vice-President	1	0	0	1	0	0	2	0	0	1	0	0	1	0	0
Secretary to Government of Federation	1	0	0	1	0	0	2	0	0	1	0	0	1	0	0
Ministers / Ministers of State	41	2	4.9	40	8	20	47	10	21.3	35	11	31.4	31	6	19.3
Ambassadors and High Commissioners	54	5	9.3	54	5	9.3	77	9	11.7	79	11	14.0	Nil	Nil	
Permanent Secretaries										29	9	31.0	25	11	44.0
Chief of Staff to the President	1	0	0	1	0	0	2	0	0	2	0	0	1	0	0
Chief Justice of the Federation	1	0	0	2	0	0	2	0	0	1	1	100	1	0	0
House of Reps	353	07	2.0	339	21	6.2	333	27	8.1	335	25	7.5	347	13	3.7
Senate	106	03	2.8	105	04	3.8	100	09	9.0	102	07	6.9	103	06	5.8
Average			**1.9**			**3.9**			**4.0**			**19.1**			**7.2**

Source: The Winihin Jemide Series – Research and Ranking Report (2016).

Percentage

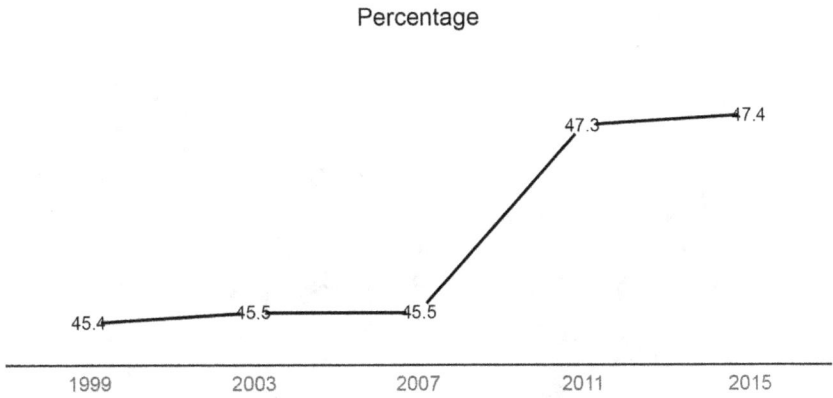

Figure 4.1 Women's Political Participation 1999–2015 (Voter Registration).

Percentage

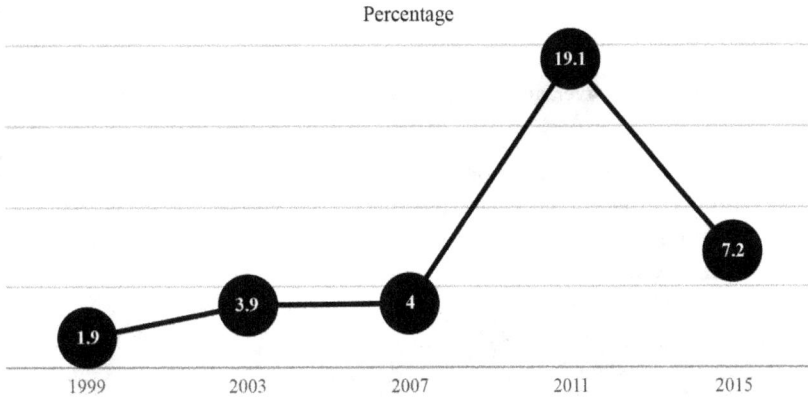

Figure 4.2 Average Percentage of Women's Representation at the Federal Level Offices.

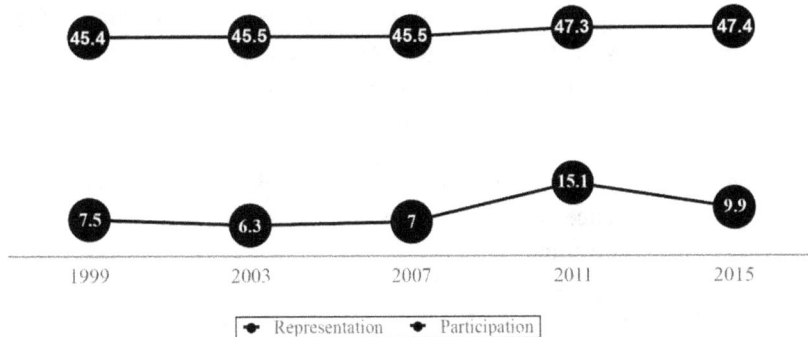

Representation   Participation

Figure 4.3 Disparity between Women's Participation and Women's Representation.

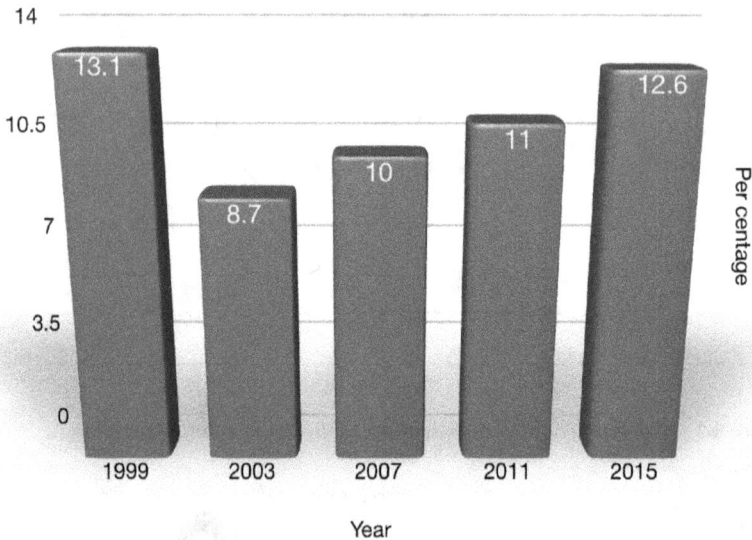

Figure 4.4   **Percentage Average of Women Representation at the State-Level Offices.**

Houses of Assembly were recorded between 1999 and 2003, out of which twenty-nine were women. On average, each state had twenty-eight members with an average of one woman in each House of Assembly. Nineteen states did not have any woman member in their state legislature, at all. There was an increase in 2007, where 48 of the 990 members of the state legislative houses were women and 51 of the 941 in 2015. NOTE: Table 4.3 shows Women Representation at State-Level Offices (Elected and Appointed by Gender).

Figures 4.2 and 4.4 show the average percentage of women representation at both federal and state offices. These figures show that, at the state level, Nigeria had the highest average percentage of women representation in 1999. While at the federal level, Nigeria had the highest average percentage of representation in 2011 with 19.1 per cent of women representation at the various offices listed. There was a tremendous increase from 4 per cent in 2007 to 19.1 per cent in 2011, yet there was a decrease by 2015 from 19.1 per cent to 7.2 per cent at the federal level.

Comparing levels of participation to actual representation in decision-making and governance, figure 4.3 depicts the disparity between women's participation in politics and women's representation at both state-level and federal-level offices. The highest level of representation was in 2011 with 15.1 per cent of women in various positions at both state and federal levels compared to the 47.3 per cent women who participated by registering to vote. This result shows a disproportional relationship between women's participation and women representation in Nigeria.

There were significant variations in the causes of women's underrepresentation across the three selected study areas. Hindrances to women's participation in politics and decision-making were rated to include a combination of factors such as social (93.7%), cultural (84.7%), political violence (86.0%), institutional design (82.6%), economic (85.0%), religious (59.9%) and legal (58.3%) (table 4.5). Significantly, overall, Nigerian women are still faced with varying social impediments that go a long way in hindering them from having symbolic and numeric representation in governance and decision-making. This finding corroborates Domingo, Holmes, O'Neil, Jones, Bird, Larson, Presier-Marshall and Valters (2015) who aver that there are multiple pathways to women's activism and that women's experience of changes at the individual level and collectively are also diverse. Several statements relating to social, cultural, political violence, institutional design and religious factors were presented to the women who responded by indicating the factors they believed hindered women's underrepresentation in governance and decision- making. These responses are presented in table 4.5.

From Table 4.5, the social factor is seen by all the respondents as the primary cause of women's underrepresentation, as 93.7 per cent of the women identified at least one variant of social factor as a cause of women's underrepresentation. Next to this social factor from the table above, is political violence as 86.0 per cent of the respondents identified at least one variant of political violence as a cause of underrepresentation. Also, 85.0 per cent of the respondents identified economic factor as a cause of underrepresentation, while 84.7 per cent identified cultural factor as a cause of underrepresentation. Of all the listed factors above, the legal factor is the least of the factors identified by the respondents as a cause of women's underrepresentation. In Anambra State, the religious factor was the least identified as a cause of women's underrepresentation.

To further gain a deeper understanding of what causes the underrepresentation of women, a qualitative analysis via in-depth interviews was conducted

Table 4.5 Factors Causing Women's Underrepresentation in Governance and Decision-Making in Nigeria

Factors	Kaduna (n=398)	Anambra (n=395)	Ondo (n=413)	Overall (n=1206)
Social	94.0	90.1	96.9	93.7
Cultural	89.2	72.4	92.0	84.7
Political Violence	92.0	71.9	93.7	86.0
Institutional Design	88.9	70.4	88.1	82.6
Economic	91.0	75.7	88.1	85.0
Religious	80.7	35.9	62.7	59.9
Legal	72.9	37.2	64.4	58.3

Source: Field Survey (2015).

among selected participants. The analysis showed that the significant factors identified as impediments to women's representation in governance and decision-making included: finance, ignorance, spousal disapproval, lack of social capital/mentorship, the timing of meetings, culture orientation, violence against women/political violence, envy and high headiness among women groups, religion, the godfather menace, education, disinheritance of women, party structure, nature of Nigerian politics, chauvinistic nature of men and corruption and insecurity. Despite these general factors identified by the respondents as common to the three geopolitical zones, there were specific impediments that were peculiar to women from each geopolitical zone identified. For instance, a respondent from Anambra State states that 'bottleneck we suffer from men, but still we are trying to mix up'. (Akure, 03)

In a similar tone, another respondent from Anambra State noted:

I don't know for any other culture, but in Igbo, a woman is meant to be under a man, whether you like it or not. Even if you are a billionaire and your husband is a shoe-maker, once you agree to marry him, you must be under him. (Akure, 04)

In addition, another respondent from Kaduna State noted: 'Men should be less chauvinistic and encourage women, especially because women are indeed concerned for all in the society' (Kaduna, 01).

Still from Kaduna State, a respondent observed: 'Women don't have enough social capital to engage in politics. By social capital, I mean they don't have the relationships, friends that they can actually use as backbones'. She further pointed out that the cultural orientation of a patriarchal society like ours (where a woman is not classified as someone who can be a leader), a woman is seen as somebody who must always be a subordinate or an associate. As such, the possibility of her coming out to vie for political positions becomes quite minimal (Kaduna, 03).

Not stopping there, she further attributed educational attainment as a significant challenge to women's representation in governance and decision-making. In contrast, educated women are always required to seek the consent of their husbands before such decisions can be taken. Also, the time of meetings was reported by almost all respondents as a significant challenge. To them, politicians always organise their meetings in the wee hours of the morning or late hours of the day, and it has usually been difficult for women to attend them; worse still, such women do not usually get the opportunity to contest for elective positions let alone being elected into office. One of the respondents from Anambra State also pointed out the issues of gender and religion, culture, party structure, harassment by men, finance and divide-and-rule tactics used by men as challenges. She also noted that the godfather menace posed a significant challenge. She states that 'if you don't have a strong godfather to stand for you, they will pull you down, no matter the amount of money you have' (Anambra, 02).

The findings are consistent with the general research survey. From the survey, finance was a significant impediment and this cuts across the three geopolitical zones but was not the most significant in Ondo State. In Ondo State, violence is reported as the most significant cause of women's under-representation in governance and decision-making. Next to that was lack of encouragement of women from society. In Anambra State, women's multiple roles and lack of support for women to participate in politics ranked next to finance as a factor causing women's underrepresentation. In Kaduna State, next to the issue of finance was the issues of violence and cultural impedi-ment, and some sociological issues were also identified as factors causing women's underrepresentation in governance and decision-making.

Geopolitical influences

H1 There is a significant relationship between geopolitical zone and women's political participation level.
H0 There is no significant relationship between geopolitical zone and wom-en's political participation level.

Table 4.6 presents a cross-tabulation of relationships between the geopolitical zone and level of women's political participation.

The results revealed that 17.8 per cent of Kaduna women had a low level of political participation, 32.2 per cent of them had a moderate level of politi-cal participation and half of them had a high level of political participation. Consider Awka women – 39.8 per cent had a low level of political participa-tion; 37.0 per cent had a moderate level of political participation and 23.3 per cent highly participated in politics. Of those from Ondo State, more than half (55.5 %) had a low level of political participation. At the same time, just 29.8 per cent of them participated in politics moderately, and the remaining 14.8 per cent highly participated in politics. The chi-square test of independence reveals a significant relationship between a geopolitical zone and level of political participation (= 172.6335, p-value<0.05).

Socioeconomic influences

H1 Socioeconomic characteristics influence women's participation in politics differently across the zones.
H0 Socioeconomic characteristics influence women's participation in politics non-differently across the zones.

Table 4.7 shows socioeconomic characteristics and level of political partici-pation by geopolitical zone.

Table 4.6   Relationship between Geopolitical Zone and Women's Political Participation Level

States from Geopolitical zones	Political Participation Level				χ^2	p-value
	Low Freq. (%)	Moderate Freq. (%)	High Freq. (%)	Total Freq. (%)		
Kaduna	71 (17.8)	128 (32.2)	199 (50.0)	398 (100)		
Anambra	157 (39.8)	146 (37.0)	92 (23.3)	395 (100)	172.6335	0.000
Ondo	229 (55.5)	123 (29.8)	61 (14.8)	413 (100)		

Source: Field Survey (2015).

Table 4.7 presents the cross-tabulation between socioeconomic characteristics and political participation of women. As regards the age group of the women, 39.1 per cent of those that belonged to the age group twenty years and below had low participation in the political activities, 34.8 per cent participated moderately and the remaining 26.1 per cent participated highly in the political activities. Among those that were in the age group twenty-one to twenty-five years, 40.7 per cent had low political participation, 30.1 per cent participated moderately in politics and 29.2 per cent participated highly in politics. Of those that belonged in the age group twenty-six to thirty years, 29.6 per cent had participated low in politics, 33.3 per cent participated moderately in politics and 37.0 per cent highly participated in politics.

The results further show that 43.0 per cent of those that belonged in the age group thirty-one to thirty-five years had a low level of political participation, 39.7 per cent participated moderately in politics and just 17.4 per cent highly participated in politics. Lastly, 37.6 per cent of those who belonged in the age group thirty-six years and above had participated low in politics, 32.3 per cent participated moderately in politics and 30.1 per cent participated highly in politics. The chi-square, however, indicates that is a significant *t* relationship between age group and political participation level (= 19.4553, *p*-value<0.05). The results reveal that women's participation is considerably high at age twenty-six years and above. This might be because of age restriction for contest into political offices.

Analysing by the marital status criterion, 36.3 per cent of those that were married had participated low in politics. In comparison, 36.3 per cent participated moderately in politics, and 27.4 per cent participated highly in politics. Among those that were widowed, 27.9 per cent participated low in politics, 37.2 per cent participated moderately in politics and 34.9 per cent participated highly in politics. Further, 21.4 per cent of those that were divorcees participated low in politics, 14.3 per cent of them participated moderately in politics and 64.3 per cent participated highly in politics. Among those that were separated, 17.4 per cent participated low in politics, 26.9 per cent participated moderately in politics and 56.5 per cent participated high in politics. Of those that were never married, 41.0 per cent had a low level of political participation, 30.6 per cent participated moderately in politics and 28.4 per cent had high-level political participation. However, the chi-square test of independence reveals a significant relationship between marital status and political participation level (= 24.2934, p-value<0.05). This result implies that the political environment is dominated majorly by single and married women.

Considering religious affiliation, 43.7 per cent of those that were Christians had low political participation, 32.5 per cent participated moderately in politics and 23.8 per cent had a high level of political participation. Among those that were Muslims, 21.0 per cent had a low level of political participation, 33.8 per cent had a moderate level of political participation and 45.3 per cent had a high level of participation. Among those that were traditional worshippers, 12.5 per cent had a low level of political participation, 50 per cent participated moderately and 37.5 per cent participated highly in politics (= 67.8686, p-value<0.05). Deductively from the results, religious affiliation influences the level of political participation of women.

The educational level of the women was also examined. Among those that had primary school education, 44.4 per cent had a low level of political participation, 29.6 per cent had a moderate level of political participation and 25.9 per cent had a high level of political participation. Among those that had secondary education, 29.9 per cent had a low level of political participation, 31.6 per cent had a moderate level of political participation and 38.5 per cent had a high level of political participation. As regards those with technically based education, 44.4 per cent had a low level of political participation, 29.6 per cent participated moderately and 25.9 per cent participated highly in political activities. Among those that had tertiary education, 40.4 per cent had a low level of political participation, 31.1 per cent participated moderately and 28.3 per cent participated highly in politics. Of those that had post-graduate education, 30.3 per cent participated low in politics, 43.9 per cent moderately participated in politics and 25.8 per cent highly participated in politics. However, the chi-square test of independence indicates a significant relationship between education and level of political participation (= 16.1214, p-value<0.05). Considering their income, among those that earned no income, 37.8 per cent had a low level of political participation, 29 per cent had a moderate level of political participation and 33.3 per cent highly participated in politics. Of those that earned between N20,001 and N40,000, 37.7 per cent had a low level of political participation, 35.1 per cent had a moderate level of political participation and 27.2 per cent highly participated in politics. Among those that earned between N40,001 and N60,000, 50.0 per cent had a low level of political participation, 39.1 per cent participated moderately and

Table 4.7 Socioeconomic Characteristics and Level of Political Participation by Geopolitical Zone

| Socioeconomic Characteristics | | Political Participation Level | | | | | | | | | | | |
| | | ANAMBRA | | | | KADUNA | | | | ONDO | | | |
Groups	Options	Low Freq. (%)	Mod. Freq. (%)	High Freq. (%)	Total Freq. (%)	Low Freq. (%)	Mod. Freq. (%)	High Freq. (%)	Total Freq. (%)	Low Freq. (%)	Mod. Freq. (%)	High Freq. (%)	Total Freq. (%)
Age group	<=20 years	9 (39.1)	11 (47.8)	3 (13.0)	23 (13.0)	12 (12.2)	43 (43.9)	43 (43.9)	98 (100)	51 (81.0)	10 (15.8)	2 (3.2)	63 (100)
	21–25 years	52 (51.0)	34 (33.3)	16 (15.7)	102 (100)	30 (17.8)	53 (31.4)	86 (50.9)	169 (100)	67 (70.5)	23 (24.2)	5 (5.3)	95 (100)
	26–30 years	20 (26.0)	31 (40.3)	26 (33.8)	77 (100)	13 (18.8)	17 (24.6)	39 (56.5)	69 (100)	31 (44.3)	24 (34.3)	15 (21.4)	70 (100)
	31–35 years	24 (36.9)	29 (44.6)	12 (18.5)	65 (100)	7 (18.8)	9 (40.9)	6 (27.3)	22 (100)	21 (61.8)	10 (29.1)	3 (8.8)	34 (100)
	36 years	52 (40.6)	41 (32.0)	35 (27.3)	128 (100)	9 (22.5)	6 (15.0)	25 (62.5)	40 (100)	59 (39.1)	56 (37.1)	36 (23.8)	151 (100)
	Statistics	$\chi^2 = 19.0179$, p-value = 0.015				$\chi^2 = 19.1442$, p-value = 0.014				$\chi^2 = 51.5475$, p-value = 0.000			
Marital status	Married	65 (36.3)	69 (38.6)	45 (25.1)	179 (100)	23 (24.2)	29 (30.5)	43 (45.3)	95 (100)	93 (41.3)	83 (36.9)	49 (21.8)	225 (100)
	Widowed	6 (37.5)	5 (31.3)	5 (31.3)	16 (100)	2 (10.0)	8 (40.0)	10 (50.0)	20 (100)	4 (57.1)	3 (42.9)	-	7 (100)
	Divorced	3 (75.0)	1 (25.0)	-	4 (100)	-	1 (14.3)	6 (85.7)	7 (100)	-	-	3 (100)	3 (100)
	Separated	1 (25.0)	1 (25.0)	2 (50.0)	4 (100)	-	5 (33.3)	10 (66.7)	15 (100)	3 (75.0)	-	1 (25.0)	4 (100)
	Never Married	82 (42.7)	70 (36.5)	40 (20.8)	192 (100)	46 (17.6)	85 (32.6)	130 (49.8)	261 (100)	129 (74.1)	37 (21.3)	8 (4.6)	174 (100)
	Statistics	$\chi^2 = 6.3830$, p-value = 0.604				$\chi^2 = 11.0057$, p-value = 0.201				$\chi^2 = 67.2729$, p-value = 0.000			
Religion	Christianity	154 (40.4)	138 (36.2)	89 (23.4)	381 (100)	24 (15.9)	53 (35.1)	74 (49.0)	151 (100)	216 (58.4)	102 (27.6)	52 (14.1)	370 (100)
	Islam	2 (22.2)	5 (55.6)	2 (22.2)	9 (100)	47 (19.2)	74 (30.2)	124 (50.6)	245 (100)	13 (31.0)	21 (50.0)	8 (19.1)	42 (100)
	Traditional	1 (20.0)	3 (60.0)	1 (20.0)	5 (100)	1 (50.0)	1 (50.0)	-	2 (100)	-	-	1 (100)	1 (100)
	Statistics	$\chi^2 = 2.8742$, p-value = 0.579				$\chi^2 = 1.8685$, p-value = 0.760				$\chi^2 = 20.0515$, p-value = 0.000			
Education	Primary	6 (66.7)	1 (11.1)	2 (22.2)	9 (100)	-	6 (54.6)	5 (45.5)	11 (100)	6 (85.7)	1 (14.3)	-	7 (100)
	Secondary	9 (29.0)	13 (41.9)	9 (29.0)	31 (100)	12 (18.8)	19 (26.7)	19 (29.7)	64 (100)	14 (63.6)	5 (22.7)	3 (13.6)	22 (100)
	Technical	22 (43.1)	19 (37.3)	10 (19.6)	51 (100)	5 (29.4)	6 (35.3)	6 (35.3)	17 (100)	11 (26.8)	12 (29.3)	18 (43.9)	41 (100)
	Tertiary	22 (43.1)	19 (37.3)	10 (19.6)	51 (100)	53 (18.6)	86 (30.2)	146 (51.2)	285 (100)	179 (61.1)	87 (26.7)	27 (9.2)	293 (100)
	Postgraduate	20 (32.8)	29 (47.5)	12 (19.7)	61 (100)	1 (4.8)	11 (52.4)	9 (42.9)	21 (100)	19 (38.0)	18 (36.0)	13 (26.0)	50 (100)
	Statistics	$\chi^2 = 8.7928$, p-value = 0.360				$\chi^2 = 11.3918$, p-value = 0.180				$\chi^2 = 48.4956$, p-value = 0.000			

(Continued)

Table 4.7 (Continued)

Socioeconomic Characteristics		Political Participation Level											
		ANAMBRA				KADUNA				ONDO			
Groups	Options	Low Freq. (%)	Mod. Freq. (%)	High Freq. (%)	Total Freq. (%)	Low Freq. (%)	Mod. Freq. (%)	High Freq. (%)	Total Freq. (%)	Low Freq. (%)	Mod. Freq. (%)	High Freq. (%)	Total Freq. (%)
Income	No income	23 (50.0)	17 (37.0)	6 (13.0)	46 (100)	50 (16.3)	98 (32.0)	158 (51.6)	306 (100)	120 (75.5)	33 (20.8)	6 (3.8)	159 (100)
	20,001–40,000	19 (48.7)	15 (38.5)	5 (12.8)	39 (100)	6 (17.1)	11 (31.4)	18 (51.4)	35 (100)	18 (45.0)	14 (35.0)	8 (20.0)	40 (100)
	40,001–60,000	16 (53.3)	11 (36.7)	3 (10.0)	30 (100)	2 (18.2)	5 (45.5)	4 (36.4)	11 (100)	14 (60.9)	9 (39.1)	-	23 (100)
	60,001–80,000	13 (39.4)	15 (45.5)	5 (15.2)	33 (100)	2 (28.6)	3 (42.9)	2 (28.6)	7 (100)	5 (41.7)	6 (50.0)	1 (8.3)	12 (100)
	80,000+	86 (34.8)	88 (35.6)	73 (29.6)	247 (100)	11 (28.2)	11 (28.11)	17 (43.6)	39 (100)	72 (40.2)	61 (34.1)	46 (25.7)	179 (100)
	Statistics	χ^2 = 16.9822, p-value = 0.030				χ^2 = 5.7979, p-value = 0.670				χ^2 = 60.4136, p-value = 0.000			
Employment Status	Working	87 (33.7)	101 (39.2)	70 (27.1)	258 (100)	21 (25.3)	27 (32.5)	35 (42.2)	83 (100)	106 (43.6)	86 (35.4)	51 (21.0)	243 (100)
	Not-Working	70 (51.1)	45 (32.9)	22 (16.1)	137 (100)	50 (15.9)	101 (32.1)	164 (52.1)	315 (100)	123 (72.4)	37 (21.8)	10 (5.9)	170 (100)
	Statistics	χ^2 = 12.4678, p-value = 0.002				χ^2 = 4.5641, p-value = 0.102				χ^2 = 36.5794, p-value = 0.000			

Source: Field Survey (2015).

27.2 per cent highly participated in politics. About 50.0 per cent of those who earned between N60,001 and N80, 000 had low political participation, 46.2 per cent had a moderate level of political participation and just 15.4 per cent participated highly in politics. Of those that earned N80,000 and above, 36.3 per cent had a low level of political participation, 34.4 per cent participated moderately and 19.2 per cent participated highly. The chi-square test revealed a significant relationship between income and level of political participation (= 22.9527, p-value<0.05). This result revealed that income was one of the variables that affected women's political participation. In addition, 36.6 per cent of those that were working had a low and moderate level of political participation each respectively, and 26.7 per cent participated high in politics. Of those that were not working, 39.1 per cent participated low in politics, 29.4 per cent participated moderately and 31.5 per cent highly participated in politics. The chi-square test reveals a significant relationship between employment status and political participation level (= 26.7236, p-value<0.05). Those that were not working had more time for political activities than those that were working.

Furthermore, 39 per cent of the upper social class had a low level of political participation, 31.2 per cent participated moderately and 29.9 per cent highly participated in politics. Among those that were in the lower class, 40.5 per cent participated low in politics, 34.3 per cent had participated moderately and 25.2 per cent highly participated in politics. Of those that were in moderate social class, 2.8 had a low and moderate level of political participation each and 3.1 highly participated in politics. Among those that refused to reveal their social class, 6.6 per cent had a low level of political participation, 47.5 per cent had a moderate level of political participation and 13.1 per cent highly participate in politics. There exists a notable relationship between social class and political participation (= 19.1037, p-value<0.05). Therefore, the results revealed that lower social class participates in political activities more than any other class. Below, the major two established causes of the exclusion of women from participatory politics will be discussed in a little more details than the others. These include social factors and violence against women.

THE IMPLICATIONS OF WOMEN'S UNDERREPRESENTATION FOR THE SOCIOECONOMIC DEVELOPMENT OF NIGERIA

Women, as political practitioners, are faced with numerous challenges at every stage of their political development. It is still a man's world, and women navigate a different societal and political landscape when compared with their male counterparts, as seen in the study. First, women politicians must deal with ambivalent reactions deeply rooted in gender stereotypes, including assertive, authoritative and dominant behaviour typical of most male politicians, which tended to be viewed as unattractive in women. Studies of attitudes towards women in traditionally male roles show that women effectively trade perceptions of competence for likeability; the more successful they appear, the less effective they are regarded. Such trends constrained women, and this affects their willingness to go all out to achieve their political aspiration. Most societal constraints of women emanate from sociopolitical ideologies and belief systems. Also, political structures, institutions, sociocultural and functional constraints put limits on women's leadership. This, the study observed, is evident in the institutional weakness seen in the party structure, such as lack of clarity in the rules for the selection of candidates. This is intertwined with the prevailing political culture of authoritarianism, male supremacy and a high level of violence and intimidation. The overall effect is to produce an ethos extremely hostile to women. Lastly, it will be challenging to enhance the democratisation of governance, which is possible through equal representation of women and men.

The study observed that low representation of women impedes and undermines the goals of equality, development, transparency and peace as well as it negatively affects the quality of democratic, electoral processes and legislative outcomes. This can be inferred from Domingo et al. (2015), who finds that women's political representation has resulted in gender-responsive legal and policy reform. According to Domingo et al. (2015), this gain includes and goes beyond women's presence in formal political positions. However, it is also often connected to women's social mobilisation and their collective organisation around gender justice.

Contrary to the above, some authors believed that low representation of women in politics does not have a significant impact on the socioeconomic development of a country. Khayria and Feki (2015) aver that, in Sub-Saharan Africa, gender inequality seems to have a weak relationship with economic performance. The implication of the low representation of women in politics for the socioeconomic development of the country is not very clear. A portion indicates that there is a positive relationship between a low representation of women and socioeconomic development, while others show that this relationship is slightly negative.

From the literature and the key-in-depth interview, there were several implications of low representation of women in politics for the socioeconomic development of the country. Given the very minimal percentage of women in governance and decision-making, it was observed in this study from various respondents that low representation of women makes it difficult to assist the community as it will be hard to lobby ministers from outside or be able to access specific amenities for community development. A respondent from Anambra State noted that low representation of women impedes the goals of equality, development and peace as women can incorporate their varying perspectives at all levels of decision-making. In addition, it is noted that a low representation undermines development and transparency.

Another implication of a low representation was that it exposed the level at which gender equality was undermined. Gender equality is helpful to the economy and society. With low representation, it indicates a dismissal of the talent and creativity of half of its population. This leads to countries losing their potential growth as a result of persisting gender inequalities evident in low representation of women in governance and decision-making. The significance of such underrepresentation in national politics is extensive.

From the study, we found that it negatively affects the quality of democratic electoral processes, and may reinforce legal and symbolic limitations on individual citizens. A respondent from Anambra State also asserted that one of the implications of low representation of women in governance and decision-making is that women will not have a significant impact on legislative outcomes and hence will not be able to promote women-friendly policy change. Therefore, making women's viewpoint visible in political decision-making will be difficult. From Ondo State, a respondent stated that 'low representation makes it difficult to change the perceptions of society and political stakeholders regarding women's capacity' (Ondo, 01). Also from Ondo State, another respondent stated that 'low representation makes it difficult to expand the pool of women willing to run for public offices as there are few examples to emulate' (Ondo, 03). From Kaduna, a respondent noted that low representation of women makes it difficult to bring women's different perspectives, views and experiences to the table that can enrich political and policy debate. This respondent noted that it hurts the socioeconomic development of the nation, as policies that can engender equality and fairness even in resource allocation will be limited. Also, from Kaduna State, another respondent observed that 'low representation negatively affects the quality of democratic electoral processes' (Kaduna, 04). The same respondent claimed that the low representation of women in politics might reinforce legal and symbolic limitations on individual citizens.

Other respondents believe that many countries with relatively low levels of socioeconomic development have outpaced developed democracies in enhancing the formal political representation of women. This generalisation has been proven by studies regarding many developing countries – including several African countries – that have much higher rates of representation of women in parliament than do some of the most developed countries such as France (12.1%), Italy (9.8%), Japan (7.3%) and the United States (13.8%) (Krook and Childs, 2010).

Chapter 5

Gender Disparity in Contemporary Nigerian Politics

Nigerian women's political activities mirror the scope of their participation in political parties in Nigeria as well as their involvement in elective positions across the three levels of government. This chapter gives hints about the positions that Nigerian women have occupied over time, especially between 1999 and 2015 within political parties in Nigeria. It also reveals the number or percentage of women in elective positions as against men. This analysis enables us to understand what has been achieved – when and where; what gaps in action or strategy exist; and what women need to do to improve upon their performances for an excellent future showing. Also, further in this chapter, the research findings of scholars concerning how Nigerian women's political power-share is configured are presented. The reports of these scholars represent a bird's-eye view of the exploits of these amazons on Nigeria's political turf.

On the patterns and levels of women's political participation, this book, using the Verba and Nie's model, identified six significant patterns of political participation, namely: inactive, voting specialists, parochial participants, communalists, campaigners and complete activists. In line with the classification by Verba and Nie, there is a variation in the pattern of participation of Nigerian women in politics such that majority were communalists (56.3%), followed by voting specialists (18.2%), inactive (10.6%), campaigners (9.2%), complete active (5.0%) and parochial participants (0.1%) in order of magnitude. This tallies with the findings of Brady et al. (1995), Lijphart (1997) and Verba et al. (1995) who aver that political participation tends to be unequally distributed among citizens. The patterns reveal that majority of Nigerian women were communalists; they participate at the local level, join organisations and participated in politics but not in partisan campaigns. This pattern is in line with Albritton's (2005) assertion that, the female gender is continually influenced by communal practice. These differences could be as a result of employment which is a crucial factor according to Iversen and Rosenbluth (2008), and cultural differences often with religion as the primary focus which is also corroborated by Norris and Inglehart (2004) and Norris (2002).

The findings of this study are consistent with the findings in Leighley (1995). Mohai (1991) on the other hand also demonstrates how these variations in participation rates were institution-specific: Blacks in environmental groups were less likely to participate in environmental politics beyond the group, while Blacks in other types of groups are more likely to participate in (general) politics beyond the group. This suggests that differences in participation levels among Whites, African Americans and Latinos reflected structural barriers or differential mobilisation patterns to participation, also relevant to the patterns observed across the selected geopolitical zones. With the observed patterns of political participation seen in the study, it corroborates other studies in extant literature, as political participation tends to be unequally distributed among citizens (Bartels, 2005; Brady et al., 1995; Griffin and Newman, 2005; Isaksson, 2010; Lijphart, 1997; Verba et al., 1995).

Many typologies of forms of political participation were identified in the literature, but this book adopts Verba and Nie's model as presented in Figure1.1, which describes six forms of political participation; indicating that all women, no matter their geopolitical zones, exhibited one form of political participation or the other (Verba and Nie, 1972). Thus the instrument was designed to first identify the forms of political participation peculiar to

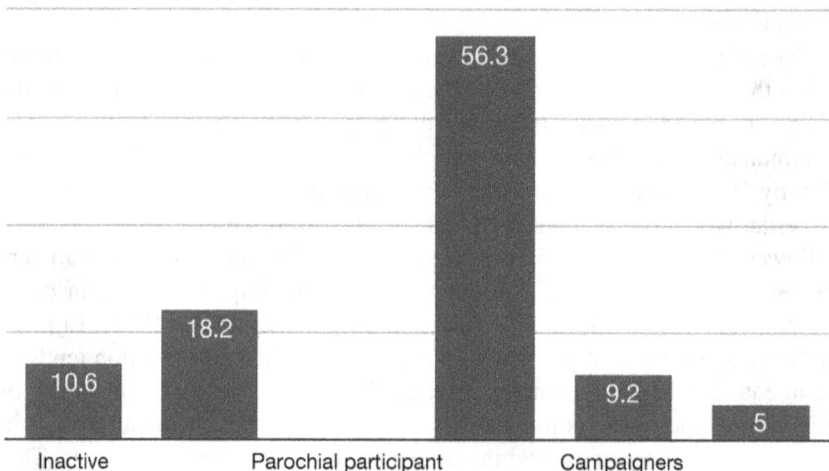

Figure 5.1   Pattern of Participation of Nigerian Women in Politics (Overall).

the geopolitical zones in Nigeria, concerning the three selected zones. Once identified, the act of participation presented in Appendix VI shows the various items summed up to arrive at each typology of participation of Nigeria women in politics. The description of women's participation in politics in Nigeria as a whole and a disaggregated description of women's participation within selected states are illustrated in figures 5.1 and 5.2, respectively, and presented in table 5.1. They present the patterns and levels of participation of women in Nigerian politics using the Verba and Nie's model as specified in the conceptual clarification.

This figure shows that, overall, 56.3 per cent of Nigerian women were more of communalists. They joined organisations (civil society organisations, CSOs – for example, political parties) and participated in politics but not in partisan campaigns.

Next to the communalists is an 18.2 per cent of Nigerian women being voting specialists – they only voted during elections but did not participate in other forms of political activities. Another set of 9.2 per cent were found to be campaigners. This set of women participated in all forms of political

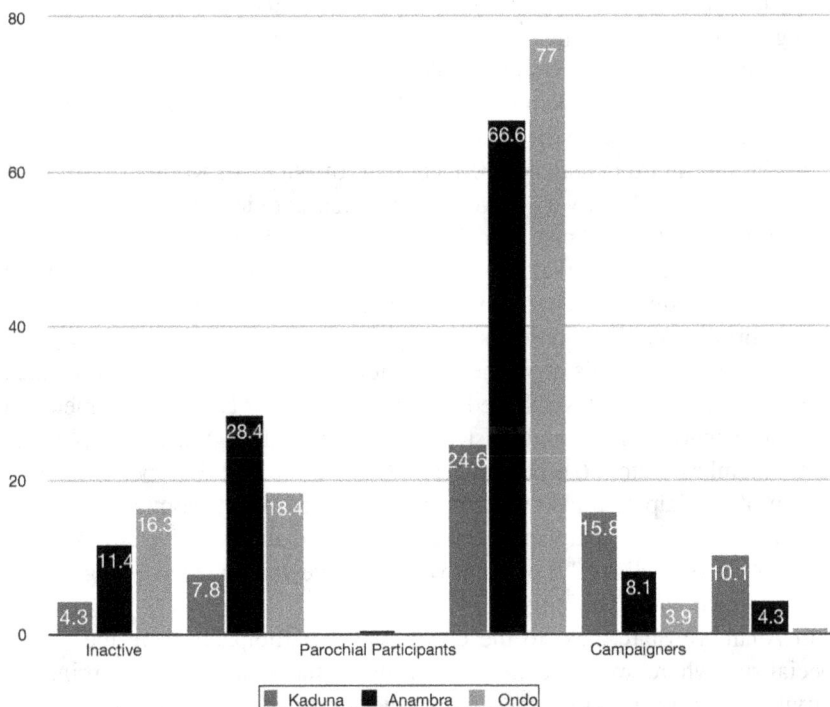

Figure 5.2   Pattern of Women's Political Participation (Disaggregated by Selected States).

Table 5.1   Pattern of Women's Political Participation

Typology of participation	Kaduna (n = 398)	Anambra (n = 395)	Ondo (n = 413)	Overall (n = 1206)
Inactive	4.3	11.4	16.3	10.6
Voting Specialist	7.8	28.4	18.4	18.2
Parochial participant	0.0	0.3	0.0	0.1
Communalist	24.6	66.6	77.0	56.3
Campaigners	15.8	8.1	3.9	9.2
Complete active	10.1	4.3	0.7	5.0

Source: FieldWork, 2015.

activities, but it did not contact government officials neither did it protest against government policies or activities. Similarly, figure 5.1 reveals that only 5.0 per cent of the women were complete activists. This set of women participated in all activities listed in section II of the questionnaire used to measure political participation level. These activities included the following: those sympathising with, or affiliated to, a political party; carrying a membership card of a political party; attending political party meetings; mobilising others to attend meetings; registering for voters card and having voters card; voting in all elections; engaging in political campaigns; contacting government officials on policy issues; protesting against government policy and wearing campaign shirt, button or wrist band. This is indicated by answering favourably to all the activities listed.

Again, the figure reveals that 0.1 per cent of Nigerian women were parochial participants. This very set of few women avoided elections and civic organisations but would contact officials regarding specific problems. Lastly, 10.6 per cent were inactive; they did not participate in any of the ten listed activities in section II of the questionnaire. Therefore, they did not participate in any form of political activities in Nigeria. Figure 5.2 shows the disaggregated patterns and levels of women's participation in politics by the selected states. In the three states selected for analysis, majority of the women fell into the category of communalist participants: Kaduna State had 24.6 per cent; Anambra State, 66.6 per cent; and Ondo State had 77.0 per cent. This pattern of participation also reveals that 15.8 per cent of women in Kaduna State were purely campaigners; 10.1 per cent were utterly active; 7.8 per cent were voting specialists; 4.3 per cent were inactive while we have no group of women as parochial participants

In Anambra State, next to the communalist participants were the voting specialists, where we have 28.4 per cent of the women whose principal activity in politics was to vote as they indicated to have voted consistently in the past elections in Nigeria. Figure 5.2 further reveals that 11.4 per cent of women from Anambra State were inactive; 8.1 per cent were campaigners;

4.3 were completely active, while 0.3 were parochial participants. Likewise in Ondo State, next to the communalists participants were the voting specialists, where we had 18.4 per cent of the women; 16.3 per cent were inactive; 3.9 per cent were campaigners; 0.7 were completely active and no woman fell into the category of the parochial participants as seen in the overall analysis in table 4.2. Those in the inactive group did little or nothing; voting specialists voted regularly but did nothing also; parochial participants contacted officials concerning specific issues; communalists engaged in political action intermittently, but were not intensely involved; campaigners were intensely involved in various campaigns; and those in the complete activists group participated in several activities identified in the questionnaire.

The qualitative analysis from IDIs with respondents shows that the forms of participation identified were voting; campaigning; contesting for political offices; contacting political officials; and lobbying and attending party meetings. This trend was reported when asked about their experience and impact of political party structures on women's political participation. The forms of political participation identified fall within the six different types of political participation identified by Verba and Nie (1972), which Albritton and Bureekul (n.d.) extended to eight in their study on how Asian minorities participated in politics. Accurately, a respondent reported that she did a door-to-door campaign and mosquito campaign. When asked what she meant by mosquito campaign, she said it means, 'Whispering. It was her former Excellency, Mrs Peter Obi that taught us to go for mosquito campaign. You leave your shop, go to another person's shop, you wouldn't even allow the person near you to hear what you are saying' (Akure, 05).

A respondent from Ondo State also noted that women participated through campaigning and real politicking. She states: 'I think there are two dimensions, we have women who campaign, dance at your rally and we have women who are politicians. So women's participation in politics must incorporate those two areas' (Ondo, 02).

Other respondents identified the process of electioneering as a means through which women participated in politics. According to a respondent, 'participation in politics has to do with the entire process of electioneering, which involves campaigning, registration, voting, contesting and funding. Women in my area are encouraged to be involved in all forms of political participation' (Ondo, 03).

A respondent from Awka noted that 'in Awka, it is women that cast votes . . . in terms of the campaign, we campaign' (Akure, 02).

In general, voting, campaigning and contesting for positions were significant forms of participation identified by almost all the respondents. Although the survey revealed that these forms of participation might not necessarily be frequent, it was observed that the majority of our respondents from the three geopolitical zones voted during the 2015 general elections. For a better sense of the role Nigerian women play in politics and governance, diverse literature is reviewed from political participation and governance from 1999 (when Nigeria restored democracy) to 2015. The role women play in politics cannot be successfully undermined, especially given that these propel a global change process. Many international organisations, non-governmental organisations and civil societies have over the years advocated for the inclusion of women in the process of governance and identified the unique contributions women can bring to the system given their make-up and needs. Pogoson (2015) attests to women's participation or denial of it in communal life, governance and decision-making. The study (2015) also examines various investments women have made in people's lives in their respective societies; how women had to battle the power structure and patriarchy, given the subordinate position ascribed to them. Pogoson (2015) concludes that there is a need to unearth the more profound and more fundamental processes of restructuring power and politics to convert political women from a minority within each political party into a majority of the citizenry and through that, improve their potential for better representation in Africa. In all, Pogoson (2015) does not, however, give adequate information on the number of women who have so far laid actual claims to the public space. That information would have helped to buttress our understanding of how far women have gone in their quest to be actively involved in governance and politics.

Adiakpan and Akpan (2014) concentrate on the efforts of women from Akwa Ibom State in politics and governance; tracing the emergence of traditional women groups with ethnic nationalities within the state and appraising the positions previously occupied by women of Akwa Ibom State origin in different levels of government. They argue that Akwa Ibom State did not have any woman as a minister or federal legislator until the emergence of the Fourth Republic but identified Late Margret Ekpo as a female member of Eastern House of Assembly in the First Republic. Since 1999 however, the state has produced two female senators and a female member of the House of Representatives. At the state level, they (Adiakpan and Akpan, 2014) note that Akwa Ibom had 1, 3, 2 and 3 women elected into the House of Assembly in 1999, 2003, 2007 and 2011 elections, respectively; while the state also had a female deputy governor from 2012 to 2015. The work further accounts for the contribution of fourteen women appointed as commissioners from the state and detailed the effort of the governor's wife.

Further, Adiakpan and Akpan (2014) evaluate the situation of women at the local government level in the Fourth Republic. Women occupied the position of chairperson, vice chairperson and councillors for some years. It shows that women got two chairpersons with seven vice chairpersons in 2008; four chairpersons with eight vice chairpersons while there were thirty-four councillors in 2012. Adiakpan and Akpan (2014) further presented the opportunities of women in appointive non-cabinet positions and also the contribution of some women as leaders and mobilisers in non-partisan, partisan and sociocultural groupings. However, Adiakpan and Akpan (2014) concentrate on Akwa Ibom State. This study does not detail women in party positions. The study failed to suggest whether women from the state have been well or underrepresented in politics. It did not also put other states of the federation in retrospect as the basis of comparing the status of Akwa Ibom State women in politics and governance. Hence, there is a vacuum for study with a national outlook, which will consider appointive, elective and party positions occupied by women in politics and governance in Nigeria.

When Agbu (2015) examined the problem of under-participation of women in Nigerian politics, he offered a psychological understanding of the discourse by presenting an overview of women's participation in the Nigerian political arena vis-à-vis that of their male counterparts with a comparison drawn from available statistics from 1999 to 2010. Agbu (2015) notes that uneven developmental and sociocultural experiences further complicate the challenges that Nigerian women encounter while venturing into politics, thus an enabling environment should be created so that more women can be encouraged to participate actively in politics. The study, however, failed to provide understanding as to how the psychological dimension, if properly annexed, can engender more participation of women in politics.

Wanting to know how women who contested for elective offices fared in that respect, Eme and Onuigbo (2015) critically reviewed the place of women in the 2015 general elections in Nigeria. The study relied on data from Nigeria's Independent National Electoral Commission (INEC); it analysed and presented them in quantitative terms. It is therein stated that from the 380 candidates nominated/cleared to contest the 2015 governorship elections in 29 concerned states, 25 were female, while of the 380 deputies, 60 were females. However, of the 15 presidential candidates, 14 were men and only 1 (Prof. Remi Sonaiya of KOWA Party) was a woman. In contrast, 10 men and 4 women were selected as the vice president. The study further avouched that for the 360 House of Representative seats, there were 10,526 male and 267 female contestants while 621 men and 122 women contested for the 109 senatorial slots. These researchers, like many other scholars, are concerned about the statistics of 2011, 2007, 2003 and 1999 general elections concerning the state of women. They categorically claim that from 1999 to 2007, there was a marginal but steady increase in political participation of women through elections and political appointments. However, with a slight decline in 2011, the women's figure cut across the board. Eme and Onuigbo (2015), relying on the initially declared results, state that only fourteen women emerged members of the House of Representatives while seven emerged senators; none emerged as governor. Their study also presents a few figures or the representation of women at the State Houses (Lagos and Adamawa). The study also identifies the general challenges of women's political participation.

Continuing, the researchers presented an analysis of women's scorecard in 2015 elections; it failed, however, to present the appointive slots which women got after the election at state and federal levels. The work also neglected the party positions occupied by women towards the elections. While the work is quantitative, it failed to reflect on what was ahead for women in the coming elections. The study also did not present the figures of women's scorecard in the election at all the State Houses of Assembly, thereby giving room for further research even on the 2015 general elections as regards the scorecard of women.

For Agishi (2014), tracing the history of women's involvement in party politics in Nigeria would give the required insight. She claims that since the emergence of indigenous political leadership in 1960, Nigerian women have remained invisible in the party system; noting specifically that women have always suffered underrepresentation in party membership and in party decision-making mechanisms. She relies on secondary data and references. Olojede (1999) avers that even in the executives of political parties, women were almost invisible, between 1957 and 1959, except for NEPU that had women in its National Executives. Agishi (2014) cites Olojede (1999) to show marginal participation of women in the decision-making of the political parties in the aborted Third Republic: NRC and SDP. She also agrees with Okoosi-Simbine (2003) cited in Pogoson (2012) who recorded that during the formation of political parties leading to the Fourth Republic, no female featured prominently in the party process. Agishi (2014) identifies the challenges of women's participation in party politics to monetisation of the political processes. She cites the case of the inability of the three female presidential aspirants under SDP to fulfil the financial requirements of their parties. The financial requirements included party tickets, personal expenses, party offices, campaign offices and expenses and financial mobilisation of voters. She identifies other challenges, including the violent nature of Nigerian party politics and discriminatory social practices.

Distraught and aghast about the scheme of things regarding women in Nigerian politics Agishi (2014) regrets that women's participation in politics, especially party politics, has been deeply constrained; hence, she suggests that parties should implement the affirmative action policy on gender equality, such that 30 per cent of party officers and candidates are certainly and non-negotiably women. She also opines that there should be a policy change through constitutional and electoral act provisions, necessitating the inclusion of women by the required percentage as a condition for registration of political parties, the composition of party executives, nomination for elections and composition of cabinets after elections.

Agishi's analytical research relies on earlier publications and other secondary sources, and focuses only on party politics but fails to consider women's involvement in the party systems in the Fourth Republic. Her paper also leaves out the elective and appointive positions reserved for women. While being historical, the study leaves out the Second Republic in its documentation, thereby creating a vacuum in her research and more opportunities for further research.

Democracy Action Group (DAG) (2014), in a quantitative empirical survey, presents a gender audit of some political parties in the Kano State of Nigeria to determine the level of women's participation and representation within the dominant political parties. The study also describes the factors hindering women from occupying essential positions in political party leadership. The survey was conducted through the interview of seventy-five respondents across five major political parties (All Progressives Congress (APC), People's Democratic Party (PDP), Labour Party (LP), National Conscience Party (NCP) and People's Democratic Movement (PDM)), dominant in the forty-four local governments of the state. DAG (2014) also relies on secondary sources, particularly from the offices of the identified political parties. The study (DAG, 2014) identifies social, cultural and religious factors as hindrances to women's political party participation and their marginalisation in party leadership. The capital-intensive nature, poverty, home responsibilities as wife and mother, lack of adequate education and violence or intimidation hinder women from participating actively in partisan political activities in Kano State.

Attempting a census of party members, DAG (2014) shows that as at 2013/2014 convention of political parties at state levels, APC female members in Kano State stood at 9,850 against 1,965,000 men while NCP claimed 4,000 female against 8,000 men, while other parties' figures were not available. Analysis at the local government level indicated that APC and PDP had the highest figures of female members in Kano State. DAG (2014) further shows that party leadership in seven positions within the same period (2013/2014) at the state level to be as follows: APC had one woman, while PDP, PDM LP and NCP had three each. The study also presented figures of women for some selected local governments, but there were no female party executives. DAG (2014) presents the hopes of the women in party leadership in Kano State; explicitly, the study does not cover women in elected and appointive political positions. It did not cover all years since the return to democracy nor eras of the First to Third Republics. Even in its analysis, detailed information on all the local government areas in Kano State and all political parties were not provided; hence room for further research.

Mofoluwawo (2014) studies discrimination against women in African politics but concentrates on Nigeria in particular. The study investigates the level of women's participation; challenges to women's participation; and suggested measures to increase women's participation in Nigerian politics. Relying on secondary data (from Women Watch) and descriptive analyses, the study presents trends in women's participation in Nigerian politics from 1999 to 2011. It reveals that 2, 4, 8 and 6 per cent of the elected seats were occupied by women through 1999, 2003, 2007 and 2011 general elections, respectively. The study involves only the Presidential, Senate, House of Representatives, Governorship and State Houses of Assembly seats. Mofoluwawo (2014) further identifies issues militating against women's participation in Nigerian politics to include sociocultural factors; economic factor; fear of marginalisation; lack of solidarity; political insecurity; harassment; violence; thuggish behaviour and intimidation of opponents; the indigene-origin criterion; and the 'step-down' phenomenon.

The study suggests approaches for increasing active women's participation in Nigerian politics to include adequate enforcement of the constitutional provisions for gender equity, women's political education and equipping, plus legislative and administrative reforms for increased access to resources. It concludes that although Nigerian women have potentials to contribute to her transformation, women discrimination remains anathema in human existence, healthy relationship and development. Mofoluwawo (2014) focuses only on seats available at general elections; without considering elective positions at the local government level. The work fails to consider the appointive positions women occupied within the studied period (1999–2011) (Mofoluwawo, 2014). This gap creates an opportunity for further research into subsequent elections in 2015 as it was limited to 1999–2011 and more in-depth empirical studies on appointive and party positions which women have occupied since the return to democracy.

The report of the Gender Audit of Political Parties in Kaduna State (2014) accounts for the status of women in five main political parties in the state. The report indicates all offices in its leadership: while women occupy four in African Democratic Congress (ADC), they only occupy those specifically designated to be occupied by women (women leaders) in APC, LP, PDP and SDP. The report is not detailed on accurate figures and stands of women within Kaduna State as regards politics and governance. At the same time, it also fails to quantify women's status in non-partisan, elective and appointive political positions in both Kaduna State and Nigeria as a whole.

Women Aid Collective (WACOL) (2014) similarly evaluated the status of women in party politics in Enugu State; it relied on data from the selected political parties' secretariats and interview of purposively selected key informants. Women in Enugu State occupy 33 per cent of leadership positions in the PDP, 29 per cent of the leadership positions in the APC, 29 per cent of the leadership positions in the All Progressive Grand Alliance (APGA), 33 per cent of the leadership positions in the Labour Party and 28 per cent of the leadership positions in the People for Democratic Change (PDC) at the state party level. It states that women are not so poorly represented within the political parties at the state level in Enugu. The study concentrates on Enugu State alone concerning the five selected political parties; it does not fully cover women's participation in all the areas of politics and governance.

Women Advocates Research and Documentation Centre (WARDC) (2014) reports the gender sensitivity of the political parties in Lagos State, Nigeria. The study relies on manifestoes, constitution and interview of members of leading political parties in Lagos State. The result indicates that all the parties recognise and are concerned about gender issues but could only sustain the practice of at least one female in every five-member committee of the parties. Specifically, it shows that only thirteen from thirty-seven executive structures are females in APC; the majority of them are male, in APGA. There is a gender imbalance in the Labour Party. Only two of thirteen executives are females in NCP while women are more actively represented in the PDP. Despite this report, WARDC (2014) presents data on Lagos State alone and also fails to include women in other political positions such as in the elective and appointive status. The study, though empirical, does not conclude based on the opinions of the respondents. More of its analysis is based on party laws and practices. The work (WARDC, 2014) also considers only happenings from 2013 to 2014, thereby creating opportunities for detailed research in this regard.

Another study conducted by Ngara and Ayabam (2013) examined the challenges and prospects of women in politics and decision-making in Nigeria. They utilised secondary data; specifically, quantitative data in publications and their work is descriptively historical and analytical. They maintain that Nigeria's precolonial history is replete with heroic exploits of women, and identified some seventeen prominent women traditional leaders across areas of present-day Nigeria. This study also identifies other prominent women who have set records in various sectors since Nigeria's independence. Their study presents tables on women figures in political positions since Nigeria's return to democracy in 1999.

They contend that women's participation in politics and decision-making witnessed an improvement over previous experiences since 1999, though it is still generally poor. Findings show that only 181 of 11,881 available positions throughout the country were won by women in 1999; with little improvement in 2003. They claimed that at the 2007 election, 1,200 women aspired for 1,532 offices, but only 660 won their primaries; contrary to this, there was a downward slope for elected women in the 2011 elections. They present that against the failure of women in elective positions in the 2011 elections, President Jonathan first appointed thirteen women, out of forty-two ministers (31%); eleven female permanent secretaries (25%); and five female advisers (38%). They (Ngara and Ayabam, 2013) further list these women and some others in private practice with milestone performance of success. They stated that the role of these women lifted the pedigree and profile of Nigerian women as hardworking, disciplined, thorough, creative, enterprising and productive.

Also, Ngara and Ayabam (2013) go on, like other scholars to identify funding, negative perception about politics, violence, cultural and religious discriminations, lack of self-confidence, low level of education as well as marginalisation in party politics as the challenges militating against women's participation in politics and decision-making in Nigeria. In furtherance of their study, they identify improvements/upward glides in women figure in politics as a great advantage for development. They observe a significant comparative growth in the interest of women in politics as a prospect as well as sterling leadership qualities and outstanding track records of achievement of some involved women. The study singled out President Jonathan's administration in upholding, to an extent, the possibility of realising the 35 per cent affirmative action. It concludes that the role women have played since 1999, coupled with an increase in women advocacy, educational/schooling level and track record of successes, guarantees prospects for women in Nigerian politics.

Critically, Ngara and Ayabam (2013) consider elective and appointive (with some employable/promotional and political) positions in Nigeria. It fails to look at the place of women in party politics. The study also ended with the 2011 elections and did not extend to 2015. Though quantitative to an extent, the paper relies on a definite secondary source and is more historical and analytical. Therefore, the study leaves an opportunity for further research with consideration of women's role within the party and the grassroots/LG politics.

Still investigating women as an epicentre of Nigeria's political pivot, Olufade (2013) while writing on Nigerian women, politics and the national identity examines the role of Nigerian women in politics and the discrimination against womenfolk especially as politics is seen as a man's turf and a 'no-go' area for women. This study, therefore, posits that women should not be left out of politics and should be allowed to contribute their quota to the development of their country. The study used a historical and descriptive approach, to highlight the roles women have played in Nigerian politics despite the patriarchal nature of the Nigerian society, from the precolonial era to date. The study, therefore, points out that equitable participation of women in politics is essential to building and sustaining democracy in Nigeria. The study also highlights the poor participation of women in Nigerian politics as a result of specific barriers such as cultural, economic and legal ones. In another vein, the study examines Nigerian women's perception of politics as a dirty game, the violence and threat associated with it as well as the demands, funding and poverty as some of the things that militate against women's participation in politics. In line with those as mentioned earlier, he also discusses conflict, and the role played by women in twenty-one major peace processes since 1992. In this regard, the study observes that where women have been involved in the peace process, they ensure that issues that affect them are addressed and included in the peace process. It also looked at a 2008 study of thirty-three peace negotiations around the world and discovered that only 4 per cent of the total participants (11 out of 280) were women. A sample of twenty-four major peace negotiations from 1992 showed that 2.5 per cent of signatories, 3.2 per cent of mediators and 7.6 per cent of negotiators are women (UN Women, 2012). It identified four key areas through which women could break down the barriers to their political and economic empowerment. These include agenda-setting, mobilising and networking, skills and information as well as spreading the word.

Olufade (2013) also made a strong case for the involvement of women in the democratic process as equal partners because they are highly committed to promoting national and local policies that address the socioeconomic and political challenges facing them, children and disadvantaged groups. Women are effective in promoting honesty in government; women are committed to peace-building; and women are associated with betterments in health, education and social development. The study recommends that Nigerian women, despite the numerous barriers faced have to create for themselves an alternative culture that will challenge the embedded traditions that eclipse the role of women. It also recommends that the Nigerian government should work towards achieving gender equality in democratic governance by increasing women's participation, and access to politics and relevant international instruments relating to full political rights for women should be ratified. This report also recommends that the government should review the existing constitutional, political and legislative framework that may hinder women's participation in politics. It also recommends that the government should include women in discussions on the electoral system reform, government proportional representation and measure their impact on gender equality. Lastly, the government should enact special measures in guaranteeing women's access to decision-making positions. Besides, women should also have equal opportunities with men during the election campaign by providing them access to public funding, access to the state media and setting campaign spending limits. In terms of the gap, the study does not take into account the giant strides that Nigeria has taken in women's participation in politics in the

Fourth Republic (1999 till date) as there have been women elected into various political positions, though still minimal. The study did not give empirical data on the level of participation of Nigerian women in politics.

Nelson (2012) discusses the dynamics and factors that limit the visibility of women in politics and governance in Nigeria. The study is a purely analytical desk-review and an extensive analysis of the trajectories of women's political participation in Nigeria, revealing a conundrum of factors that limit women's political advancement. These include the contestable notion of citizenship, monetisation of politics, prevailing cultural attitudes, poor socio-economic conditions, corruption and the violent nature of Nigerian politics. It further reviews issues on gender relations in the Nigerian society, stating the creative capability of Nigerian women working tirelessly for high productivity. In evaluating the stand of women in politics in Nigeria, the same study presents a description of roles women have played in Nigeria's political landscape from the pre-independence era until recent times. Categorically, Nelson (2012) states that throughout the military rule in Nigeria, only three women were appointed ministers at the national level, eleven were appointed commissioners at the state level and only two were appointed as sole administrators of local governments. Aside from this, he shows figures of women in 1992 elections to include a woman senator and twelve members of the House of Representative. The study, like many others, indicates that from the 1998 election that ushered in the Fourth Republic, women statistics stood at three senators, twelve members of House of Representative, one deputy governor, one Speaker at a State House and twelve members of State Houses of Assembly. These are Nelson's (2012) figures for 2003 and 2007, as presented in other literature.

While Nelson's (2012) is a descriptive study and presents some figures on women elected in the Fourth Republic, the study does not show the statistics of women for appointive positions in governance at all tiers of government. It also fails to present statistics on women's stand within the political parties in Nigeria. Nelson's (2012) work differs from others by presenting the status of women during the military era on which many authors are silent. The exclusion of appointive and party positions held by women in this study gives room for further research.

Viewing empowerment from another perspective, Luka (2012) empirically examines the role of Nigerian women in politics as an imperative of empowerment in Nigeria. He notably presents that the proportion of seats occupied by women in the National parliament never exceeded 3.1 per cent and 5 per cent for federal cabinets in 1999. It further shows that 30 per cent of the ministers in 1999 under President Obasanjo were women with two advisors, nine assistants and eight permanent secretaries. Luka (2012) further indicates that women were appointed as commissioners at the state level. He categorically states that from 1999 to 2011, no woman was elected into the office of the president or governor in any state. This study further proves this by presenting a statistical illustration of elective political seats occupied by women (1999–2011) at the federal and state levels. This work avers that out of a total of 469 seats in the Federal Parliament (Senate and House of Representatives), only fifteen women (representing 3.19 per cent in 1999) were successful but that increased to twenty-five seats in 2003 representing 5.33 per cent – to thirty-four seats in 2007 representing 7.24 per cent. However, there was a slight decline in 2011 to thirty-three seats, representing 7.03 per cent. He further stated that 1, 2, 6 and 1 were elected as deputy governor in 1999, 2003, 2007 and 2011 elections, respectively. While Luka (2012) is more quantitative in the statistical analysis of the 2011 elections, he fails to project hope or prospect of women in the 2015 elections. His study neglects the party positions occupied by women within the study duration. The study focused on the elective and appointive political positions attained by women at the federal and state levels. However, the data for the state excluded figures on its appointive positions. The study, like many others, sidelined the elective, appointive and party positions occupied by women at the third tier of government (local government). Also, the study did not account for the downward slope in women participation in the federal legislature in 2011 against the 2007 elections. Thus, this gap creates room for further research in this area of women in politics.

Odi (2012) analyses the opportunities and challenges to the full realisation of democracy as being a function of the participation in political and other civic processes. The study claims that there is a low level of political and civic participation by women in Nigeria; this has hindered them from contributing their quota to the development and consolidation of the nation's democracy. The study states that though women's civic participation is evident in histories of nationalities that make up the country, the current status of women has not measured up with the global standard. It further claims that although women play multiple roles within the family, community and society, there still exists gender discrimination in the public sphere where women are marginalised in electoral processes, and underrepresented in critical sectors of the economic, political and social institutions.

Assuming a quantitative bent, the study in question analyses women-to-men statistics of membership of Nigeria's National Assembly 1980–1992, 1999–2007, State Houses of Assembly 1999–2007 and local government chairperson for 2003. The study indicates 1 of 56 and 3 of 442 for women in Senate and House of Representatives in 1980, respectively. It shows 1 of 90 and 14 of 575 for women in Senate and House of Representatives in 1992, respectively. It further presents 2.8, 3.7 and 8.3 per cent to be women in Senate for 1999, 2003 and 2007, respectively, while 3.6, 6 and 7 per cent of the members were women in the House of Representatives in 1999, 2003 and 2007, respectively. Figures on the combinations of the State Houses of Assembly indicated 12 to 966, 39 to 912 and 54 to 936 for women to men in 1999, 2003 and 2007, respectively. It finally presents figures for local governments indicating 8 women from 765 chairpersons and 143 from 8,667 councillors. Odi (2012) indicates that thirty-two women were elected into the national assemblies of the country from the 2011 general elections. It identifies and describes the challenges and factors militating against women having equal participation with men in politics and decision-making. The identified factors include cultural practices, violence and intimidation; lack of finance; nature of party formation; non-adoption of the affirmative action in the constitution; and other laws in the country as well as non-domestication of the CEDAW ideals. While claiming that solutions are pursued through women advocacies and some government supports, the study observes that a lot still needs to be done to improve women's political participation and civic enjoyments.

Odi (2012) identifies women at the local government level, but it neglected women's status in appointive and party positions. The study again only presents figures from 1999 to 2007 in detail, neglecting details of women in the National Assembly in 2011 and 2015. It also fails to compare the statistics as the basis for the projection of future elections in Nigeria. The work though presented the women as chairpersons and councillors at the local government level, was limited to 2003; it did not present those of 1999, 2007 and other years, opportunities for further research have been left by Odi (2012) in these areas.

Looking at this subject from a fresh angle, Ogbogu (2012), in an empirical study, examined the role of women in politics and the sustenance of democracy by dissecting women's challenges, experiences and contributions in the democratic processes. She examined how women shatter the ceiling that limits/marginalises them and proffers strategies that can assist them to realise their political leadership potentials in Nigeria. The data were gathered by a survey through questionnaire administration on 700 randomly selected female politicians, activists and professionals in government as well as dominant political parties across Nigeria's six geopolitical zones. The questionnaire survey was supported with an interview of ten purposively selected respondents in key political leadership positions across Nigeria.

Going rather quantitative, Ogbogu (2012) presents figure on slots occupied by women in Nigeria's National and States Assemblies for 1999, 2003 and 2007. She indicates that for 1999, 2003 and 2007; 1.2, 4 and 5.5 per cent of members of State Houses of Assembly were women; 3.6, 6 and 7 per cent of members of House of Representative were women; while 2.8, 3.7 and 8.3 per cent of the senators were women, respectively. This survey indicates exclusion from informal political party network as the main challenge to women. At the same time, it recognises other problems to include religion, finance, multiple roles of women, education and training, inherited and bio-logical weaknesses as well as cultural barriers. The interview elaborated on the specific contributions of women to politics and sustenance of democracy in Nigeria. It further recommends some strategies adopted by women in breaking barriers that hinder their participation in politics and democracy in Nigeria. It proposes party network, mobilisation, agenda change, negotiation, and awareness among other strategies to overcome women's challenges in political participation. Ogbogu (2012) is an empirical study which surveyed opinions on women's contributions to politics and democracy in Nigeria; it does not present other executive positions occupied by women in Nigeria. The study fails to consider the positions of women within the political parties and also fails to present data on the stand of women in appointive positions. This gap presents the opportunity for thorough investigation and documenta-tion of the role of women in Nigerian politics from 1999 to 2015.

Taking another view of the anticipated centrality of women in administra-tion and politics, Sani (2012) succinctly describes the involvement of women in political and non-political leadership positions in Nigeria. The study con-ceptualises women's political participation and overview of the pre-indepen-dence and post-independence roles of women in governance. In respect to the pre-Fourth Republic era, Sani (2012) presents figures along with many other authors on the status of women in politics and elaborates on the performance of each head of state and president within the same period. This work further avouches that the 2011 election did not witness any improvement for women in elective positions. However, in the appointive slots, women were said to be above the global benchmark of 30 per cent with the President Jonathan administration being the highest with women appointees. In summary, Sani (2012) explains that there have been sixty-one female ministers from 1979 to 2012; nineteen female senators from 1999 to 2012; and forty-eight female members of the House of Representatives from 1999 to 2012. Sani (2012) states further that there was one female governor through judicially created opportunity, in history of Nigeria, eleven female deputy governors from 1999 to 2012 and a considerable percentage of women in other sectors such as the judiciary and the corporate/private sectors.

Sani (2012) documents the profile of individual women in leadership positions (appointive and elective) between 1999 and 2011 but neglects the contributions of women at the party level. The work also does not cover all the years in the Fourth Republic; neither did it fully elaborate on all the appointive positions under other presidents aside Jonathan. Therefore, there exist opportunities for further research into women's political participation in party positions and grassroots political role of women. Under a different

lens, Fapohunda (2011) examines the issue of gender in peacekeeping operations and the attempt at increasing and improving the role of women in this
category of operations. The paper states the institutional as well as political
contexts within which they have been implemented. The study reports that
out of the 77,117 UN peacekeeping personnel in 2008, only 2 per cent were
females – which implies that there is yet to be an achievement of gender balance in peacekeeping operations. The study employs a descriptive and analytical approach of relevant literature to understand better the challenges that
stand in the way of achieving gender balance. It also suggests key policy and
implementation strategies that could contribute to the growing discourse on
gender issues, especially in peacekeeping. It additionally seeks to find ways
of advocating for women in peacekeeping and development and validating
the need for goals of achieving gender balance in peacekeeping and development. As a bonus, it seeks to provide the necessary information, support and
encouragement to those who share an interest in women's advancement ideals, with the ultimate aim of fostering institutional transformation.

The study under consideration discovers that despite different resolutions,
plans of action and declarations to achieve gender balance – such as the
Windhoek Declaration, the Namibia Plan of Action and Resolution 1325 –
much is yet to be achieved. The study also discovers that between 1957 and
1979, out of the total number of 6,250 troops that participated globally in
peacekeeping operations, only 5 were females representing 0.8 per cent. Also,
between 1957 and 1989, out of the 19,980 troops, there were only 20 females
which accounted for 0.1 per cent. In 2006 out of 84,320 troops, 1,235 were
females accounting for 1.88 per cent, in 2007 of the 70,639 troops 1,034
were female representing 1.44 per cent, while in 2008 out of a total of 75,323
troops, 1,734 were females accounting for 2.25 per cent.

This same study also discussed the role of women in peacekeeping, gender mainstreaming in peace support operations, female recruitment in peace
support operations as well as the incentives and disincentives for female
peacekeepers. It also addresses female in mission leadership, mission-specific
recruitment policies and practices and the impact of women peacekeepers.
Not the least, it addresses training and capacity-building activities, as well.
The study also discovers that female involvement in peacekeeping missions
can trigger positive changes for women in countries where they serve by
providing examples of female leadership. The study also concludes that
the presence of women in military and civilian positions can help to defer
misconduct and unprofessional behaviour. It was also identified that certain
factors affect gender mainstreaming in peacekeeping operations such as lack
of resources and lack of funds. Fapohunda (2011) recommends that in order
to boost female participation in peacekeeping troop, contributing countries
should take measures that will bring about institutional changes such as

recruitment policies and incentive for female peacekeepers. There should also be functional gender-based units in peacekeeping operations. Besides, there should be the installation of effective monitoring, evaluation and reporting processes on the progress, achievements and challenges to female participation in peacekeeping programmes as they arise. Recruitment and selection should take gender balance into account, and as such, international declarations and treaties such as the Windhoek Declaration should be implemented.

Providing conceptual and theoretical analyses, Fayomi and Ajayi (n.d) explore the role of women in political leadership in Nigeria by examining the two key concepts of politics and leadership and the issue of providing clarification on the two concepts. The study also examines the various theories of leadership and discusses them briefly. They are:

(i)   The Great Man theory
(ii) The Trait theory
(iii) The Behaviourist theory
(iv) The Situational theory
(v)   The Contingency theory
(vi) The Transactional theory
(vii) The Transformational theory.

The study explores the role of women in political leadership in Nigeria by making use of the historical and descriptive approach. The study looks at the antecedents of women in political leadership in Nigeria. It explores the role of women in precolonial Nigeria citing examples such as Queen Amina, Queen Kambasa, Efunsetan Aniwura and Madam Tinubu. It identifies women leaders' roles in Nigerian politics in the colonial era, such as of Madam Olajumoke, Obasa, Madam Okwei, Mrs Olufunmilayo Ransome-Kuti and the Aba women who led the Aba riots of 1929. Fayomi and Ajayi (n.d) identify the various ways women leadership has helped in mitigating and confronting the effect of bad policies. The study also looks at the political leadership of women in the postcolonial era. It discovers that though the roles of women have changed, it still shows a low participation level in leadership in Nigeria. The study highlights that between 1960 and 1965, there were only four women legislators in the House of Assembly while the military regime that came into power reduced women's participation to peripheral roles. The study also found that out of a total of 1,297 local government positions worldwide in 1990, women won just 206. The Abacha regime produced 3 female senators, 12 House of Representatives members out of a total of 360 and States Houses of Assembly had just 12 women out of 990 members and out of the 8,810 councillors across the nation, 143 were women while out of the 774 local government chairpersons, the nation had only 12 women. The study also discovered that from 1960 to 1999 only, about 3.1 per cent of elected political office holders were women and 5 per cent of all appointive positions were women. The study also pointed out that out of all the 11,881 positions available throughout the country in 1999, women only won 181.

Fayomi and Ajayi (n.d) state that despite efforts at ensuring a significant increase in the number of women in leadership positions, the 2003 election produced just 8.8 per cent of women's representation in the National Assembly. The study also shows that there was significant improvement regarding women's participation in political leadership as reflected by the appointment of women into essential leadership and administrative positions. It also shows that, of all the forty-two ministers appointed by the Goodluck Jonathan administration before 13 September 2013, thirteen were women representing 31 per cent. The study shows that women contribute to national development when allowed to do so. Despite the significant strides made by the country, the study observes that Nigeria is still lagging in women representation in leadership positions and recommends that the country should adhere to the global benchmark of 35 per cent affirmative action.

From yet another perspective, Olojede (1999) conducted a historically empirical study on women and democratic governance in Nigeria, considering the lessons from the Second and Third Republics. She avers that 120 top Nigerian women managers revealed that even top professional women are apathetic towards the political process. From the study, about 96.7 per cent of the respondents who occupied the first three positions in public and private sectors indicated a lack of interest in party politics. Findings showed that gender inequality exists in political participation and well-educated women groups challenge the initial belief that education by itself abolishes gender differences. Olojede's (1999) studies, though empirical, did not cover the Fourth Republic. It also concentrated on women in top positions in public and private, professional practices, thereby leaving out the grassroots women. It generally did not look at the women in elective, appointive and party positions, thereby leaving room for further study and empirical research with a concentration on women in Nigerian politics in general.

Besides, Pogoson (2015) attests to women's participation or lack of it in communal life, governance and decision-making. She examines various investments women have made in people's lives in their respective societies and how women had to battle the power structure and patriarchy given the subordinate position ascribed to them. Pogoson (2015) concludes that there is a need to unearth the more profound and more fundamental processes of restructuring power and politics to convert political women from a minority within each political party into a majority of the citizenry, thus improving the potential for representation in Africa.

Lamidi (2014) uses the national 2008 Nigeria Demographic and Health Survey (NDHS) to examine various determinants of women's decision-making power across the six geopolitical regions in Nigeria. He identifies factors that affect and relate to women's household decision-making power in Nigeria. These include education, household wealth, women employment (professional and non-professional), age, age at first union formation, urbanisation, identification with Islamic and other religions as well as polygamy. He also identified essential distinctions in these predictors on women household decision-making power across the zones.

The UN Women Nigeria office (2014) examines the sociocultural determinants of voting patterns in Nigeria and by utilising a mixed method of qualitative and quantitative research with the use of gender lens. The body discovered a consistent voting pattern across the various states, indicating that common factors and cultural idiosyncrasies of particular geopolitical zones affect both men and women on their political choices. Also, Awofeso and Odeyemi (2014) unveil the extent to which culture impedes the political participation of women in Nigeria and propose suggestions to make up the situation. Udokang and Awofeso (2013) use the feminist and gender theory broadly to explain the subservient situation women find themselves in, concerning men – and the need to seek equality between men and women in all ramifications. Quadri and Agbalajobi (2013) compare women's participation in politics in Nigeria between 1999 and 2011. They note that though women had participated in politics in varying degrees at different periods, the nature of politics, lack of party support for female politicians combined with the internalised ideas on the appropriate roles of women in the society continue to aid their underrepresentation in political decision-making.

Further, the British Council (2012) emphasises that women's participation in politics has more comprehensive benefits and impact, generally. The body noted that in Northern Nigeria with about a quarter of all the country's population and the most significant figure of women among the zones, it has the lowest number of women candidates and women elected to public offices in the 2011 general elections. It concluded that the regional differences could indicate that some specific factors were at play in Northern Nigeria.

Probing further but in a different direction, Ladbury (2011) identifies youth gangs hired by politicians to intimidate rivals and the general populace as a significant (security) concern; he further noted that regional differences could be explained in part by women in the South that have had the franchise for a long time (since 1960) while women in the North were not allowed to exercise the franchise until 1979. Salihu (2011), Transformation Education for Girls in Nigeria and Tanzania (TEGINT) (2011), UNDP (2011) and United Nations Children's Fund (UNICEF) (2011), all studies of specific Nigerian communities, emphasise the vital role of patrilineal kinship and patronage networks in helping men articulate power by mobilising active ties for the political process. Most of the studies are unclear on the extent to which patronage networks penetrate or dominate party structure or if women are incorporated into, or excluded from, such networks.

In another breath, Oni and Agbude (2011) examined specific factors responsible for the low level of women's political participation in Ogun State. Through the use of quantitative and qualitative research methods, they discovered that the level of education, financial status, patriarchal system and male domination in the society have been the culprits. They also discovered that the three historical legacies of religious heritage, legacies of colonial and military administration and family responsibilities significantly contributed to women's low political participation in Ogun State. This study also examines whether these reasons were peculiar to the South-West, where Ogun State is located or cut across the other geopolitical zones of Nigeria.

FACTORS HAMPERING WOMEN'S PARTICIPATION IN POLITICS: SOCIETAL STRUCTURES

About half of the Nigerian population are women, and they play vital roles in many spheres of life. However, despite their significant contributions and number, they suffer discriminations that have not been adequately addressed. Discriminations against women have not been recognised as they should have been due to some cultural stereotypes: abuse of religion, traditional practices and patriarchal cum societal structures. As a result, Nigerian women have, therefore over the years, become targets of violence of diverse forms, based on their positions in promoting transformative politics. This section will, therefore, first examine the theoretical perspective of the discrimination and inequality suffered by women; second, it will assess the current status of women in politics and the various efforts made by them for their political empowerment; and third, it will identify problems women face in their quest to participate in politics, and last suggest possible keys to their political empowerment.

According to Akinyode-Afolabi and Arogundade (2003) cited in Agbalajobi (2010) women constitute over half of the world's population, contribute meaningfully to society and play vital roles as mothers, producers, home-managers, community organisers and sociocultural and political activists.

The political activist roles of women emerged through women groups and movements who have stood against historical gender discrimination and inequality. Before the current dispensation of the emergence of these movements, gender roles were divided between the male and female sexes. These roles, according to Akinyode-Afolabi and Arogundade (2003) cited in

Agbalajobi (2010), can be broadly classified into productive and reproductive gender roles. According to Rosaldo and Lamphere (1974, 20–22):

> From those societies we might want to call most egalitarian to those which sexual stratification is most marked, men are the locus of cultural value. Some area of activity is always seen as exclusively or predominantly male and therefore overwhelmingly and morally important.

As a consequence, women have for long suffered various forms of gender discrimination, inequality and exclusion, especially in the area of politics.

Sex-role socialisation assigns distinct and often unequal work and political positions to biological sexes, turning them into socially distinct groups. Gender economists see this as the sexual division of labour. This concept is central to the Nigerian political system where sexes are assigned to different complementary tasks, now inherent in the labour market and the political scene (Agbalajobi, 2010).

Debates and arguments concerning women participation in politics have centred on the cultural classification of women as the weaker sex and place them in a subordinate position to men in the nation's political system. The British, as the colonial masters, through the 1922 Sir Hugh Clifford Constitution disenfranchised women. The 1922 Constitution thus made the distinctions more prominent, although there were instances of traditional gender inequality even before the British institutionalised it. Women were still leaders in commerce and held political positions such as Iyalode, Iyaloja and Iyalaje in Yorubaland. Some women became regents, and a few became Oba.

Nevertheless, the 1922 Clifford Constitution nailed the political coffin for women and institutionalised gender discrimination in ways unimaginable. However, in Yorubaland, these women holding leadership titles still practised their roles according to tradition. However, all other women had no say in any form of politics, according to the 1922 Constitution. Women wanted to participate, and they started forming unofficial alliances and movements, which mostly were responsible for the increase in political participation of women. Kira (2003) recognised an important variable responsible for the increase in women participation other than women movements. In her study, she concludes that 'women would be even more supportive of electing more women to public office if they were knowledgeable as men about the extent of women's under-representation' (Kira, 2003, 367) Kira (2003) cited in Agbalajobi (2010) went further to distinguish women 'descriptive' representation from 'substantive' representation. *Descriptive representation* refers to the representation of their respective constituencies, whereas *substantive* refers to representation based on gender (the prioritising of the pursuit of women's interests by female representatives). Thus, is women's participation substantive – for the pursuit of the interest of women; is women's participation descriptive – for the pursuit of the interest of their constituency; or is women increase in political participation a movement in itself? This section is aimed at evaluating women's participation in politics and those factors responsible for increase in participation and those that hamper participation. This section is also to determine if substantive representation is fundamental to women participation or not. Finally, the section is to determine other intervening variables that affect women's increase in political participation, and which inform their intention to do so.

Political participation here entails various variables of participation but voting in elections and contesting elective (public) offices. This is quite different from representation. Representation entails elective/public offices held in relation to other aspects of representation. For instance, the increase of votes cast by women in elections from 10 to 40 per cent of total votes cast in eight years signifies a form of increase in participation. However, when the number of women holding public offices – as compared to that of men – is relatively lower, there is underrepresentation. That is, there may be an increase in participation of women and yet underrepresentation of women in politics; or there could be a high representation of women in politics and yet a low level of participation, depending on the standards used to measure participation. However, the former is rather common. In his work 'The Objectives of Man and the Nature of their Political Relations', Chapman (1993, 11) cited in Agbalajobi (2010) was able to discover that

> men are the major determinants of political actions and inactions generally concerned with the perpetuation of power of the state. When women compete with men for access to political power, they do so on the terms already established by men for competition among themselves. The success of women in politics like that of any group cannot be achieved within a system without displacing or replacing the existing elite. Moreover, a change in values which cannot occur independently in the socio-economic as well as political relations, without apparent involvement of women in the political process through holding of various offices (positions) and make known their ambition through consciousness and practical involvement in the political scene a condition, which if absent, allows or facilitates the political elites dominated by and govern women remain the same.

VIOLENCE AGAINST WOMEN (VAW) IN POLITICS

Violence Against Women (VAW) has become the most widespread form of abuse worldwide, affecting approximately one-third of all women in their lifetime. This phenomenon and the threat of such violence exercised through individuals, communities and institutions in both formal and informal ways, violate women's human rights, constrain their choice and negatively impact on their ability to participate in, contribute to and benefit from development. Therefore, VAW is unacceptable under any social, political, economic or cultural circumstance at all levels. This is because it contributes to the erasure and marginalisation of women which invariably means women will be missing in political leadership significantly.

VAW's participation is a prevalent phenomenon in Africa and has been part of human history. Women in Africa, like their counterparts in other parts of the world, suffer various forms of violence irrespective of age, class, religion or social status. 'Violence is an extremely complex phenomenon that has its roots in the interaction of many factors – biological, social, cultural, economic and political – and which is mostly caused by unequal power relations' (Bisika, 2008). Violence is a significant obstacle to women's growth and development as it hinders their progress in achieving development (Abama and Kwaja, 2009). The United Nations also sees VAW as an obstacle to the achievement of the objectives of equality, development and peace. In their view, it violates and impairs or nullifies the enjoyment by women of their human rights and fundamental freedom.

Accordingly, VAW encompasses but is not limited to, 'physical, sexual and psychological violence occurring in the family, within the general community or violence perpetrated or condoned by the state wherever it occurs' (UN Women, 1995).

VAW is not only a manifestation of unequal power relations between men and women; it is also a mechanism for perpetuating gender inequality (Bisika, 2008). This violence, which is reinforced by discriminatory cultural, social and economic structures, devastates lives, fractures communities and stalls development (Sani, 2020, 287). Nigeria is often referred to as the 'Giant of Africa', because of its large population and relatively vibrant economy. With approximately 206 million inhabitants, Nigeria is the most populous country in Africa and the seventh most populous country in the world (Worldometer, 2020). The percentage population of total female in Nigeria was last measured at 49.07 in 2015, according to the World Bank. The National Demographic and Health Survey of 2008 showed that 28 per cent of Nigerian women have suffered one form of violence or the other. VAW is institutionalised through family structures, wider social and economic frameworks and cultural cum religious traditions. It is a widely accepted method for controlling women.

Moreover, it is mostly overlooked by law enforcement agencies and is also ignored by those in power. It examines the nexus between VAW and their participation in Nigerian politics. Cognisance is also at this moment given to forms of VAW in Nigerian politics across the selected geopolitical zones.

VAW effectively disenfranchises women from leadership positions as their participation in politics is hampered. The variation in the forms of VAW across Nigerian geopolitical zones is noted, while the impact of the VAW on women involvement /participation in political activities is also examined.

Using a theoretical framework that combines feminist and cultural theory perspectives in the analysis of violence, we recognise the concept of VAW and political leadership, and also identify forms of VAW in Nigerian politics across the selected geopolitical zones. VAW effectively disenfranchises women from leadership positions as their participation in politics is hampered. According to Bowman (2003), 'Several theories of domestic violence are reflected in the works undertaken by activists rather than academics that have analysed the problem of domestic violence in Africa'. Elizabeth Schneider posits that 'the theoretical grounding of domestic violence work has important implications for the remedial strategies chosen to address the problem, and especially whether it is seen as an aspect of a larger struggle for gender equality'.

According to Bowman (2003), five general categories of theory appear in the literature on domestic violence in Africa. (1) rights theories; (2) feminist theories; (3) cultural explanation; (4) society-in-transition explanation; and (5) culture-of-violence explanation. Here, the feminist theory and the cultural explanation will be used in explaining the phenomenon. Bowman believes explicitly that feminist explanations are frequent in the domestic violence literature in Africa. The reason is that it is difficult to avoid interpreting domestic violence in Africa in terms of pervasive gender inequality. Traditional African societies are patriarchal in their customs and traditions, and therefore a woman holds a subordinate position. This inequality has remained institutionalised in African customary law. For example, women have no rights to inherit from their husband under most African systems of customary law; they are not regarded as sharing ownership of marital property and are also excluded from ownership of land. Therefore, the struggle against domestic violence is seen as just one part of a much broader context, the struggle for gender equality.

The second theory adopted for this analysis is that which relates to the emphasis of the power of tradition and norms. In support of this proposition, Atinmo (2000) describes interviews at the Social Welfare Office in the Ibadan region of Nigeria, at which police officers 'remind wives that Yoruba culture allows men to beat women'. Other cultural explanations are more indirect, pointing, for example, to the uneven distribution of power within traditional African marriages, the impact of polygamy, the forthrightness and acceptance of male promiscuity, the power of the extended family over the married couple and the almost universal institution of bride price as underlying the widespread abuse of wives. Bride price makes it difficult for women to leave an abusive husband except such families the women are from are willing to return the amount paid.

The cultural theory of domestic violence is not attributing violence as endemic in African societies. However, it is pointing to the fact that there is a close link between violence and the enforcement of conformity to traditional roles for women and dominance for their husbands. Bowman (2003) says the theory sees violence as emerging almost inevitably out of a society that treats women as property, socialises women to be passive, reduces their bargaining power through the institution of polygamy and the like. This section, therefore, merges the cultural argument with those based on gender equality.

GENDER-BASED VIOLENCE AND THE POLITICAL PARTICIPATION OF WOMEN: FORGING A NEXUS

Violence is a significant obstacle to growth, development and the participation of women in politics. VAW, in particular, hinders progress in achieving development (Abama and Kwaja, 2009). It violates and impairs the enjoyment by women of their human rights and fundamental freedom (Akinboye and Agbalajobi, 2013). Violence against Women and Girls (VAWG) is the most widespread form of abuse worldwide, affecting one-third of all women in their lifetime (Mukasa, 2015; DFID, 2013). According to the 1995 Beijing Declaration and Platform for Action (BPfA) report, the UN Declaration on the Elimination of VAW (UN, 1993) and the Inter-American Convention on the Prevention, Punishment and Eradication of VAW (UN Women (1994)), cited in Kamau and Nzomo (2012), VAW is any act of gender-based violence as a result of 'physical, sexual or psychological harm or suffering to women, including threats of such acts, coercion or arbitrary deprivation of liberty, whether occurring in public or in private life'. This definition covers dowry-related death, sexual abuse of female children, marital rape, female genital mutilation (FGM) and other traditional practices harmful to women such as spousal violence and violence related to exploitation (Krantz and Garcia-Moreno, 2005; Kamau and Nzomo, 2012).

VAW is one of the most widespread and universal violations of human rights. They know no geographical boundaries, no age limit, no class distinction and no cultural differences (Mukasa et al., 2014; The World Health Organization (WHO), London School of Hygiene and Tropical Medicine, and South African Medical Research Council, 2013; Heise and Garcia-Moreno, 2002). VAW has substantial implications for gender equality, social inclusion and the participation of women in governance (Bill & Melinda Gates Foundation, 2015). Gender-based violence (GBV) reflects and reinforces inequality between men and women and compromises the health, dignity, security and autonomy of the victims (Vernellia, 2003; Izumi, 2007; Akinboye and Agbalajobi, 2013).

VAW manifests at every level of society, from interpersonal and familiar relationships, through communities and right up throughout society, including via the state (Mitchell, 2012). Women are at risk of violence from both intimate partners and strangers (WHO, London School of Hygiene and Tropical Medicine, and South African Medical Research Council, 2013; Ellsberg and Heise, 2005; Heise and Garcia-Moreno, 2002). It is difficult to access reliable data for gender-based violence because this crime often goes unreported by both victims and police (Heise et al., 2002; Watts and Zimmerman 2002). However, recent data shows that in Sub-Saharan Africa, about 13 per cent and 45 per cent proportion of women at some point in their lives are assaulted by their intimate partners and strangers (Mukasa et al., 2014).

VAW and girls can take many forms. Human trafficking, female genital mutilation/cutting, violence against children – particularly sexual violence against girls – are all forms of VAW. As regards human trafficking, data show that known victims are overwhelmingly women and girls, and the estimated share of girls among total trafficking victims has doubled, from 10 per cent in 2004 to 21 per cent in 2011 (UN Office on Drug and Crime (2014). Violence against children is also widespread, with 26 to 38 per cent of girls and 9 to 21 per cent of boys having experienced sexual violence before age eighteen (UNICEF, 2014).

VAW exacts a high toll in terms of health and economic costs. This has a negative susceptibility on the ability of women to participate fully in politics. VAW exacts enormous, indirect costs as well. These costs, while hard to measure, inevitably have a profound impact on the political economy of any society because women's capability and quality of life diminishes. Women who undergo one form of abuse or the other, are often socially isolated, which prevents them from participating in community and even income-generating activities, and perhaps most importantly, robbing them of the social interaction that might empower them to end the abuse (Buvinic, Morrison and Shifter as cited in Morrison and Biehl, 1999).

In Nigeria, there have been various cases of violence in the process of participating in politics in one form or the other. One form of such violence is the electoral violence. Electoral violence either sponsored or occasioned spontaneously are related to social and economic concerns such as political instability, competition for resources, and religion and ethnic distrust facilitating anger and leading to little or no respect for the rule of law. Other causal factors of electoral violence are winner-loser power relations, weak security or law enforcement capacity, communal tensions and presence of willing protesters. Electoral violence in Nigeria is predominantly carried out by gangs characterised mostly by illiterate, unemployed and poor young men who are openly recruited, financed and sometimes, armed by politicians, state officials and party officials or their representatives (Aniekwe and Kushie, 2011, 20). In almost all elections in Nigeria since the 1965 elections and especially after the rebirth of democracy in 1999, there has been several pre-electoral or post-electoral violence (Onwudiwe and Berwind-Dart, 2010).

More so, election campaign is associated with gangster violence and vandalism, fake promises, deceit, insults, confrontations and intimidation which fuel pre-election and post-election violence in the country (Ehinmore and Ehiabhi, 2013, 50). The spread of rumour and inflammatory messages about an election or its outcome could be an immediate trigger of electoral violence, as the case of Nigeria's 2011 elections (Harwood and Campbell, 2010; Ofili, 2011, 3). The political scenario in the country is reserved for the bold that can freely participate in active party politics (Ehinmore and Ehiabhi, 2011). All these cause psychological violence to the women as their 'feminine' traits are characterised as being gentle, soft-spoken and motherly.

Gender-based election violence is primarily directed towards women as a result of their aspirations to seek political office, their link to political activities or simply their commitment to vote. Okumu (2008) referred to political VAW as 'political rape'. From his perspective, political rape occurs when men subdue women due to their ego and when the women try to get what traditionally or naturally belongs to the domain of men. Violence is used to intimidate or control them (Okumu, 2008, 82). Some of them are pressured to step down in favour of a male candidate and could be victims of threats and physical violence. Though violence is also equally used against male aspirants by their fellow men, they have more significant effects on women aspirants.

The Nigerian presidential election of 16 April 2011 was, unlike the previous elections, well organised and credible but still witnessed post-electoral violence, especially in the Northern region. The targets of attacks were mainly PDP leaders and supporters; state institutions and individuals who were non-Muslims. More so, some members of the National Youth Service Corps (NYSC) were attacked (Orji and Uzodi, 2012, 41). INEC recruited NYSC members to serve as ad-hoc election staff in their communities of deployment since they are non-natives. However, this call to duty portrayed the Youth Corps members as part of the election officials. This unfortunate perception, as well as the fact that most of the NYSC members deployed to Northern states were non-natives and non-Muslims, set them up as prime targets.

Two female Corps members were raped before being killed, while an unspecified number of other female Corps members were raped and assaulted by protesters in Gadau village. The case of the female NYSC members reflects the assault experienced by several other women during the protests (*Tribune*,

2011). The chairman of the CPC in Borno State, Zana Shettima, also claimed that supporters of the party were targeted and shot by security operatives in Maiduguri (Liman, 2011). Over 100 civilians, mostly women and children who were fleeing protests in Kaduna were reportedly stopped, arrested by soldiers and detained at an Army post in Zaria. They were detained for days in an area that lacked adequate ventilation and were deprived of food and water for a long time before they were released (Liman, 2011, 3).

The 2011 post-election violence witnessed sexual abuse, although the gravity of the sexual violence associated with the protests may have been under-reported. Bauchi State Police Commandant confirmed this when he announced that 'an unspecified number of female Corps members were raped, molested and assaulted by irate youths in Gadau village'. (Orude, 2011, 5; Mohammed, 2011, 10) The culture of silence around sexual abuse, insufficient reporting mechanism, the attitude of security agents towards victims of sexual abuse and difficulty in identifying perpetrators of sexual abuse in the context of violence limits availability of information (Amnesty International, 2006).

Physical assault was a frequent and well-reported aspect of the 2011 post-election violence. The media was replete with stories of individuals, who were maimed, injured and beaten by protesters. A large number of people suffered bodily harm inflicted with dangerous weapons such as machetes, cutlasses and arrows (Asemota, 2011). Gunshot injuries were widespread, according to reports from various hospitals (Binniyat, 2011, 7). While there is no official figure on the number of victims that suffered assault and physical injury, figures from various sources suggest that physical assault was the most common form of violence experienced during the protests.

A local human rights defender told Amnesty International (2011): 'The pattern of the killings now is extremely worrying, with attacks on women, children and the elderly' (2011, 13). Gender-based electoral violence has in no small dimension determined women's participation in politics.

Chapter 6

Strategies for an Increased Representation of Nigerian Women in Governance

The quest to increase women's representation in political decision-making and governance in Africa and particularly in Nigeria constitutes an almost non-negotiable desideratum. As a result of the need to achieve gender equity, it becomes particularly essential to determine where the country is with regard to gender equity in Nigeria; only then can governments, development agencies and advocacy groups adequately plan for parity and fairness. This chapter has opened enriching information about achieving improved political participation for women, and it is expected to generate data that will be useful to politicians, policymakers, women advocacy groups and gender activists. The chapter will further form a basis for disseminating information and reference materials on the strategic mechanism that would enhance the continued participation and representation of women in decision-making as well as governance in Nigeria.

The strategies for increased representation of women in governance and decision-making in Nigeria are multifaceted. Training, networking and mentoring; orientation and enlightenment; legislative and value changes; and financial support and empowerment are some of the basic strategies for an increased women's participation in politics and decision-making. This is because of the multidimensional challenges women face in their quest to participate in politics and to have substantive, symbolic representation in governance. In line with this finding, Krook and Norris (2014) note that efforts to promote women's representation revolve around quota. However, it does not exhaust the list of options available for recasting the political recruitment process to motivate more women to consider a political career, encourage political parties to select more female candidates or enhance women's prospect of electoral success.

117

At the first European Summit on Women in Decision-Making in 1992, it was noted that women represented half the potential talents and skills of humanity and their underrepresentation in decision-making portended a loss to the society as a whole (Athens, 1992). With the inclusion of women's political representation and their empowerment – and that of the girl child – in the fifth Sustainable Development Goals (SDGs), women's political empowerment is a high-priority issue in international development coopera-tion (Mosedale, 2014). It is therefore imperative to identify strategies that will enhance substantive and symbolic participation and representation which will engender women's political empowerment.

At this moment, the total percentage of women in political offices in Nigeria is put at a shy 7 per cent (Gabriel, 2015). Despite provisions in the Beijing Declaration and Platform for Action of 1995, which recommended that governments should support at least 30 per cent affirmative action for women in the political space, and the recommendation in the National Gender Policy establishing a benchmark of 35 per cent for women's representation in public office, very little has been achieved in this regard (Oloyede, 2016). Although there is a relatively high level of women's participation in politics at low levels of the political structure, there is a low-level representation of women at high levels of the political structure. This raises a fundamental question as to why there is disparity between participation and representa-tion, interrogates its reality and demands an urgent and unconditional redress.

The low representation of women has been ascribed to an array of barriers that the women in Nigeria face in their quest for full participation in various aspects of social life. Some of the challenges are associated with entrenched cultural attitudes, which hinder women's participation in public life as well as in politics. Others include the apparent lack of internal democracy in the political parties which has remained the trend in Nigeria since the 1999 general elections, where some women indicated their interest as aspirants. However, few were selected as candidates (Akpan, 2015).

This disparity creates problems that should be resolved urgently. One of these problems is that it creates an extensive reservoir of the population who are rarely going to find political fulfilment – many women always attend ward meetings and vote at elections but never get to hold political positions. The second problem is that, owing to the few number of women who are even-tually appointed into top positions of power and decision-making, women issues (such as women-friendly policies and provisions of public good) hardly ever get to the front burners of the policy arena nor are they given the attention they deserve. Other implication of women's low participation at high levels of politics is denial of economic empowerment which politics brings. At the same time, they continue to lack the social prestige the high office confers.

Women's participation or representation in politics reveals vital information about them and their ability to make choices concerning their lives, and act on them. It also positively correlates with more inclusive governance and better economic outcomes as politics plays significant role in the economy (Krook, 2010). It is therefore imperative to understand the patterns of participation – why disparity exists between participation and representation – and to shed light on the constraints they face. This is because unleashing the talents of women can bring powerfully positive changes and increase the likelihood of better outcomes for the nation (Rosenbluth et al., 2015). Women, according to Schreiber (2015), cited in (Rosenbluth et al., 2015), are more likely to act in a bipartisan manner and bring up new ideas and new issues to the policy table, therefore, increasing women's representation. It could also have a positive impact on governance and decision-making, and bring about policy outcomes which are more inclusive of the whole population.

In seeking reliable solutions to the problem of women's low participation and underrepresentation in politics, this chapter (critically engaging with the literature, research findings from interviews and other dependable sources) here offers a few well-considered strategies for improving the participatory experience of womenfolk in Nigerian politics in particular, and in the global political sphere in general.

STRATEGIES

Women's Internal Coordination: Training, Mentoring, Networking and Modelling

According to Krook and Norris (2014), civil society has gone a long way to ensure certain targets are set and strategies adopted to see them come to reality. One of such ways is media campaign. To Krook and Norris (2014), media campaigns are variegated but have the fundamental aim and target of playing up the current lack of gender balance, and the need to elect more women. Evidence of its workability is given in the cases of the Czech Republic and Turkey. In the Czech Republic's 2006 elections, a poster campaign was mounted by the group 'Fórum 50%' in subways and streets to appeal to the sentiments and feelings of women.

According to Krook and Norris (2014), the message implied that while there were some differences among men in politics, there was little real 'choice' among candidates – who still were almost exclusively men. This approach helped more women to come to political ascendancy in Czechoslovakia.

In Turkey, the 'Association to Support Women Candidates, KA.DER', vouchsafed similar innovative campaigns. In preparation for the general elections in 2007, the group created posters of popular businesswomen and female artists wearing a tie or moustache, asking 'Is it necessary to be a man to gain access into parliament?' In the 2009 local elections in Turkey, the women made use of billboards to portray the domination of men in politics. This strategy has also worked in many other parts of the world. The United Nations Development Programme (UNDP) (2016) adopted gender mainstreaming strategies to ensure that the parliament as a whole considered all of its policies and processes from a gender perspective. This was done by having dedicated gender equality committees. In countries such as Canada, Dominican Republic, France, Belgium, Monaco, Republic of Korea, Moldova, Pakistan, India and Spain dedicated gender equality committees were set up.

Still focusing on the participation of women and their internal coordination, training, mentoring, networking and modelling, it is necessary to refer to the persuasions of Egwu (2015). He fixed attention on the participation of women in the 2015 general elections in Nigeria by noting that despite the equal right with men granted by the constitution, the political climate was still not favourable to women, and which in turn was responsible for their low participation in politics in the country. The study examines the political status of women from the precolonial period to 2015 and explains why the challenges faced by them politically are neglected. The study employs the descriptive approach in achieving the objectives postulated earlier. The study discusses the historical participation of women in Nigerian politics and classifies it into three periods which are the precolonial, colonial and postcolonial. It gives examples of women in politics in the precolonial period. The study also notes that colonial policies were not favourable to women – and which were the reasons for various protests by women during the colonial period, and low participation in politics. The study also looks at the role of women in the postcolonial period and highlights those women that made notable impacts.

In addition, the study observes that out of the forty-seven million voters who registered for the 1999 elections, twenty-seven million were women, and out of the total 11,117 elective positions, only 631 women contested winning only 180 positions. The study also discovered that out of the 978 seats available for the State Houses of Assembly, men occupied 966, leaving women with only 12 seats. In 2003, out of the 951 seats, women won 39, representing 4 per cent while in 2007, women occupied 54 seats out of a total of 990 (5.5%).

By retrospective analysis, and contrary to the previous pattern, there was a drastic decline in 2011 as women won just 12 out of 990 seats accounting for only 1.21 per cent. In 2015, women won sixty seats which represented 6.1 per cent of the total seats. Regarding the House of Representatives, out of a total of 360 seats, women won thirteen, representing 3.6 per cent in 1999. In 2003, women won 21 out of 339 seats (3.6%); in the 2007 general elections, women won 25 seats (7%), while in 2011, out of 360 available seats women only won 19 (5.27%). In 2015, women won a total of 14 seats (3.89%). In the Senate, women occupied 3 (2.8%) out of a total of 109 seats; in 2003 women won 4 seats (3.7%) and in 2007, women occupied 9 out of 109 seats (8.3%) while they won only 7 (6.4%) in 2011. In the 2015 general elections, women won 8 (7.34%) of the total seats. The study also shows that there were no female deputy governors in 1999; two in 2003; six in 2007; and one in 2011. While appraising the 2015 general elections, the study identified that out of the 68,833,476 registered voters, there were 45,888,984 women and 22,944,984 men. Despite the high number of registered female voters, the country is still primarily dominated by men in elective offices. It also discovered that though 49 per cent of registered voters were women, only 7 per cent are in governance.

The icing on the cake of the study is the identification of the challenges to women's participation in politics in Nigeria. It shows that Nigerian women have the lowest representation of 5.9 per cent in the national legislature when compared to other African countries. Nigeria also has the lowest female representation in governance in the world with 7 per cent! Some of the challenges identified by the study include the following:

1. Lack of confidence, on the part of the women.
2. Lack of superiority complex in women.
3. Lack of trust among women.
4. Fear of success or rejection among Nigerian women.
5. Fear of popularity and shyness among Nigerian women.

These challenges, however, are such that could be easily overcome through a formidable women's coordination scheme. The study concomitantly recommended:

1. Women should aspire more for elective positions, campaign seriously and win.
2. Women should put up strong arguments to push forward their case for improved representation in politics and should base such arguments on the various national and international declarations and conventions on gender equality.
3. Women should use various organisations and forums as a rallying point for collective action politically and draw attention to gender issues in politics.
4. There should be campaigns and advocacy.

Education and Training, Mentoring
and Counselling as Strategy

In a survey of the three geopolitical zones of Nigeria, results show that 92.7 per cent of the respondents from Ondo State believed that adequate training of women would increase the representation of women in governance; likewise, 89.4 per cent of the respondents from Kaduna State agreed. In Ondo State and Kaduna State, training was seen as a very viable tool to increase women's representation in governance as the majority of the respondents noted this.

Similar to training and women development is the issue of networking, mentoring, counselling and role modelling. For this, 91.6 per cent of the respondents from Ondo State pointed to the significant role of networking and mentoring as an essential strategy that would lead to an increase in women's representation in governance. The distribution of viewpoints of women reveals that training, networking and mentoring, engendering policies guiding political participation, were predominant in the survey. This reveals the importance of education in society. From the qualitative data, each respondent was asked to identify strategies that would increase women's representation in governance. They pointed out the following: civic education, community grassroots sensitisation, gender mainstreaming policy – via lobbying, mobilising support from home, reduction of cost of campaigning and constitutional enactment. A respondent from Anambra State noted the need for civic education as a viable tool through which women's participation can be enhanced. She said:

> Do you know this thing could even be institutionalised even in schools? If it could be institutionalised in schools from primary schools under civic education, it will help to ensure from early childhood, these issues of gender discriminations are taken care of. To eliminate gender discrimination, there is need to re-orientate the people, especially the custodians of the culture. (Akure, 04)

This position was also corroborated by a respondent from Ondo State who noted the importance of sensitisation that should be done at any opportunity available. Given the failure of women who came out seeking elective positions but did not grow through the ranks, a respondent noted that women must start their political career especially for those seeking elective positions, from the grassroots. The respondent thought that women should not merely troop out to canvass for positions without learning the rules of the game or without starting from the grassroots. This is the issue about mentoring, counselling and role modelling, which are practical forms of training and education.

According to the respondent, this is one major challenge confronting some Nigerian women vying for political positions. She said:

> The issue of progression is something that we hammer on. You don't just come out no matter how educated you think you are and say you want to start from the top. If you look at the history of majority of women, especially Professor Sonaya of KOWA Party, I expected Sonaya to have started from the beginning, and then build herself to the top. You don't just wake up one day and say you want to be Nigerian President. That is one thing we preach to women here in Kaduna State, that yes you want to become something, but start from the beginning. Let your ward recognise you and make you a Counsellor. When your ward has recognised you, then let your local government recognise you and then the state will recognise you or your constituency, and then eventually you become undeniable visible to all. (Kaduna, 03)

According to Agbalajobi (2010):

> [The] Forum of Nigerian Women in Politics (FONWIP) is an example, whose central objective is to promote women empowerment and eradication of all forms of violence and discrimination against women. It supports women in decision making in both the public and private sector. The group organises seminars on empowerment and inequality, among other things. It is influential in its agenda; it requested that government should yield to 30% female representation in government appointments; made several attempts to increase official awareness on gender issues in public policies and conduct of workshops for women who aspire to run for public offices.

In other words, there is a need for a support network of role models, through the identification of aspirants and pairing them with established women politicians; playing a mentoring 'role and providing capacity building training to young or aspiring female politicians', (Agbalajobi, 2010) to encourage women. It may also be useful to consider building a coalition of NGOs and grassroots women associations that coordinate the support and advocacy for women aspirants.

Intervention of the United Nations and Other International Organisations

The principles, policies and actions towards ending gender inequality in Nigerian politics have been advanced and undertaken with the influence of international organisations by both government and non-governmental organisations. On its part, the United Nations (UN) has championed several declarations and conventions aimed at ending all forms of political discrimination against women. Among such documents that prohibit women discrimination are the following:

i The Universal Declaration of Human Rights.
ii The International Convention on Civil and Political Rights (ICCPR).
iii The Convention on the Elimination of all Forms of Discrimination against Women (CEDAW)

Following conferences in Copenhagen, Nairobi, Vienna, Cairo and Beijing, women participation in discussions on development has become a recurrent issue as women access to decision-making and full participation in public affairs is now recognised as a fundamental condition for democracy and for attaining sustainable development, as real democracy is characterised by full and equitable participation of women in both formulation and implementation of decisions in all spheres of public life. Moreover, no state can claim democracy if half of its population are excluded from decision-making processes. The United Nations also has programmes and agencies dedicated to uplifting the status of women in political affairs, for example, the Fourth Conference of Women held in Beijing, China in 1995, with the theme 'Equality, Development and Peace Contriving Strategies' towards the active liberation and empowerment of women with its overall aim of annulling those practices and values that discriminate against women. The United Nations is also taking steps to increase the number of women representation in legislative bodies around the world, and improve women's social, economic and political status, which is essential for the achievement of both a transparent and accountable government. The United Nations also takes steps to ensure and encourage women towards realising their abilities and utmost importance in the political and social development such that they will be significantly represented in the decision-making bodies in every organisation. It politically educates and empowers women to take active part in the political process as party members, leaders, voters and candidates.

The United Nations, as a coordinating world body, however, has its limitations mainly because of its avowal and regulation prohibiting it from meddling in the affairs of member nations. If this was not the case, it would be easy to enforce all declarations and agreements of the General Assembly and conventions on member nations. This would have made a significant difference in guaranteeing that all member nations comply with, for example, the affirmation action. Be this as it may, the United Nations still reserves the initiative to demand, through subtle – rather than legal – means, the compliance of member states to all its declarations, memoranda of understanding and walk the talk of every conference decision.

National Government's Tasks: Faithfulness
to Commitments, as a UN Affiliate

It has been established that gender parity is desirable, and this will positively rub off on national development. Efforts have been made, but results on hand probably point to the insufficiency of these efforts. National governments and political parties must give vent to their promises and what is contained in the instrument signed as well as what is contained in national constitutions, party constitutions and manifestoes.

On a positive note, most policy documents of political parties now enshrine women representation. However, unfortunately, in most political parties, this simply remains an ideal. Most political parties have thus far not implemented those ideals. It is in this regard that political parties need to be compelled and sensitised to increase women's participation, especially in crucial decision-making organs of the parties. The provision of gender-sensitive rules, policies and programmes of the United Nations and other international organisations is not enough. The said provisions must be implemented to the letter. The most critical intervention needed would be to establish a level playing ground for political competitors, across gender lines. This can only happen if the leadership is committed to affirmative action and women empowerment, as has been the case in Rwanda (Gatimu and Ndung' u I, 2016). In the case of Nigeria, implementing the 35 per cent affirmative action for women means more women will be involved in governance processes in Nigeria. It is not enough to have 35 per cent affirmative action in our National Gender Policy. The National Assembly must provide legislation that mandates political parties to reserve 35 per cent of positions for women. When quota laws are vague, they leave political parties to apply them as they deem fit, often failing to achieve the intended purpose.

There is an urgent need for national governments to respect, and be faithful to, the allegiance they swore to, as members of the United Nations. In this respect, national governments could engage relevant stakeholders such as the Independent National Electoral Commission and political parties in introducing and enforcing the observance and implementation of quotas, as agreed to at the UN conventions, after all, other regulations regarding, for example, the minimum age or academic qualification of a political office contestant are religiously adhered to.

Elimination of Political Violence and Violence against Women

In this subsection is a form of political-related strategy. As shown in chapter 5, it is evident from the analysis of reports collected across the three geopolitical zones of Nigeria – as in some other parts of Africa, South-East

Strategies for an increased representation of women

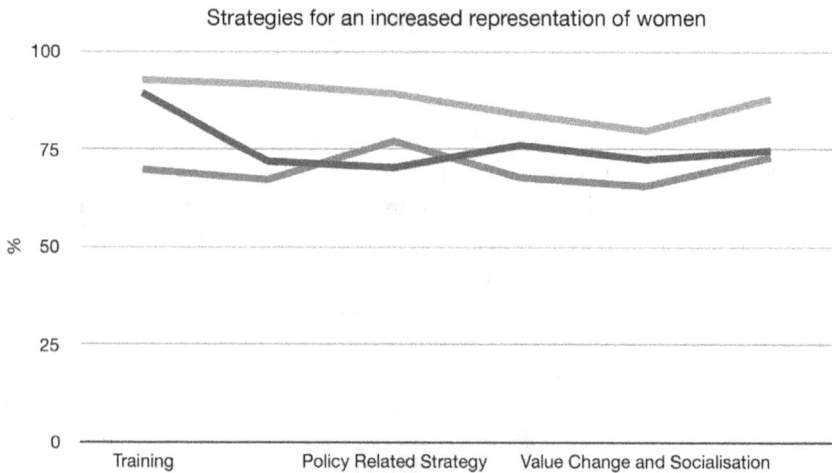

Figure 6.1   Strategies for an Increased Representation of Women.

Asia, South Asia, the Middle East, South-Eastern and Eastern Europe and the Balkans – there is a spike in political violence targeted at women ranging from wartime sexual violence to attacks on female civilians and crackdowns on female-led protests. The report shows twice as many cases reported during the first quarter of 2019 (261 incidents) as during the first quarter of 2018 (125 incidents). This form of violence targets women from all walks of life and not just those active in politics. It is as such obvious that the threat of political violence towards women is on the increase. For particularity reference, on 19 November 2019, in Nigeria, Kogi State to be specific, a People's Democratic Party women leader was burnt to death during post-election violence – just a single example of tens of such other attacks on women in Nigeria during, before or after elections. It is generally difficult for women to swim in the murky waters of Nigerian politics (Charles and Ikenna 2009, 119). Fear of all forms of gender-based violence is thus one of the reasons most cited by women political aspirants as their primary obstacle in electoral politics. In 2003, for example, there were party clashes, political assassinations and community unrests, especially in the Niger-delta area. In 2007, electoral violence was more of a surety such that people kept away from the polls, as in Rivers State where violent threats resulted in low voter turnout and there were several political kidnappings alongside violence (Onwudiwe and Berwind-Dart, 2010). All these give us an understanding of how violence – and violence against women – is a form of political violence which inhibits women's political participation and women's civic engagement.

Violence against women is widespread across the world, and it represents a universal violation of women's rights, notwithstanding the age, class distinction, cultural affiliations or where the women may have come from (Mukasa et al., 2014). It does, as such, make some sense to create an awareness of the political and legal rights of women while also encouraging them to claim them. Also, creating an environment that allows for women to engage in decision-making processes sustainably and effectively free from political harassments and violence is pivotal and critical. Finally, in this regard, the establishment of legal funds to enable women politicians prosecute occasions of perceived political injustice, in their quest for inclusion in the political calculation of their communities will be a significant incentive.

Dismantling Entrenched, Obnoxious, Sociocultural Structures and Patriarchy

The male pre-dominated political environment has pre-conditioned the environment that their female counterparts compete with them in. Consciousness and involvement of women could change the values, to enable a political environment to be freer for women, that is 'the fact of women's underrepresentation, if made known to the public, could shape political behaviour' (Duerst-Lahti and Verstegen, 1995).

Throughout recorded history in all parts of the world, women have been subjected to domination by men. This is as a result of persisting cultural stereotype, abuse of religious and traditional practices and patriarchal and societal structures in which men dominate economic, political and social power. The role women have historically played has been that of the followers of male political leaders. This form of discrimination is not merely an African or Nigerian phenomenon but a global one. The only difference is that it has lasted for so long in this part of the world as other developed nations of the world are moving towards gender equality and equity. Women are unjustifiably discriminated against in many ways. For instance, in some courts and police stations in Nigeria today, women who propose to stand surety for accused persons, who have secured bail, are routinely disqualified simply because they are women. Even though all over the world today, democracy has become a vital tool for attaining sustainable development, the impact of the definition of democracy remains elusive. Political participation which is sine qua non of democracy and allows for diversity of opinions and participation of both men and women cannot thrive by excluding the women folk that constitute half of the world's population. According to Anifowose (2004) some established democracies such as Britain and the United States of America's democratic 'polyarchies', for a long time, were in fact, male 'polyarchies' and struggled to keep women away from voting (Anifowose, 2004).

While Anifowose (2004) submits that identifying how male domination originated cannot be fathomed or traced historically, he believes that one highly plausible explanation is to be found in physiological differences. Men are generally heavier, taller and even physically more durable than women and therefore more capable than women to enforce their will through physical violence and threat of violence. Women, on the other hand, are vulnerable because of their role of childbearing and nursing. In addition, discrimination and subjection of women is further enforced by custom, traditional practices, beliefs and the law, behind which stood the coercive force of the state. In sum, the critical point is that discrimination against women has its root in the nature of our societies which celebrate men as being unique, stronger and fit for the public space. In contrast, women are feeble and weak and meant to stay within private boundaries. This norm has affected how women are perceived and has led to a deficient level of political engagement (Agbalajobi, 2010). Given this, the rather opprobriously odious and obnoxiously antiquated patriarchal structure of African states, and indeed of Nigeria in particular, should be prosecuted and dumped in the yard of history while new dawn of hope that beacons from modern civilisation should replace it, ensuring that women have as much right as their male counterparts to feature in human affairs – including, but not limited to politics.

Implementation of Quotas and Proportional Representation

Researchers have identified quota as a viable tool to increase the selection and election of women. Many researchers, such as Krook and Zetterberg (2014), have looked at the significance of quotas and have also variously classified the type of representation it offers. Various scholars examined the susceptibility of quotas for political engagement, with quotas encouraging more women to stand for election and also to incentivise political parties to target women's votes (Buckley, 2016; Allen and Cutts, 2018). Murray (2012) observes how quotas can help women pull down barricades between them and public office. Childs (2004) reported that this group of women thought that their presence encouraged other women to become politically active and encouraged them to contact their political representatives more frequently. Others who worked on quota emphasised the need to look beyond the numbers and assess the impact of an increased number of female representatives on political outcomes (Krook and Childs, 2008; Krook and Messing-Mathie, 2013; Krook and Zetterberg, 2014; Paxton and Hughs, 2016).

There are three different types of quotas here identified: constitutional, electoral and party examined by Franceschet et al. (2012). The goal of most quota systems is to garner up to 30 per cent female representation, even though similar laws introduced in France essayed and targeted 50 per cent representation. This target, however, is yet to be achieved. Rather than proposing any specific target in Belgium, their approach targets a systematic percentage rise – which expects women political leadership to go up incrementally over the years. Some scholars such as Krook (2009) and Murray (2012, 2014) categorised electoral gender quotas into three dimensions: reserved seats, party quotas and legislative quotas.

On the other hand, reserved seats are policies that make room for women in political groups. They are usually enacted through constitutional reforms that establish separate electoral roles for women, designate separate districts for female candidates or allocate women's seats to political parties based on their proportion of the popular vote. They guarantee women's presence by revising the mechanisms of election to mandate a minimum number of female representatives. These measures first appeared in the 1930s in India, but have been adopted as recently as 2009 in Egypt. Indeed, they have become an increasingly prominent solution in countries with deficient levels of female parliamentary representation. They are concentrated geographically in Africa, Asia and the Middle East, for example, in countries such as Rwanda, Uganda, Bangladesh, Pakistan, Jordan and Afghanistan.

Party quotas are the prerogatives adopted voluntarily by political parties to require a certain proportion of women among their parties' candidates (Krook, 2009; Murray, 2012). In contemporary Nigeria, major parties often sound this mantra, but it only remains mere dreams that have never seen the light of day in any of the parties. Party quotas are introduced through changes to individual party statutes, and they introduce new criteria for candidate selection to encourage the party elite to recognise existing sentiments and consider alternative spheres of political recruitment. Given their origins with parties, these quotas differ from reserved seats in that they concern slates of candidates, rather than the final proportion of women elected. They were first adopted in the early 1970s by various left-wing parties in Western Europe. Today they are the most common type of gender quota, appearing in political parties worldwide. In countries such as the United Kingdom, Sweden and Germany, they continue to be the most common strategy employed – including more countries in Western Europe. On many occasions, however, they also frequently coexist with legislative quotas in Latin America in states such as Brazil, Dominican Republic and Mexico.

Lastly, legislative quotas are measures passed by national parliaments that require all parties to nominate a certain proportion of female candidates. They differ from reserved seats in that they apply to candidate lists, rather than the final proportion of women elected. Legislative quotas involve reforming the constitution or the electoral law to alter the meanings of equality and representation that inform candidate selection processes by legitimising affirmative action and recognising 'gender' as a political identity. Similar to party quotas, legislative quotas address selection processes, rather than the number of women elected. Unlike party quotas, however, they are mandatory provisions that apply to all political groupings, rather than merely to those who choose to adopt quotas. Legislative quotas typically call for women to constitute between 25 and 50 per cent of all candidates. They are the newest type of gender quota, appearing first in the early 1990s, but have become increasingly common as more countries are adopting quota policies. With some notable exceptions, these measures tend to be found in developing countries, particularly in Latin America, for example, in Argentina, Brazil and Mexico; in post-conflict societies, primarily in Africa, as in Burundi and Liberia; the Middle East, as in Iraq; and Southeastern Europe, as in Kosovo and Bosnia–Herzegovina.

Notwithstanding the potentialities and promises of the various quota measures highlighted above, Krook (2009) discussed some limitations to electoral quota from the perspective of various scholars. She avers that there are many people, including some feminist voices, raising strong and convincing objections to quotas per se as a strategy for increasing women's political representation (Bacchi, 2006). There is a great deal of opposition to quotas as they have been seen by many as undemocratic especially since they violate the notion that there should be 'free choice' in who is nominated or elected to political office. Many other opposing voices vociferate discontent and aversion for quotas because they deny equal treatment to men and women, in that there is usually no open competition for seats between them, adding that it represents a form of discrimination against men. Again, many claim that quotas are some form of condescension to women because they tend to infer that women are not capable of winning office without receiving this undue help.

Furthermore, another school sees quotas as contradicting roles in the principle of self-interest in politics. More specifically, quotas for women appear to challenge the status of the same male politicians and party leaders who pass these policies, as they require that men cede seats to women as a group. Several authorities firmly endorse electoral gender quotas as a strategy to increase the fortune and number of women candidates and concomitantly increase women's political representation (Krook and True, 2012; Buckley et al., 2016; Norris and Dahlerup, 2015; Krook and Norris, 2014; Dahlerup, 2007; Dahlerup and Friedenvall, 2005). Quota is now in use in many countries across the world.

Dahlerup (2006) did a global study to compare gender quotas with the aims to investigate under what circumstances gender quotas do increase women's representation – and why they sometimes fail. According to Norris and Dahlerup (2015), every country would adopt a quota system most sympathetic to their particular political circumstances.

CONCLUSION

The promise of a renewed hope – evidenced in a litany of global successes, through strategic interventions identified in this work – is received for women's meaningful and full participation in contemporary Nigerian political initiatives and enterprise. These identified strategies include women's internal coordination, featuring training, mentoring, networking, modelling, seminars, the intervention of the United Nations and other international organisations, and consideration of quotas and proportional representation. While the potential gains of all but quotas have been somewhat highlighted above, this chapter may be concluded by looking at the gains of quotas across the globe.

Gender quotas, despite difficulties, have worked in a great many climes. In one electoral cycle between 2011 and 2016, women's political representation in Dáil Éireann has risen to 22 per cent, a six percentage point increase. This compares favourably to the five percentage point increase achieved across five electoral cycles between 1992 and 2011 (Buckley et al., 2016). Ireland provides an example of a place where gender quotas have worked. Without doubt, gender quotas contributed to an increase in women's candidate selection and election in the 2016 general elections in Ireland. They helped create a cultural shift in political parties whereby women party members and their electoral ambitions were no longer overlooked. Norris and Dahlerup (2015) also gave examples of successful implementation of gender quotas in several countries across the globe. Examples include South Africa, Argentina, Latin America, Ireland, Netherlands and Italy.

McGing (2019) argues that:

> the use of electoral gender quotas means that the Global South has now over-taken the Global North as world leaders in women's parliamentary representation. This is a rapid turnaround on the situation just 20 years ago where the Scandinavian countries and the Netherlands were at the top of the world rankings for women's representation.

In addition, McGing affirms that electoral gender quotas have significantly advanced women's access to parliamentary politics at a global level.

According to Maguire (2018), in France (women hold 39 per cent of parliamentary seats); however electoral law stipulates that the number of candidates for each sex should not differ by more than 2 per cent. In Spain, there is a legal requirement for candidate lists to comprise at least 40 per cent of each sex. This has produced 39 per cent of parliamentary seats which are held by women. Mexico has a quota of men and women, which must comprise at least 40 per cent of the candidates of the same gender, with the constitutional provision for political parties to ensure gender parity in the make-up of candidates for political office. This has produced 42 per cent of parliamentary seats, which are held by women. Ireland introduced legislation in 2012, which stated that at least 30 per cent of candidates should be women and which rose to 40 per cent in 2019. Even though Ireland has not been able to achieve this, it has women occupying 22 per cent of parliamentary seats. In Australia, the Australian Labour Party applies a quota of 40 per cent for each of the sexes for pre-selection for public office at both state and federal levels. This is evident in 29 per cent of parliamentary seats that are held by women. Canada has different quota implementations across the leading political parties with 28 per cent of parliamentary seats held by women. The ruling Liberal Party has had a target of women constituting 25 per cent of its MPs since 1993; the figure now stands at 30 per cent. The Conservative Party has 20 per cent representation among MPs as a result of the New Democratic Party's target of 50 per cent that was set since 1985. Now, it has reached 41 per cent. In general, 28 per cent of Canadian MPs are female! Sweden has a high proportion of female MPs. This can be associated with the present coalition of three parties (Social Democratic Party, the Left Party and the Green Party) all having 50 per cent minimum quotas for women on party candidate list for over twenty years. The Moderate Party, which is the main opposition party, had introduced a gender quota system since 2009. This has engendered positive result with 44 per cent of parliamentary seats held by women in Canada. Germany also has a variation in the quota provisions by the political parties although women hold 36 per cent of parliamentary seats. The Christian Democratic Union (CDU), which has the most number of parliamentary seats, has a party statute which states that at least a third of candidates and party officials should be women. If this is not the case, then internal elections have to be repeated. The second largest party, the Social Democratic Party (SDP) has, since 1996, imposed a higher requirement, with candidate list needing to have 40 per cent of each gender. The last example given by Maguire (2018) is that of South Africa, where women hold 41 per cent of parliamentary seats. As far as local councils are concerned, electoral law stipulates that parties must seek to ensure that 50 per cent of candidates on party lists are women. However, there are no legal sanctions for non-compliance. Since 2009, the ruling party, the African National Congress (ANC) has had a 50 per cent gender quota for both local and national elections (Maguire, 2018).

The Nigerian quota-implementation experience is also an encouraging one that however needs polishing. Agishi (2014) considers the challenges and the way forward for women's participation in party politics in Nigeria. In her view, party politics is the launching pad into political positions in most democracies. Like many authors, she maintains that very few women have participated in the management of Nigerian public institutions such as the political parties. She claims that the 2011 elections still witnessed the marginalisation of women in party politics. Citing the case of the total rejection of the only female presidential aspirant (Sarah Jubril) in the People's Democratic Party, she argues that there is the need for political parties to support their women. The foregoing arguments only reinforce the practical usefulness of quotas as an empirically dependable means of shoring up women's participation and representation in contemporary global politics.

About the survey carried out in the three geopolitical zones of Nigeria, the report in Anambra State shows the need to engender policies guiding activities of political parties. This was seen as the most crucial strategy that would lead to an increase in the representation of women in governance, according to the respondents. This is because 77.1 per cent of the respondents identified the need for quota provisions and the need for gender policy to be put to work at all levels of participation. These are generally seen as an affirmative action of laws allocating quotas for women to assist in the promotion for gender balance in public life. Quotas are considered as a legitimate means of securing this end. In many countries, the exclusion of women in politics is as a result of many reasons – financial, cultural, traditional and political. Playing up this fact and the reasons that have made it so implies that quotas should not be seen as discrimination towards men and cannot be branded unconstitutional as most quotas are formulated under neutral basis. The Law (Nigerian) provides for a maximum of 60 per cent and a minimum of 30 per cent representation for either sex, which was implemented as a result of the Beijing Conference. The conference agreed that 30 per cent of public seats and positions should be reserved for women. Nigeria records an increase of 78 per cent progress in women's election into public offices from 1999–2007.

In the Fourth Republic, which started on 29 May 1999, the Nigerian political terrain witnessed an increase in the number of women political appointees as few women emerged as Chairpersons of Local Government Councils. Lagos State produced a female Deputy Governor in the person of Senator Bucknor Akerele. In the Senate, there were three women, namely Chief (Mrs) Florence Ita-Giwa representing Cross River State South Senatorial District; Mrs Stella Omu from Delta State and Hajia Khairat Abdul-Rasaq representing the FCT. In the Executive Councils, former president Obasanjo also appointed several women in the Federal Executive Council (Agbalajobi, 2010). Former president Jonathan also appointed some women in his cabinet.

It is evident that there has been an increase in the number of positions staffed by women in Nigerian political affairs, but it remains a far cry from what was the vogue in the 1950s. This has been made possible by the quota allocation system as approved by the United Nations to be implemented in global politics. It can, therefore, be seen that the practice of the quota system assists in reducing the low level of women participation in politics, a real solution to a patriarchal society. It also stereotypes the presence of women, which changes the face of decision-making, thereby providing opportunities for substantive input. This technique contributes in no small measure in improving female intention to participate in Nigerian politics despite the prevailing political structure and societal norms, as 'a woman's experience is needed and necessary in political life and policymaking in order to represent the entire society' (Phillips, 1995). Quotas are therefore not meant to discriminate but compensate women for those things that obstruct them from making headway in their political career.

Finally, women participation in Nigerian politics is an issue of significant concern. Women have been put at the backburner politically for years. This has engendered a consciousness of women underrepresentation in public life. However, it has been shown that the intention of most women to participate in politics is basically to support their female folk. This is their substantive responsibility, and it is even on this platform that most women emerge as public office holders successfully. They use the platform of women movements as a veritable platform to seize political power and consolidate the power on this same platform. Be it as it may, there is an increase in women participation on these bases (even though marginal and rather sluggish). Women movements – keying into strategies outlined in this book – are promised the achievement of gender equality and equity, sooner than later.

Acronyms

ABN	Association for Better Nigeria
ABU	Ahmadu Bello University
ACN	Action Congress of Nigeria
ADC	African Democratic Congress
AF	African Union
AG	Action Group
AI	Amnesty International
ANC	African National Congress
ANPP	All Nigeria Peoples Party
APC	All Progressives Congress
APGA	All Progressives Grand Alliance
APPRRW	African Protocol on People's Rights and the Rights of Women
APRM	African Peer Review Mechanism
BCN	British Council Nigeria
BPfA	Beijing Platform for Action
BPfA	Beijing Declaration and Platform for Action
CBCGE	Community-Based Committees on Gender Equity
CD	Campaign for Democracy
CAP	Common African Position
CDU	Christian Democratic Union
CEDAW	Convention on the Elimination of All Forms of Discrimination against Women
CP	Conservative Party
CPC	Congress for Progressive Change
CSO	Civil Society Organisation
CSW	Commission on the Status of Women

DAG	Democracy Action Group
FCC	Federal Character Commission
FCT	Federal Capital Territory
FEC	Federal Executive Council
FGM	Female Genital Mutilation
FMG	Federal Military Government
FONWIP	Forum of Nigerian Women in Politics
FWCW	Fourth World Conference on Women
GA	General Assembly
GAD	Gender and Development
GBV	Gender-Based Violence
GEWE	Gender Equality and Women Empowerment
HS	Heads of State
HG	Heads of Government
HRC	Human Rights Commission
IDI	In-depth Interview
ICCPR	International Convention on Civil and Political Rights
ICPD PoA	International Conference on Population Development Plan of Action
IDEA	Institute for Democracy and Electoral Assistance
INEC	Independent National Electoral Commission
IPU	Inter-Parliamentary Union
KII	Key-Informant Interview
LAC	Legal Aid Council
LGA	Local Government Area
LMWA	Lagos Market Women's Association
LP	Labour Party
LP	Liberal Party
MDGs	Millennium Development Goals
MLA	Mass Literacy Agency
NADECO	National Democratic Coalition
NAPTIP	National Agency for the Prohibition of Trafficking in Person
NBS	National Bureau of Statistics
NCCCGE	National Consultative and Coordinating Committee on Gender Equity
NCNC	National Council of Nigeria and Cameroun
NCWD	National Centre for Women Development
NCWA	National Council on Women Affairs
NCP	National Conscience Party
NDHS	Nigeria Demographic and Health Survey
NEC	National Electoral Commission

NEEDS	National Economic Empowerment and Development Strategy
NEMG	Nigerian Election Monitoring Group
NEPAD	New Partnership for African Development
NEPU	Northern Elements Progressive Union
NERDC	Nigerian Educational Research and Development Council
NGC	National Gender Commission
NGOs	Non-Governmental Organisations
NGP	National Gender Policy
NDHS	Nigeria Demographic and Health Survey
NLC	Nigerian Legislative Council
NNDP	Nigerian National Democratic Party
NOA	National Orientation Agency
NPC	National Population Commission
NPC	National Planning Commission
NPP	Nigerian People's Party
NPW	National Policy of Women
NRC	National Republican Convention
NTTGE	National Technical Team of Gender Experts
NUC	National Universities Commission
NYSC	National Youth Service Corps
PDC	People for Democratic Change
PDM	People's Democratic Movement
PDP	People's Democratic Party
PwD	Persons with Disabilities
RECs	Regional Economic Communities
SADC	South African Development Community
SAMRC	South African Medical Research Council
SDGs	Sustainable Development Goals
SDGEA	Solemn Declaration on Gender Equality in Africa
SDP	Social Democratic Party
SEEDS	Strategies for Ecology Education, Diversity and Sustainability
SNA	Sole Native Authority
TEGINT	Transformation Education for Girls in Nigeria and Tanzania
UBE	Universal Basic Education
UN	United Nations
UNDP	United Nations Development Programme
UNICEF	United Nations Children's Fund
UPN	United Party of Nigeria
UNSC	United Nations Security Council
UDHR	Universal Declaration of Human Rights
VAW	Violence Against Women

VAWG	Violence Against Women and Girls
WACOL	Women Aid Collective
WARDC	Women Advocates Research and Documentation Centre
WGDD	Women and Gender Development Directorate
WHO	World Health Organization
WID	Women in Development
WiLDAF	Women in Law and Development in Africa
WIN	Women in Nigeria
WPA	World Plan of Action
WU	Women's Union

Bibliography

Abama, E. and Kwaja, C. M. 2009. 'Violence against women in Nigeria: How the millennium development goals addresses the challenges', *The Journal of Pan African Studies*, 3(3), pp. 23–34.

Adamu, F. 2006. Women's struggle and the politics of difference in Nigeria. Available from http://web-fu-berlin.de/gpo/pdf/tagunga/fatima_1_adamu.pdf (Accessed 18 May 2020).

Adeleke, J. O. 2013. 'Violence and women participation in politics: A case study of Ekiti State, Nigeria', *International Journal of Sociology an Anthropology,* 5(1), pp. 26–34.

Adiakpan, I. and Akpan, R. 2014. 'Akwa Ibom Women: Contribution to politics and governance', in E. U. Eno-Abasi, E. E. Felicia and M. U. Inyang (eds.), *Nigeria's Centenary: 100 years of Akwa Ibom women's imprint in national development.* Uyo, Nigeria: Centre for Gender Studies, University of Uyo.

Agagu, A. A. 2007. 'Political socialization, political culture and political behaviour in Nigeria', in F. Omotoso (eds.), *Readings in political behaviour.* Ibadan: Johnmof Printers Ltd.

Agbalajobi, D. T. 2010. 'Women's participation and the political process in Nigeria: Problem and prospects', *African Journal of Political Science and International Relations,* 4(2), pp. 15–82.

Agbu, J. 2015. 'Under-participation of women in Nigerian politics: A psychological perspective', in A. Momoh (eds.), *Democracy and socioeconomic issues in Nigeria.* Nigeria: Visart Printing and Publishing Company Nigeria Limited.

Agishi, T. V. 2014. 'Women participation in party politics in Nigeria: Challenges and the way forward', *Arabian Journal of Business and Management Review* (Nigerian Chapter), 2(4), pp. 95–100.

Aina, O. I. 2012. 'Two halves make a whole: Gender at the crossroads of the Nigeria development agenda', *Inaugural Lecture Series.* Ile-Ife, Nigeria: Obafemi Awolowo University Press.

Akinboye, S. 2004. 'Challenges and prognosis of gender equality in Nigerian politics', in S. O. Akinboye (eds.), *Paradox of gender equality in Nigerian politics 2004.* Lagos: Concept Publications Limited, pp. 232–246.

Akinboye, S. and Agbalajobi, D. T. 2013. 'Gender-Based violence and the quest for sustainable development in Nigeria', in F. Toyin and B. Bridget (eds.) *The power of gender the gender of power: Women's labor, rights, and responsibilities in Africa.* Trenton, NJ: African World Press.

Akindele, S. T., Adeyemi, O. O. and Aluko, K. 2011. 'The myth and reality of women in politics: A discourse of the core issues', *African Journal of Political Science and International Relations,* 5(4), pp. 190–207.

Akinyode-Afolabi, A. and Arogundade, L. 2003. Gender Audit- 2003 elections and issues in women's political participation in Nigeria. A Publication of Women Advocates Research and Documentation (WARDC). www.boellnigeria.org.

Akpan, E. S. 2015. 'Men without women: An analysis of the 2015 General Election in Nigeria'. Available at https://www.inecnigeria.org/wp-content/uploads/2019/02/Conference-Paper-by-Nse-Etim-Akpan.pdf (Accessed 21 June 2020).

Albritton, R. and Bureekul, T. 2005. 'How Asian minorities participate in politics', *paper presented for an Asian Barometer Conference on Democracy and Citizen Politics in East Asia,* June 17–18, Taipei, Taiwan.

Allen, P. and Cutts, D. 2018. 'How do gender quotas affect public support for women as political leaders?' *West European Politics,* 41(1), pp. 147–168.

Almond, G. A. and Verba, S. 1963. *The civic culture: Political attitudes and democracy in five nations.* Princeton: Princeton University Press.

Alsharif, A. 2011. *Saudi King gives women right to vote, Reuters.* Available at https://www.reuters.com/article/us-saudi-king-women/saudi-king-gives-women-right-to-vote-idUSTRE78O10Y20110925 (Accessed 21 June 2020).

Alstott, L. 2004. *No exit: What parents owe their children and what society owes parents.* New York: Oxford University Press.

Aluko, Y. A. 2011. 'Gender and women political leadership in Nigeria', *The Nigerian Journal of Sociology and Anthropology,* 9, pp. 37–55.

Alvarez, M. L. 2013. 'From unheard screams to powerful voices: A case study of women's political empowerment in the Philippines'. 12th National Convention on Statistics (NCS) EDSA Shangri-la Hotel, Mandaluyong City, October 1–2, 2013.

Alwin, D. F., Cohen, R. L. and Newcomb, T. M. 1991. *Political attitudes over the life span: The Bennington women after 50 years.* Wisconsin: Wisconsin University Press.

Amadi, L. and Amadi, C. 2015. 'Towards institutionalizing gender equality in Africa: How effective are the global gender summits and conventions? A critique', *African Journal of Political Science and International Relations,* 9(1) pp. 12–26.

Amnesty International. 2006. *Nigeria: Rape–the Silent Weapon.* Available at https://www.amnesty.org/en/documents/AFR44/020/2006/en/ (Accessed 22 June 2020).

Amnesty International Publications. 2011. *Nigeria loss of life, insecurity and impunity in the run-up to Nigeria's elections.* London: Amnesty International Publications.

Anderlini,S. N. 2007. *Women building peace: What they do, why it matters.* London: Lynne Rienner.

Aniekwe, C. C. and Kushie J. 2011. 'Electoral violence situational analysis: Identifying hot-spots in the 2011 general elections in Nigeria.' National Associations for Peaceful Elections in Nigeria (NAPEN), http://www.ifes.org/Content/Projects/Applied-Resea rch-Center/Criss-Cutting/Election-Violence-Education-and-Resolution.asp.

Anifowose, R. 2004. 'Women political participation in Nigeria', in S. Akinboye (eds.), *Paradox of gender equality in Nigerian politics*. Lagos: Concept Publications limited, pp. 204–218.

Anugwam, E. E. 2009. 'Women, education and work in Nigeria', *Educational Research and Development*, 4(4), pp. 127–134.

Arowolo, D. and Aluko, F. 2010. 'Women and political participation in Nigeria', *European Journal of Social Sciences*, 14(4), pp. 581–593.

Asemota, A. 2011. '7 Killed, 65 Churches Burnt in Katsina', *Sunday Sun Lagos,* 24 April, p. 8.

Atinmo, M. 2000. 'Sociocultural implications of wife beating among the Yoruba in Ibadan City, Nigeria', in F. Oyekanmi (ed.), *Men, women and violence: A Collection of Papers from Codesria Gender Institute 1997*'. Dakar, Senegal: Council for the Development of Social Science Research in Africa (CODESRIA).

Atkeson, L. R. and Rapoport, R. B. 2003. 'The more things change the more they stay the same: Examining differences in political communication, 1952–2000', *Public Opinion Quarterly,* 67(4), pp. 495–521.

Attoe Effah, S. A (nd) 'Women in the development of Nigeria since Pre- colonial Times'. Available at www.onlinenigeria.com/links/LinksReadprint.asp?blurb=15 0 (Accessed 13 June 2020).

Awe, B. 1992. *Nigerian women in historical perspective*. Lagos: Sankore Publishers Limited.

Awofeso, O. and Odeyemi, T. I. 2014. 'Gender and political participation in Nigeria: A cultural perspective', *Journal of Research in Peace, Gender and Development*, 4(6), pp. 104–110.

Babatope, E. 1995. *The Abacha Regime and the June 12 Crisis: A struggle for Democracy*. Lagos: Ebino Topsy.

Bacchi, C. 2006. 'Arguing for and against quotas: Theoretical issues', in D. Dahlerup (ed.), *Women, quotas, and politics*(. New York: Routledge, pp. 32–51.

Badmus, I. A. 2006. 'Political parties and women's political leadership in Nigeria: The case of PDP, the ANPP and the AD', *A Journal of African Studies; Ufahamu*, 32(3), pp. 55–91.

Bari, F. 2005. 'Enhancing participation of women in development through an enabling environment for achieving gender equality and the advancement of women', *Women's political participation: issues and challenges*. Bangkok, Thailand, 8–11 November. Thailand: United Nations, Division for the Advancement of Women (DAW) *Expert Group Meeting*, pp. 77–81.

Barlow, M. and Selin, S. 1987. *Women and arms control in Canada*. Ottatwa: Canadian Centre for Arms Control and Disarmament.

Barnes, T. D. and Burchard, S. M. 2012. '"Engendering" politics the impact of descriptive representation on women's political engagement in Sub-Saharan Africa', *Comparative Political Studies*, 46(7), pp. 767–790.

Bartels, L. M. 2005. *Economic inequality and political representation*. Mimeo: Princeton University.

Bill and Melinda gates Foundation. 2015. *No Ceilings: The full participation report* Available at http://www.noceilings.org/about/(Accessed 20 June 2020).

Binniyat, I. 2011. 'Post-presidential election mayhem: On Sunday alone. We had 300 patients with Bullet Wounds –hospital', *Sunday Vanguard Lagos*, 23 April. Available at http://www.vanguarddngr.com/200/04/election-mayhem-on-s unday-alone-we-had-300-patients-with0bullet-wounds-hospital (Accessed 22 June 2020).

Bisika, T. 2008. 'Do social and cultural factors perpetuate gender-based violence in Malawi?', *Gender & Behaviour,* 6(2), pp. 1884–1896.

Boehmer, E. 2005. *Stories of women gender and narrative in the Post-Colonial Nation*. Manchester University Press.

Bourne, P. A. 2010. 'Unconventional political participation in a middle-income developing country', *Current Research Journal of Social Science,* 2(2), pp. 196–203.

Bove, A. 2020. 'The limits of political culture: An introduction to G. W. F. Hegel's Notion of Bildung', in A. Bove (ed.) *Questionable returns.* Vienna: IWM Junior Visiting Fellows Conference, Vol. 12, pp. 2.

Bowman, C. G. 2003. 'Theories of domestic violence in the African Context', *American University Journal of Gender Social Policy and Law,* 11(2), pp. 847–863.

Brady, H. E., Verba, S. and Schlozman, K. L. 1995. 'Beyond SES: A resource model of political participation', *American Political Science Review*, 89(2), pp. 271–294.

Brake, E. 2004. 'Rawls and feminism: What should feminists make of liberal neutrality?', *Journal of Moral Philosophy* 1, pp. 293–309.

Bratton, M. 1999. 'Political participation in a new democracy, institutional consideration from Zambia', *Comparative Political Studies,* 32, pp. 549–588.

Briere, J. 2004. 'Violence against women, outcome complexity and implications for assessment and treatment', *Journal of Interpersonal Violence,* 19(11), pp. 252–276.

Brint, M. 1991. *A genealogy of political culture.* Boulder: Westview.

Brison, S. J. 1997. 'Outliving oneself: Trauma, memory, and personal identity', in D. T. Meyer (eds.), *Feminists rethink the self.* New York: Routledge, pp. 12–40.

British Council Nigeria. 2009. 'Nigeria: The next generation- Literature Review'.

British Council Nigeria. 2012. Gender in Nigeria Report 2012. *Improving the lives of girls and women in Nigeria: Issues, policies, action* (2nd edn.). Johannesburg: UK Aid from the Department of International Development.

Brown, N. E. 2014. 'Political Participation of Women of colour: An Intersectional Analysis', *Journal of Women, Politics & Policy,* 35(4), pp. 315–348.

Brownmiller, S. 1984. *Femininity.* New York: Simon & Schuster.

Buckley, F., Galligan, Y. and McGing, C. 2016. 'Women and the election: Assessing the impact of gender quotas', in M. Gallagher and M. Marsh (eds.) *How Ireland Voted 2016: The election that nobody won.* Camden: Palgrave Macmillan, pp. 185–205.

Bulloch, A., Kroeck, G., Kundu, S., Newhouse, W. and Lowe, K. B. 2012. 'Women's political leadership participation around the world: An institutional analysis', *The Leadership Quarterly,* 23(3), pp. 398–411.

Burns, N. 2007. 'Gender in the aggregate, gender in the individual, gender and political action', *Politics & Gender*, 3, pp. 104–124.

Burns, N., Schlozman, K. L. and Verba, S. 1997. 'The public consequences of private inequality: family life and citizen participation', *American Political Science Review*, 91, pp. 373–389.

Burrell, B. 2004. *Women and political participation. A reference handbook.* Santa Barbara: ABC-CLIO Inc.

Campbell, M. and Stapenhurst, C. F. 2005. 'Developing capacity through networks lesson from anticorruption parliamentary coalitions', *World Bank Institute*. Washington DC, January. Washington DC: World Bank. Available at http://doc uments.worldbank.org/curated/en/967181468329457031/pdf/330890CEbrief1101 Jan050Networks.pdf (Accessed 22 June 2020).

Carnevale, A. and Stone, S. 1994. 'Diversity beyond the golden rule', *Training and Development*, 48(10), pp. 22–40.

Carothers, T. 2016. Democracy support Strategies: Leading with Women's Political Empowerment. Massachusetts, NW. 14 September. Massachusetts: Carnegie Endowment for International Peace.

Central Intelligence Agency. 2013. 'The World Factbook. The work of a Nation. The Center of Intelligence. [online] https://www.cia.gov/library/publications/the-world- factbook/fields/2119.html (Accessed 22 June 2020).

Centre for Gender, Women & Children in Sustainable Development. 2014. Sociocultural determinants of voting patterns in Nigeria: Reference to women's participation and representation.

Chambers, C. 2008. *Sex, Culture, and justice: The Limits of Choice.* University Park: Pennsylvania State University Press.

Charles, I. E. and Ikenna, M. A. 2009. 'Electoral process and gender discrimination in Nigeria. A case study of 2003 and 2007 general elections', *Journal of Sustainable Development in Africa*, 10(4), pp. 113–128.

Charlotte, R. 2011. *Why are so few women in top local government jobs?* Available at http://www.theguardian.com/local-government-network/2011/sep/13/few-wo menlocal-government-jobs (Accessed 21 June 2020).

Childs, S. 2004. *New labour's women MPs.* New York: Routledge.

Childs, S. and Krook, M. L. 2008. 'Critical mass theory and women's political representation', *Political Studies* 56(3) pp. 725–736.

Chingwete, A., Richmond, S. and Alpin, C. 2014) 'Support for African women's equality rises. Education, jobs & political participation', *Afrobarometer*, 27 March 2014.

Clayton, A. 2015. 'Women's political engagement and quota-mandated female representation: Evidence from a randomized policy experiment', *Comparative Political Studies*, 48(3), pp. 333–369.

Clayton, A., Josefesson, C. and Wang, V. 2016. 'Quotas and women's substantive representation: Evidence from a content analysis of Ugandan plenary debates' *Politics & Gender*, 13(2), pp. 1–29 and pp. 276–304.

Coffé, H. and Bolzendahl, C. 2010. 'Same game, different rules? Gender differences in political participation', *Sex Roles*, 62, pp. 318–333.

Cole S. 2011. 'Increasing women's political participation in Liberia: Challenges and potential Lessons from India, Rwanda and South Africa,' International Foundation for Electoral Systems (IFES), Washington, D.C., U.S.A. 19 August.

Cornell, D. 1998. *At the heart of freedom: Feminism, sex, and equality.* Princeton: Princeton University Press.

Cornwall, A. 2008. 'Unpacking 'participation': Models, meanings and practices', *Community Development Journal,* 43(3), pp. 269–283.

Creswell, J. W. 2003. *Research design: Qualitative, quantitative and mixed method. Rhetoric of research and methodology.* Thousand Oaks: Sage Publication Inc.

Creswell, J. W. and Poth, C. N. 2018. *Qualitative inquiry & research design: Choosing among five traditions.* Thousand Oaks: Sage Publications Inc.

Cudd, A. 2006. *Analysing oppression.* New York: Oxford University Press.

DAG. 2014. 'Entrenching Kano women in political parties for political empowerment'. Survey Report submitted to *Voice for Change (V4C), Maitama, Abuja, Nigeria.* Democracy Action Group.

Dahl, R. 1998. *On democracy.* New Haven: Yale University Press.

Dahl, R. A. 1971. *Polyarchy: participation and opposition.* New Haven: Yale University Press.

Dahlerup, D. and Freidenvall, L. 2005. 'Quotas as a "fast track" to equal representation for women', *International Feminist Journal of Politics,* 7(1), pp. 26–48.

Dahlerup, D. 2006. *Women, quotas and politics* (1st ed.) London: Routledge.

Dahlerup, D. 2007. 'Electoral gender quotas: Between equality of opportunity and equality of result', *Representation,* 43(2), pp. 73–92.

Dahlerup, D. 2007. Electoral gender quotas: Between equality of opportunity and equality of result. *Representation,* 43(2), pp. 73–92.

Dalton, R. J. 2008. 'Citizenship norms and the expansion of political participation', *Political Studies,* 56, pp. 76–98.

Dalton, R. J., Sickle, A. and Weldon, S. 2009. 'The individual-institutional nexus of protest behavior', *British Journal of Political Science,* 40, pp. 51–73.

Darcy, R., Welch, S. and Clarke, J. 1994. *Women, election and representation.* Nebraska: University of Nebraska Press.

Das, S. P. 2005. 'Human rights: A gender perspective', *The Indian Journal of Political Science,* 66(4), pp. 755–772.

Dawson, R. E. and Prewitt, K. 1969. *Political socialization.* Boston: Little, Brown and Company.

DFID. 2013. Violence against women and girls CHASE Guidance note series. Department for International Development Available at <https://www.gov.uk/government/publications/violence-against-women-and-girls-chase-guidance-note-series-guidance-note-4> (Accessed 21 June 2020).

Dessler, G. 2005. *Human resource management.* New Jersey: Prentice Hall.

Dibie, R. and Okere, J. S. 2015. 'Government and NGOs performance with respect to women empowerment', *Africa's Public Service Delivery & Performance Review,* 3(1), pp. 92–136.

Diop, C. A. 1978. *The cultural unity of Negro Africa.* Chicago: Third World Press XI.

Domingo, P., Holmes, R., O'Neil, T., Jones, N., Bird, K., Larson, A., Presier-Marshall, E. and Valters, C. 2015. *Women's voice and leadership in decision-making*, Overseas Development Institute. Available at https://www.odi.org/sites/odi.org .uk/files/odi-assets/publications-opinion-files/9627.pdf (Accessed 22 June 2020).

Duerst-Lahti, G. and Verstegen, D. 1995. 'Making something of absence: The "Year of the Woman" and women's representation', in G. Duerst-Lahti and R. M. Kelly (eds.), *Gender power, leadership, and governance.* Ann Arbor: University of Michigan Press, pp. 213–238.

Dunn, A. 2007. 'Champions of participation: Engaging citizens in local governance', *An International Learning Report prepared for the Citizenship DRC, 08.*

Easteal, P. 1994. 'Violence against women in the home: How far have we come? How far to go?', *Family Matters,* 37, pp. 86–93.

Edwards, J. 2015. 'Where next for progress on women's rights?'. Institute of Development Studies. Available at www.ides.ac.uk/opinion/where-next-for-pr ogress-on-women-s-rights (Accessed 18 June 2020).

Egwu, J. U. 2015. 'Women Participation in the 2015 general elections in Nigeria', *International E-journal of Advances in Social Sciences*, 1(3), pp. 395–403.

Ehinmore, O. M. and Ehiabhi, O. S. 2013. 'Electoral violence and the crisis of democratic experiment in postcolonial Nigeria', *Journal of Arts and Humanities (JAH),* 2(5), pp. 46–51.

EISA. 2006. *South Africa: Women's representation quotas.* Available from: http://www.eisa.org.za/WEP/souquotas.htm.

Ekpenyong, O., Ibiam O. E. and Agha, E. O. 2015. Politics in Nigeria: To what extent has the gender agenda gained momentum?', *IOSR Journal of Humanities and Social Science (IOSR-JHSS),* 20(5), pp. 1–10.

Ellsberg, M. and Heise, L. 2005. 'Researching violence against women', *WHO and Program for Appropriate Technology in Health* (PATH), p. 12. Available at https ://apps.who.int/iris/bitstream/handle/10665/42966/9241546476_eng.pdf?sequen ce=1 (Accessed 14 June 2020).

Eme, O. I. and Onuigbo, R. A. 2015. 'An analysis of Nigerian women's score card in 2015 Polls', *Singaporean Journal of Business Economics and Management Studies,* 4(4), pp. 17–29.

Enaibe P. U. 2012. 'Need to promote women education and participation in politics for sustainable national development', *International Journal of Educational Research and Development,* 1(1), pp. 1–5.

Ersson, S. and Lane, Jan-Erik. 2008. 'Political culture', in Daniele Caramani (ed.), *Comparative politics.* Oxford: Oxford University Press, pp. 419–444.

Erunke, C. E. and Shuaibu, U. A. 2013. 'The role of women in Nigerian politics: Addressing the gender question for an enhanced political representation in the Fourth Republic', *International Journal of Gender and Women's Studies,* 1(1), pp. 45–55.

Evans, G. and Rose, P. 2007. 'Support for democracy in Malawi: Does schooling matter?', *World Development,* 35, pp. 904–919.

Ezeilo, J. 2012. 'Gender analysis of Nigerian political parties: Progress and stagnation'. Unpublished Paper.

Fapounda, T. M. 2011. 'Integrating women and gender issues in peace and development', *International Journal of Peace and Development Studies*, 2(6), pp. 162–170.

Fayomi, O. O. and Ajayi, L. Y. 2015. 'An exploratory study of women in political leadership in Nigeria', *World Academy of Science, Engineering and Technology, International Journal of Economics and Management Engineering*, 2. Available at https://pdfs.semanticscholar.org (Accessed 21 June 2020).

Federal Ministry of Women Affairs and Social Development. 2006. *National gender policy*. Abuja: Federal Secretariat.

Ford, L. E. 2002. *Women and politics: The pursuit of equality*. Boston: Houghton Mifflin Company.

Fox R. L. and Lawless J. L. 2004. 'Entering the arena? Gender and the decision to run for office', *American Journal of Political Science*, 48(2), pp. 264–280.

Franceschet, Susan, Krook, Mona Lena, Piscopo, Jennifer M. (eds). 2012. *The impact of gender quotas*. New York: Oxford University Press.

Francis, L. P. 1998. 'In defense of affirmative action', in S. M. Cahn, *In affirmative action and the university: A philosophical inquiry*. Philadelphia: Temple University Press.

Fridkin, K. and Kenney, P. 2007. 'Examining the gender gap in children's attitudes toward politics', *Sex Roles*, 56(3), pp. 133–140.

Gabriel, C. 2015, June 19. *Electoral positions: Why Nigeria records more women losers than winners*. Vanguard.

Gabriel, C. 2015. 'Elective positions: Why Nigeria records more women loses than winners', *Vanguard*, May. Available at https://www.vanguardngr.com/20 15/05/elective-positions-why-nigeria-records-more-women-losers-than-winners/ (Accessed 23 June 2020).

Gambo, S. and Lenshie, N. E. 2013. 'Gender politics, media and democracy in Nigeria', *Journal of International Politics and Development*, 11(1&2), pp. 1–220.

Gatimu, S. and Ndung'u, I. 2016. 'Kenyan Politics: where have all the women gone?' *ISS Today*. Available at http://www.issafrica.org/ISS-today/kenyan-politics-where -have-all-the-women-gone (Accessed 12 August 2019).

Geisler, G. 2004. *Women and the remaking of politics in Southern Africa. Negotiating autonomy, incorporation and representation*. Uppsala: Nordic Africa Institute.

George-Genyi, M. 2010. 'The place of women in a decade of return to democracy in Nigeria, 1999- 2009', in V. Egwemi (ed.), *A decade of democracy in Nigeria, 1999-2—0 issues, challenges and prospects of consolidation*. Aboki Publishers.

Goetz, A. and Hassim, S. (eds). 2003. *No Shortcuts to Power: African women in politics and policy making*. Zed Books LTD and David Philip Publishers.

Gordon, J. 1992. 'Getting started on diversity work', *Training*, 29(1), pp. 26–31.

Gottfredson, L. 1992. 'Dilemmas in developing diversity programs', in Jackson, S. and Associates (eds.), *Diversity in the workplace: Human resources initiatives*. New York: Guildford Press.

Green, K. 2006. 'Parity and procedural justice', *Essays in Philosophy*, 7(1), pp. 18–28.

Griffin, J. D. and Newman, B. 2005. 'Are voters better represented?', *The Journal of Politics*, 67(4), pp. 1206–1227.

Habboush, M. 2011. *United Arab Emirate (UAE) Nationals Ask: Why can't we all vote?* Available at https://www.reuters.com/article/us-emirates-elections-campaign /uae-nationals-ask-why-cant-we-all-vote-idUSTRE78K33F20110921https://www. reuters.com/article/us-emirates-elections-campaign/uae-nationals-ask-why-cant -we-all-vote-idUSTRE78K33F20110921 (Accessed 21 June 2020).

Hamadeh-Banerjee, L. and Oquist, P. 2000. *Overview: women's political participation and good governance: 21st century challenges.* New York: United Nations Development Programme.

Harrison, L. and Munn, J. 2007. 'Gendered (non)participants? What constructions of citizenship tell us about democratic governance in the twenty-first century', *Parliamentary Affairs*, 60, pp. 426–436.

Harwood, A. and Campbell, J. 2010. 'Opinion: Text messaging as a weapon in Nigeria'. *Global Post*, September 22. Available at https://www.pri.org/stories/2010 -09-22/opinion-text-messaging-weapon-nigeria (Accessed 20 June 2020).

Heise L., Ellsberg, M., Gottemoeller, M. 2002. 'A global overview of gender-based violence', *The International Journal of Gynecology & Obstetrics* 78(Suppl 1), S5–S14. doi:10.1016/S0020-7292(02)00038-3.

Heise, L. and Garcia-Moreno, C. 2002. 'Violence by intimate partners' in E. G. Krug et al. (eds.), *World Report on violence and health.* WHO, p. 89.

Henn, M. and Foard, N. 2012. 'Young people, political participation and trust in Britain', *Parliamentary Affairs,* 65, pp. 47–67.

Hickey, G. and Kipping, E. 1996. 'A multi-stage approach to the coding of data from open-ended questions', *Nurse Researcher* 4, pp. 81–91.

Hillman, B. 2017. 'Increasing women's parliamentary representation in Asia and the Pacific: The Indonesia experience', *Asia and the Pacific Policy*, 4(1), pp. 38–49.

Hines, A. M. 1993. 'Linking qualitative and quantitative methods in cross cultural survey research: Techniques from cognitive science', *American Journal of Community Psychology*, 21(6), pp. 729–746.

Hoare, J. and Gell, F. (eds.). 2009. 'Women's leadership and participation: Overview', in J. Hoare and F. Gell (eds.), *Women's leadership and participation: Case studies on learning for action* (pp. 1–18). Oxfam GB/Practical Action Publishing.

Hogstrom, J. 2012. 'women's representation in national politics in the world's democratic countries: A research note', *Journal of Women, Politics & Policy*, 33(3), pp. 263–279.

Hooghe, M. and Stolle, D. 2004. 'Good girls go to the polling booth, bad boys go everywhere: Gender differences in anticipated political participation among American fourteen-year-olds', *Women & Politics*, 26(3), pp. 1–23.

Hsieh, H. F. and Shannon, S. 2005. 'Three approaches to qualitative content analysis', *Qualitative Health Research*, 15(9), pp. 1277–1288.

Human Right Education and Monitoring Center. 2014. Women & political representation. Handbook on increasing women's political participation in Georgia. EMC. OSCE office for Democratic Institutions and Human Rights (ODIHR), Poland.

Igbuzor, O. 2008. Promoting gender equality for sustainable development using the National Gender Policy. Available on http://www.gamji.com/article6000/NEWS7 860.htm.

Ihonvbere, J. and Shaw, T. 1998. *Illusions of power: Nigeria in transition*. New Jersey: Africa World Press.

Ikpeze, V. C. 2002. 'Understanding affirmative action as aid to Women's Human Rights in Nigeria', in H. Ibrahim (eds.), *Bar Perspectives, a Quarterly Publication of the Nigerian Bar Association (NBA)*. Abuja: Nigerian Bar Association (NBA), pp. 54–580.

INEC. 2019. Political Parties. Available at https://inecnigeria.org/political-parties/ (Accessed 18 June 2020).

Inglehart, R. and Norris, P. 2003. *Rising tide: Gender equality and cultural change around the world*. Cambridge: Cambridge University Press.

International IDEA. 1997. 'Politics—Women in Focus on the political participation of Women beyond Numbers', A workshop. http://archive.idea.int/women/links .htm.

International IDEA. 2000. Democracy in Nigeria: Continuing Dialogue (s) for Nation Building. International IDEA.

IPU. 2017. *Women in national parliaments*. Available at http://archive.ipu.org/wmn -e/classif.htm (Accessed 21 June 2020).

Isa, F. G. 2003. 'The optional protocol for the convention on the elimination of all forms of discrimination against women: Strengthening the protection mechanism of women's human rights', *Arizona Journal of International and Comparative Law*, 20(2), pp. 291–321.

Isaksson, A. S. 2010. 'Political participation in Africa: Participatory inequalities and the role of resources', *Working Papers in Economics*. University of Gothenburg, August. Gothenburg: Equis Accredited, pp. 1–25.

Isiugo-Abanihe, U. 2002. 'Quantitative research techniques', in U. A. Isamah Isiugo-Abanihe and J. Adesina (eds.), *Currents and perspectives in sociology*, Malthouse Social Science Studies. Lagos: Malthouse, pp. 52–72.

Iversen, T. and Rosenbluth, F. 2008. 'Work and power: The connection between female labor force participation and female political representation', *Annual Review of Political Science*, 11, pp. 479–495.

Izumi, K. 2007. 'Gender-based violence and property grabbing in Africa: A denial of women's Liberty and security', in G. Terry and J. Hoare (eds.), *Gender-based violence*. Oxford: Oxfam GB, pp. 14–23.

Jaggar, A. M. 1983. *Feminist politics and human nature*. Sussex, England: The Harvester.

Jaggar, V. Held (eds.), *Feminists rethink the self, Feminist theory and politics series*. Oxford: Westview Press, pp. 12–39.

Jasper, J. M. 2005. 'Culture, knowledge, and politics', in T. Janoskiu, R. R. Alford, A. M. Hicks and M. A. Schwartz (eds.), *The handbook of political sociology*. Cambridge: Cambridge University Press, pp. 115–134.

Jochum, V., Pratten, B. and Wilding, K. 2005. *Civil renewal and active citizenship: A guide to the debate*. London: NCVO.

Johari, J. C. 1982. *Comparative politics*. New Delhi: Sterling Publishers.

Johnson, R. B. and Onwuegbuzie, A. J. 2004. 'Mixed methods research: A research paradigm whose time has come', *Educational Researcher*, 33(7), pp. 14–26.

Aiyede, Emmanuel Remi (2012). 'Special issue: Nigeria's 2011 elections', *Journal of African Elections*, 11(1), pp. 74–99.

Kaimenyi, C., Kinya, E. and Samwel C. M. 2013. 'An analysis of affirmative action: The two-thirds gender rule in Kenya', *International Journal of Business, Humanities and Technology*, 3(6), pp. 91–97.

Kamau, N. and Nzomo, M. 2012. 'Violence and women participation in electoral process challenges and prospects for the 2013 Elections in Kenya', *African Research and Resource Forum (ARRF)*, Elections dispatch no.7, ISSN: 2012-2007.

Karam, A. 1998. *Women in parliament: Beyond numbers.* Stockholm, Sweden: International Institute for Democracy and Electoral Assistance (IDEA).

Karl, M. 1995. *Women and empowerment: Participation and decision-making.* New Jersey: Zed Books.

Kassa, S. 2015. 'Challenges and opportunities of women political participation in Ethiopia', *Journal of Global Economics* 3(4), pp. 1–7.

Kew, D. 2004. 'The Third Generation of Nigerian civil society: The Rise of Non-governmental Organizations in the 1990s', in A. A. Agbaje, L. Diamond and E. Onwudiwe (eds.), *Nigeria's struggle for democracy and good governance.* Ibadan: Ibadan University Press.

Khayria, K. and Feki, R. 2015. 'Gender inequality and economic development', *Business and Economics Journal* 6(4). Available at https://www.researchgate.net/publication/283482318_Gender_Inequality_and_Economic_Development (Accessed 21 June 2020).

Kiley, J. 2014. As GOP celebrates win, no signs of narrowing gender, age gaps. Available at https://www.pewresearch.org/fact-tank/2014/11/05/as-gop-celebrates-win-no-sign-of-narrowing-gender-age-gaps/ (Accessed 21 June 2020).

Knuttila, M. and Kubik, W. 2000. *State theories.* London: Zed Books.

Kolawole, S. 2011. 'Two youth corpers murdered in cold blood while on national Service', *This Day,* 23 April. Available at http://www.thisdaylive.com/articles/two-youth-corpers-murdered-in-cold-blood-while-on-national-service/90142 (Accessed 21 June 2020).

Kolawole, T. O., Abubaka, B. M., Owonubi, E. and Adebayo, A. A. 2012. 'Gender and party politics in Africa with reference to Nigeria', *Online Journal of Education Research*, 1(7), pp. 132–144.

Krantz, G. and Garcia-Moreno, C. 2005. 'Violence against women', *Journal of Epidemiology and Community Health,* 59(10), pp. 818–821.

Krejcie, R. and Morgan, D. 1970. 'Determining sample size for research activities', *Educational and Psychological Measurement*, 30, pp. 607–610.

Kroeber A. L. 2018. *Culture: A Critical review of concepts and definitions.* Classic reprint. London: Forgotten Books.

Krook, M. L. 2006. 'Reforming representation: The diffusion of candidate gender quotas worldwide', *Politics & Gender,* 2(3), pp. 303–327.

Krook, M. L. 2009. *Quotas for women in politics.* New York: Oxford University Press.

Krook, M. L. 2010. 'Women's representation in parliament: A qualitative comparative analysis', *Political Studies*, 58(5), pp. 886–908.

Krook, M. L. 2015. 'Gender and elections: Temporary special measures beyond quotas'. *Conflict Prevention and Peace Forum CPPF Working Papers on Women in Politics:* No. 4.

Krook, M. L. and Childs, S. 2010. *Women, gender and politics.* Oxford: Oxford University Press.

Krook, M. L. and Jacqui, T. 2012. 'Rethinking the life cycles of international norms: The United Nations and the global promotion of gender equality', *European Journal of International Relations,* 18(1), pp. 103–127.

Krook, M. L. and Messing-Mathie, A. 2013. 'Gender quotas and comparative politics: Past, present, and future research agendas', *Politics &Gender,* 9(3), pp. 299–303.

Krook, M. L., and Norris, P. 2014. 'Beyond quotas: Strategies to promote gender equality in elected office', *Political Studies,* 62(1), pp. 2–20.

Krook, M. L., and True, J. 2008. 'Global strategies for gender equality: The United Nations before and after Beijing', in *Annual International Studies Association Conference.*

Krook, M. L., and True, J. 2012. 'Rethinking the life cycles of international norms: The United Nations and the global promotion of gender equality', *European Journal of International Relations,* 18(1), 103–127.

Krook, M. L. and Zetterberg, P. 2014. 'Electoral quotas and political representation: Comparative Perspectives', *International Political Science Review,* 35(2), pp. 3–11.

Kukah, M. H. 2003. *Democracy and civil society in Nigeria.* Ibadan: Spectrum Books.

Ladbury, S. 2011. Religion, exclusion and violence in northern Nigeria. Final Report for DFID, 31 January 2011.

Lamidi, E. O. 2014. Determinants of women's decision-making power in Nigeria. Paper presented at the *Annual meeting of the American Sociological Association,* Hilton San Francisco Union Square and Parc 55 Wyndham San Francisco. Available at http://citation.allacademic.com/meta/p723738_index.html.

Lee, R. A. 1999. 'The evolution of affirmative action', *Sage Journals,* 28(3), pp. 393–408.

Leighley, J. 1995. 'Attitudes, opportunities and incentives: A field essay on political participation'. *Political Research Quarterly,* 48(1), pp. 181–209. doi:10.2307/449127.

Lewu, A. Y. 2005. 'Women in Nigerian politics', in H. A. Saliu (ed.), *Nigeria under democratic rule (1999-2003)* 2. Ibadan: University Press plc.

Liebowitz, J. and Ibrahim, J. 2013. 'A capacity assessment of Nigerian political parties', *Democratic Governance for Development (DGD) Programme,* UNPD Nigeria, January 2013.

Lijphart, A. 1997. 'Unequal participation: Democracy's unresolved dilemma', *The American Political Science Review,* 91, pp. 1–14.

Liman, I. 2011. 'We Lost over 400 in Southern Kaduna–Hausa/Fulani', *Daily Trust,* 25 April. Available at http://www.dailytrust.com.ng/index.php/news/17737-we-lo st-over-400-in-southern-kaduna--hausafulani?device=iphone (Accessed 25 June 2020). (WEBSITE Does not work).

Lindberg, S. I. 2004. 'Women's empowerment and democratization: The effects of electoral systems, participation and experience in Africa', *Studies in Comparative International Development*, 39, pp. 28–53.

Lovenduski, J. 2005. *Feminizing politics*. Cambridge, UK: Polity Press.

Luka, R. C. 2012. 'Women and political participation in Nigeria: The imperative of empowerment', *Journal of Social Sciences and Public Policy*, 3, pp. 24–37.

Maguire, S. 2018. Barriers to Women Entering Parliament and Local Government, institute for Policy Research Report 2018. University of Bath.

Malhotra, A., Schulte, J., Patel, P. and Petesch, P. 2009. *Innovation for women's empowerment and gender equality*. North Washington, D.C.: International Centre for research on Women (ICRW).

Mama, A. 1995. 'Feminism or femocracy, state feminism and democratisation in Nigeria', *African Development*, 20(1), pp. 37–58.

Mama, A. and Margo, O. 2008. 'Conflict and women's activism', *Feminist Africa*, 10, pp. 1–8.

Markham, S. 2013. 'Women as agents of change: Having voice in society and influencing policy', *Gender Equality & Development*, Women's Voices, Agency & Participation Research Series 2013 No. 5.

Martin, O. 2013. *The African Union's mechanisms to foster gender mainstreaming and ensure women's political participation and representation*. Stockholm, Sweden: International Institute for Democracy and Electoral Assistance (IDEA).

Matland, R. E. and Montgomery, K. A. 2003. 'Recruiting women to national legislatures: A general framework with applications to post-communist Democracies', in R. E. Matland and K. A. Montgomery (eds.), *Women's access to political power in post-communist Europe*. New York and Oxford: Oxford University Press, pp. 20.

Matland, R. E. and Montgomery, K. A. (eds.). 2003. *Women's access to political power in post-communist Europe*. Oxford: Oxford University Press, pp. 321–342.

Matland, R. E. and Studler, D. T. 1996. 'The contagion of women candidates in single-member district and proportional representation electoral systems: Canada and Norway', *Journal of Politics*, 58(3), pp. 707–733.

Mba, N. E. 1982. *Nigerian women mobilized, women's political activity in southern Nigeria, 1900-1965*. Berkeley: University of California.

Mba, N. E. 1989. 'Kaba and Khaki: women and the militarized state in Nigeria', in J. L. Parpart and K. A. Staudt (eds.), *Women and the state in Africa*. USA: Lynne Rienner Publisher, Inc.

McEwan, C. 2000. 'Engendering citizenship: Gendered spaces of democracy in South Africa', *Political Geography*, 19, pp. 627–651.

McGing, C. 2019. 'Electoral quotas and women's rights', in *International Human Rights of Women*. Springer, pp. 175–192.

McLean, C. 2002. 'The merit of merit', *Report/Newsmagazine*, 29(8), pp. 34–36.

Meyers, D. 2004. *Being yourself: Essays on identity, action, and social life*. Maryland: Rowman and Littlefield.

Migirou, K. 1998. 'Towards effective implementation of international women's human rights legislation', in A. Karam (ed.), *Women in parliament: Beyond numbers*. Stockholm, Sweden: International IDEA.

Mofoluwawo, E. O. 2014. 'Social, cultural and economic discrimination to women participation in African politics: The case of Nigeria', *International Journal of Learning and Development,* 4(1), pp. 169–175.

Mohai, P. 1991. 'Black environmentalism', *Social Science Quarterly,* 71(4), pp. 744–765.

Mohamed, M. W., Tanko, Y. D. and Mukhtar, I. 2015. 'The myth and reality of women's political marginalisation in Nigeria', *International Journal of Humanities and Social Science Invention,* 4(2), pp. 1–15.

Mohammed, A. 2011. '11 Corps members died in Bauchi violence- Police', *Daily Trust,* 25 April, http://www.dailytrust.com.ng.

Mohammed, A. 2014. 'Universal challenge: Unleashing the transformative power of women', *The African Women's Journal,* (7). Keeping the African Women's Decade Alive. African Women in Power/Politics.

Mohammed, H. D. 1985. 'Women in Nigeria history: Examples from Borno Empire, Nupeland and Igboland', in Women in Nigeria (eds.), *Women in Nigeria today.* London: Zed Books.

Morrison, A. and Lorento, B. M. (eds.). 1999. *Too close to home: Domestic violence in Latin America.* Washington, DC: Inter-America Development Bank.

Mosedale, S. 2014. 'Women's empowerment as a development goal: Taking a feminist standpoint', *Journal of International Development,* 26, pp. 1115–1125.

Motevalli, G. 2013. Afghanistan's first female Mayor proves critics wrong. Available at http://www.theguardian.com/world/2013/feb/24/afghanistan-first-female-mayor (Accessed 21 June 2020).

Mukasa, S. 2015. *Banning gender-based violence in Nigeria–a major step forward.* Available at https://www.huffpost.com/entry/banning-genderbased-viole_b _7293920 (Accessed 21 June 2020).

Mukasa, S., McCleary-Sills, J., Heilman, B. and Namy, S. 2014. Review of Australian aid initiatives in the Pacific aimed at ending violence against women. Available at https://www.dfat.gov.au/about-us/publications/Pages/review-of-australian-aid -initiatives-in-the-pacific-aimed-at-ending-violence-against-women (Accessed 21 June 2020).

Munroe, T. 2002. *An introduction to politics: Lectures for first-year students.* Jamaica: University of the West Indies Press.

Murray, R. 2012. 'Parity and legislative competence in France', in S. Franceschet, M. L. Krook and J. Piscopo (eds.), *The impact of gender quotas.* Oxford: Oxford University Press, 2012.

Nanette, P. and Cheryl, E. C. 1999. 'Empowerment: what is it?' *Journal of Extension,* 37(5). Available at https://www.joe.org/joe/1999october/comm1.php (Accessed 21 June 2020).

National Democratic Institute. 2010. *Democracy and the challenge for change: A guide to increasing women's political participation.* Washington DC: National Democratic Institute.

Ndujihe, C. 2011. 'How Nigeria is shared under Johnathan', Vanguard, 05 November. Available at https://www.vanguardngr.com/2011/11/how-nigeria-is-shared-under-j onathan/ (Accessed 21 June 2020).

Nelson, E. E. 2012. 'Democracy and the struggle for political empowerment of women in Nigerian', *International Journal of Advanced Legal Studies and Governance*, 3(1), pp. 85–99.

Next Generation Nigeria. www.nextgenerationnigeria.org/2009/06.

Ngara, C. O. and Ayabam, A. T. 2013. 'Women in politics and decision-making in Nigeria: Challenges and prospects', *European Journal of Business and Social Sciences*, 2(8), pp. 47–58.

Nilges, T. 2005. 'Gender inequality in politics', *Human rights: A gender perspective*, Vol. 1.

NOI Polls. 2014. *2 in 10 Nigerians Claim They Have Political Party Affiliation.* Available at https://noi-polls.com/2-in-10-nigerians-claim-they-have-political-part y-affiliation/ (Accessed 21 June 2020).

Norris, P. 2002. *Democratic phoenix: Reinventing political activism.* Cambridge: Cambridge University Press.

Norris, P. and Dahlerup, D. 2015. 'On the fast track: The spread of gender quota policies for elected office'. *Faculty Research Working Paper Series.* Harvard Kennedy School, July 2015.

Norris, P. and Inglehart, R. 2003. 'Cultural barriers to women's leadership: A worldwide comparison', *Journal of Democracy*, 26, pp. 1–30.

Norris, P. and Inglehart, R. 2004. 'Cultural barriers to women's leadership: A worldwide comparison', *Journal of Democracy*, 26, pp. 1–30.

Norris, P., and Dahlerup, D. 2015. On the fast track: The spread of gender quota policies for elected office.

Nwabueeze, B. O. 1989. 'Our March to Constitutional Democracy'. The 1989 Guardian Lecture Lagos, delivered on July 24.

Nwankwo, Clement and Domingo, Pilar. 2010. Review of the International assistance to Political Party and Party System Development. Case Study Report: Nigeria. Overseas Development Institute (ODI), London.

Nzomo, M. 2003. 'The 2002 General Elections in Kenya: Women's Performance and prospects in parliamentary politics', *Journal of Social and Religious Concern*, 18(1–2). Available at http://web.peacelink.it/wajibu/18_issue/p2.html (Accessed date January 2020).

Obadiya, John Olusheye. 2009. Nigerian Women and Development: Yesterday, today and tomorrow. http://www.Obadiyajohn.blogspot.com/2009/11/nigerian-women-a nd-development.html?m=1.

O'Barr, J. 1984. 'African women in politics', in M. Hay and S. Stichter (eds.), *African women south of the Sahara.* New York: Longman Group.

Odah, A. O. 2007. *2007 Elections and challenges on Nigeria.* Available at: www .allafrica.com (Accessed 25 June 2020) (invalid website).

Odi, M. 2012. 'Women's political and civic participation in Nigeria: Opportunities and challenges to the full realization of democracy'. Paper presented at Fifth Convening of the *International Women's Democracy Network, World Movement for Democracy's Seventh Assembly, Lima, Peru* (October, 2012).

Ofili, P. E. 2011. Provocative discourse and violence in Nigeria's 2011 Elections, *Africa Portal*, No. 17. Available at http://www.africaportal.org/sites/default/fil

es/Backgrounder%20No.17-Provocative%20Discourse%20&%20Violence%20in %20Nigeria's%202011%20Elections.pdf (Accessed 15 April 2018).

Ogbogu, C. O. 2012. 'The role of women in politics and in the sustenance of democracy in Nigeria', *International Journal of Business and Social Science,* 3(18), pp. 182–191.

Ogundipe- Leslie, M. 1985. 'Women in Nigeria: Problems and realities', in D. L. Badejo (eds.), *Women in Nigeria today.* London: Zed Books LTD.

Ogunniyi, O. J. and Dosunmu A. G. 2014. 'Historical background and impact of women's involvement in formal education in Nigeria', *European Scientific Journal (Special Edition),* 1, pp. 188–192.

Ojo, J. S. 2013. 'An assessment of gender inequality in democratic politics in the Fourth Republic in Nigeria (1999-2003)', *International NGO Journal,* 8(7), pp. 138–145.

Ojo, O. E. 2004. 'The military and political transition', in A. B. Agbaje Adigun, Larry Diamond and Ebere Onwudiwe (eds.), *Nigeria's struggle for democracy and good governance.* Ibadan University Press.

Okibe, H. B. 2016. 'Marginalisation of women by women in the contest for elective positions in Nigeria: A reconstruction paradigm', *The International Journal of Humanities & Social Studies,* 4(7), pp. 236–245.

Okin, S. M. 1989. *Justice, gender and the family.* New York: Basic Books.

Okonjo, K. 1975. 'The role of women in the development of culture in Nigeria', in R. R. Leavitt (ed.), *Women cross-culturally: Change and challenge.* France: Mauton Publisher, pp. 31–40.

Okonjo, K. 1976. 'The dual political system in operation, Igbo women and community politics in mid-Western Nigeria', in N. J. Hafkin and E. G. Bay (eds.), *Women in Africa.* California: California Stanford University Press, pp. 45–58.

Okoosi-Simbine, A. T. 2007. 'Women marginalisation and politics in Nigeria: A review \ essay', in I. O. Albert, D. Marco and V. Adetula (eds.), *Perspectives on the 2003 elections in Nigeria.* Ibadan: Stirling-Herden Publisher Ltd.

Okoosi-Simbine A. T. 2012. 'Gender politics and the 2011 elections', *Journal of African Elections,* 11(1), pp. 74–99.

Okoronkwo-Chukwu, U. 2013. 'Female representation in Nigeria: The case of the 2011 General Elections and the Fallacy of 35% Affirmative Action', *Research on Humanities and Social Sciences,* 3(2), pp. 39–47.

Okpilike, F. M. E. and Abamba, G. O. 2013. 'Sociological explanation of male dominance in Nigerian party politics: Implication for education', *British Journal of Education, Society and Behavioural Studies,* 3(2), pp. 154–162.

Okumu, D. 2008. '(Re) Configuring gender-based violence on 'political rape'', in Kamau (ed.), *Perspectives on gender discourse: Enhancing women's participation.* Nairobi: Heinrich Böll Stiftung, East & Horn of Africa Office, pp. 77–88.

Olatunde, D. 2010. Women and the political history of Nigeria. wiredspace.wits.ac .za.

Ologbenla, D. K. 2003. 'What is good for the goose is not good for the gander: Real issues in gender discrimination in Nigerian public administration', *Institute of Public Administration of Nigeria (IPAN),* 1(2), pp. 1–23.

Olojede, I. 1999. 'Women and democratic governance: Lessons from second and third republics', in H. A. Saliu (ed.), *Issues in contemporary political economy of Nigeria*. Ilorin: Sally and Associates, pp. 243–255.

Oloyede, O. 2016. Monitoring participation of women in politics in Nigeria. Being a conference paper. http://unstats.un.org/unsd/gender/Finland_Oct2016/Documents/Nigeria_paper.pdf.

Olufade, A. O. 2013. 'Nigerian women, politics and the national identity question', *African Educational Research Journal,* 1(3), pp. 161–170.

Omitola, O. and Lalude, G. 1998. 'Women and political participation state sponsored participation, mass-based or organization participation', *Ife Journal of Social Science Review*, Conference Proceedings July 1998.

Omotola, J. S. 2007. 'What is this gender talk all about after All? Gender, power and politics in contemporary Nigeria', *African Study Monographs*, 28(1), pp. 33–46.

Oni, S. and Agbude, G. 2009. 'Determinants of political participation amongst women in Ogun State, Nigeria', *Journal of Library Information Science & Technology,* 1(4), pp. 1–20.

Oni, S. and Joshua, S. 2012. 'Gender relations in Nigeria's democratic governance', *Journal of Politics and Governance*, 1(2/3), pp. 4–15.

Onwudiwe, E. and Berwind-Dart, C. 2010. 'Breaking the cycle of electoral violence in Nigeria', Washington, DC: United States Institute of Peace. Available at https://www.usip.org/sites/default/files/SR263-Breaking_the_Cycle_of_Electoral_Violence_in_Nigeria.pdf (Accessed 22 June 2020).

Opara, I. 2015. 'Olabisi: Government policies on women are only okay on paper', *The Guardian,* 7 February. Available at https://guardian.ng/sunday-magazine/c104-sunday-magazine/olabisi-government-policies-on-women-are-only-okay-on-paper/ (Accessed 21 June 2020).

Orji, N. and Uzodi, N. 2012. 'The 2011 post-election violence in Nigeria', Policy and Legal Advocacy Centre (PLAC) with from Open Society Initiative for West Africa, pp. 12.

Orude, P. 2011. '11 corps members killed in Bauchi, female raped', *Sunday Sun,* 24 April.

Osinulu, C. and Mba, N. (eds.). 1996. *Nigerian women in politics 1986-1993*. Lagos: Malthouse Press Limited.

O'Toole, T., Marsh, D. and Jones, S. 2003. 'Political literacy cuts both ways: The politics of non-participation among young People', *The Political Quarterly*, 74(3), pp. 349–360.

Oyekanmi, F. D. 2004. 'Socio-economic dimensions of gender equality', in S. O. Akinboye and V. I. Adeleke (eds.), *Paradox of gender equality in Nigerian politics*. Lagos: Concept Publications.

Panda, S. 1995. *Gender environment and participation in politics*. New Delhi: M.D. Publications.

Paquette, D. 2015. 'Gender equality', *Washington Post.*

Parpart, J. 1988. 'Women and the state', in D. Rothchild and N. Chazan (eds.), *The precarious balance: State and society in Africa*. Boulder: Westview Press.

Pateman, C. 1970. *Participation and democratic theory*. Cambridge: Cambridge University Press.

Pattie, C., Seyd, P. and Whiteley, P. 2003. 'Citizenship and civic engagement: Attitudes and behaviour in Britain', *Political Studies*, 51(3), pp. 443–468.

Paxton, P. and Hughes, M. M. 2016. *Women and politics and power: A Global perspective*. Washington, D.C.: CQ Press.

Paxton, P., Kunovich, S. and Hughes, M. M. 2007. 'Gender in politics', *Annual Review of Sociology*, 33, 263–284.

Paxton, P. M., Hughes, M. M., and Barnes, T. 2020. *Women, politics, and power: A global perspective*. Rowman & Littlefield Publishers.

Pearce, D. 1978. 'The feminization of poverty: Women, work and welfare', *Urban and Social Change Review,* 11(1,2), pp. 28–36.

Peters, A. 2006. Electoral gender quotas: Undemocratic, unfair and inefficient? Unpublished manuscript.

Peterson, S. V. and Runyan, A. 1999. *Global gender issues* (2nd ed). Colorado: Westview Press.

Phillips, A. 1991. *Engendering democracy*. Cambridge: Polity Press.

Phillips, A. 1995. *The politics of presence*. Oxford: Polity Press.

Phillips, A. 2004. 'Defending equality of outcome', *Journal of Political Philosophy*, 12, pp. 1–19.

Pietila, H. and Vickers, J. 1990. *Making women matter: The role of the United Nations*. London: Zed Books.

Pogoson, A. I. 2012. 'Gender, political parties and the reproduction of patriarchy in Nigeria, A Reflection on the democratisation process 1999-2011', *Journal of African Elections*. Special Issues: Nigeria's 2011 Elections, 11(1), pp. 100–122.

Pogoson, A. I. 2013. 'Women participation in electoral processes: the Nigerian Experience', *The Nigerian Electoral Journal. Special Issue,* 5(1), pp. 4–33.

Pogoson, A. I. 2015. 'The face of 'Eve' in Nigerian politics: Laying claim to the public space', in A. Momoh (ed.), *Democracy and socioeconomic issues in Nigeria*, Nigeria: Visart Printing and Publishing Company Nigeria Limited.

Potter, W. and Levine-Donnerstein, D. 1999. 'Rethinking validity and reliability in content analysis', *Journal of Applied Communication Research*, 27, pp. 258–284.

Priya, N. 2013. Women in power: Beyond access to influence in a post-2015 world. London: VSO International.

Pye, L. W. and Verba, S. (eds.), *Political culture and political development*. Princeton, NJ: Princeton University Press, 1965.

Quadri, M. O. 2013. 'Gender policy of Nigerian political parties: A study of Action Congress of Nigeria (ACN) and People's Democratic Party (PDP)', *The Nigerian Electoral Journal* (Special Issue), 5(1), pp. 4–33.

Quadri, M. O. and Agbalajobi, D. T. 2013. 'A comparative analysis of women's performance in the Nigerian political process: 1999-2011 elections', *African Journal of Institutions and Development (AJID)*, 8(1–2), pp. 123–138.

Rai, S. M. 2005. 'Equal participation of women and men in decision-making process, with particular emphasis on political participation and leadership'. *Background Paper Prepared for the Expert Group Meeting of the Division for the Advancement of Women (DAW)*, United Nations held 24–27 October 2005 in Addis Ababa.

Randall, V. 1987. *Women and politics- An international perspective*. Macmillan Education.

Rapoport R.B. 1981. 'The sex gap in political persuading: Where the 'structuring principle' works', *American Journal of Political Science*, 25, pp. 32–48. doi: 10.2307/2110911.

Rhode, D. 1994. 'Feminism and the state', *Harvard Law Review*, 107, pp. 1181–1208.

Rhode, D. 1997. *Speaking of sex: The denial of gender inequality*. Cambridge: Harvard University Press.

Riley, C. E., Griffin, C. and Morey, Y. 2010. 'The case for 'everyday politics': Evaluating neo-tribal theory as a way to understand alternative forms of political participation, using electronic dance music culture as an example', *Sociology*, 44(2), pp. 345–363.

Robinson, C. 1996. *Language use in rural development: An African perspective*. Berlin: Mouton de Gruyter.

Rodney, W. 1972. *How Europe underdeveloped Africa*. London/Dar es Salam: Bogle L'Ouverture Publications/Tanzania Publishing House.

Rosaldo M. Z. and Lamphere, L. (eds.). 1974. *Women, culture and society*. Stanford University Press.

Rosenbluth, F., Kalla, J., and Teele, D. 2015. *The female political career*. The World Bank.

Rossett, A. and Bickham, T. 1994. 'Diversity training', *Training*, 31(1), pp. 40–46.

SADC. 2012. Women in politics and decision making. www.sadc.int/issues/gender/women-politics/.

Salihu, A. 2015. 'Framing engagement: Women in an imperfect political system, Lessons from the 2007 elections', in A. Momoh (ed.), *Democracy and socioeconomic Issues in Nigeria*. Abuja: Friedrich Ebert Stiftung.

Salihu, A. (ed.). 2011. Nigeria women's trust fund: Politics strategy and sustainability. Available at https://nigerianwomentrustfund.org/publications/nigerian-women-trust-fund-politics-strategy-and-sustainability-2011/ (Accessed 21 June 2020).

Sani, H. 2012. *Women and leadership*. Abuja, Nigeria: Hans International School.

Sapiro, V. 1983. *The political integration of women: Roles, socialization and politics*. University of Illinois Press.

Sani, M. A.(2020. 'Preventing and mitigating violence against women in elections in Nigeria', in Chris Jones, Pregala Pilley and Idayat Hassan (eds.), *Fighting corruption in African contexts: Our collective responsibility*. New Castle: Cambridge Scholars Publishing, pp. 284–295.

Schlozman, K. L., Burns, N. and Verba, S. 1994. 'Gender and the pathways to participation: The role of resources', *Journal of Politics*, 56(4), pp. 963–990.

Schlozman, K. L., Burns, N. and Verba, S. 1999. 'What happened at work today? A multistage model of gender, employment, and political participation', *Journal of Politics*, 61(1), pp. 29–53.

Schmidt, G. 2006. 'Violation of women rights seen from a Kenyan perspective', *Master's Thesis*. Maryknoll Institute of African Studies.

Sheldon, K. 2015. 'Women and African history,' *Oxford Bibliographies.*

Shettima, K. A. 1995. 'Engendering Nigeria's Third Republic', *African Studies Review,* 38(2), pp. 61–98.

Sinha, N. 2007. *Empowerment of women through political participation.* Delhi: Kalpaz Publishers.

Smith, P. 2004. 'Liberalism as an Antidote to Stereotyping. Varieties of feminist liberalism', in Amy R. Baehr (ed.), *Varieties of feminist liberalism.* Lanham, MD: Rowman & Littlefield, pp. 21–36.

Sodaro, M. J. 2001. *Comparative politics: A global introduction.* New York: McGraw-Hill Higher Education.

Soetan, F. 1998. 'Women and democratisation in Nigeria: Theory, evidence and policy implications', *Ife Journal of Social Science Review. Conference,* Proceedings July 1998.

Sowell, T. 2004. *Affirmative action around the world: An empirical study* (1st ed). Yale University Press.

Stanford Encyclopedia of Philosophy. 2007. *Liberal feminism* (First published Thru Oct 18, 2007; Substantive Revision Mon Sept 30, 2013) http://plato.stanford.edu/ entries/feminism-liberal/.

Stange, M. Z. and Oyster, C. K. (eds.). 2011. *The multimedia encyclopedia of women in today's World.* New York: Sage Publications.

Staudt, K. 1986. 'Stratification: Implications for women's politics', in C. Robertson and I. Berger (eds.), *Women and class in Africa.* New York: Holmes and Meier.

Staudt, K. 1989. 'The state and gender in colonial Africa', in S. Charlton, J. Everett and K. Staudt (eds.), *Women, state and development.* Albany: SUNY Press.

Taiwo, O. J. and Ahmed, F. 2015. Geographical analysis of voter apathy in presidential elections between 1999 and 2011 in Nigeria', *African Geographical Review,* pp. 1–21. DOI: 10.1080/19376812.2015.1009381.

Tanko, N. M. and Best, K. C. S. 1990. 'The role of women in small scale industry: A case study of Plateau State of Nigeria', in I. L. Bashir and O. Ojowu (eds.), *Policy issues in small scale industrial development in Nigeria.* Jos: Centre for Development Studies, University of Jos.

Tashakkori, A. and Teddlie, C. 1998. *Mixed methodology: Combining qualitative and quantitative approaches.* Thousand Oaks: Sage Publications.

Taylor, S. 2002. 'When affirmative action is nothing but discrimination', *National Journal,* 34(38), pp. 2685–2689.

TEGINT Report. 2011. *Transforming education for girls in Nigeria: Baseline research summary report.* Available at: https://actionaid.org/publications/2011/transforming -education-girls-nigeria-baseline-research-summary-report (Accessed June 21 2020).

Teorell, J., Torcal, M. and Montero, J. R. 2007. 'Political participation: Mapping the terrain', in J. W. van Deth, J. R. Montero, A. Westholm (eds.), *Citizenship and involvement in European democracies: A Comparative analysis.* London and New York: Routledge, pp. 334–357.

The Electoral Commission. 2004. 'Gender and political participation', *Research Report,* April. https://www.electoralcommission.org.uk/sites/default/files/electoral _commission_pdf_file/Final_report_270404_12488-9470__E__N__S__W__.pdf.

The Nation. 2019. 'Celebrating martyrs of democracy in politics', *The Nation*, June 12, 2019.

The Winihin Jemide Series. 2016. Research and ranking report on female representation at state/local government levels in Nigeria from 1999 to 2015. https://winihin-jemideseries.org/ (Accessed 19 May 2020).

Torto, B. T. 2013. 'Affirmative action and women empowerment in Ghana: Challenges to a growing democracy', *Conflict Trends,* 1, pp. 41–49.

Tremblay, M. 2007. 'Democracy, representative, and women: A comparative analysis', *Democratization*, 14(4), pp. 533–553. DOI: 10.1080/13510340701398261.

Tripp, A. M., Casimiro, I., Kwesiga, J. and Mungwa, A. 2009. *African omen's movements: Changing political landscapes.* New York: Cambridge University Press.

True, J., George, N., Niner, S., and Parashar, S. 2014. 'Women's political participation in Asia and the Pacific', *Social Science Research Council/Working papers: Conflict Prevention and Peace Forum, CPPF Working Papers on Women in Politics*, No. 3.

Tsikata, D. 2009. *Affirmative action and the prospects for gender equality in Ghanaian politics.* Abantu: Women in Broadcasting and the Friedrich-Ebert-Stiftung.

Tuana, N. and Tong, R. 1995. *Feminism and philosophy.* Westview Press.

Turner, E. T. and Oshare, M. O. 1994. 'Women uprisings against the Nigerian oil industry in the 1980s' in T. Turner and B. J. Ferguson (eds.), *Arise Ye mighty people!: Gender, class, and race in popular struggles.* Africa World Press, p. 132, 123–160.

Udokang, J. C. and Awofeso, O. 2013. *Political ideas: An introduction.* Lagos Nigeria: MacGrace Publisher.

UNDP. 1993. *Human development report.* New York: UNDP.

UNDP. 2005. Human Development Women's political participation: Issues and challenges. EGM/WPD-EE/2005/EP. Report 12. www.hdr.undp.org.

UNDP. 2010. 'Women's representation in local government in Asia-Pacific'. *Status Report 2010.* pp. 8.

UNDP. 2012. *Gender equality and women's empowerment in Public Administration: Uganda case study.* New York: UNDP.

UNDP Nigeria. 2011. Human development report Nigeria, 2008-9. UNDP Abuja.

UNICEF. 2011. Cross sectional survey, August 2011.

UNICEF. 2014. Female Genital Mutilation/Cutting: what might the future hold? Available at https://www.unicef.org/media/files/FGM-C_Report_7_15_Final_LR .pdf (Accessed 21 June 2020).

United Nation. 2001. *Short history of CEDAW Convention.* United Nations Department of Public Information. Available at www.un.org/womenwatch/daw/ cedaw/history.htm (Accessed 16 Jan 2015).

United Nation General Assembly. 1993. Resolution 48/104 Declaration on the Elimination of Violence against Women, 1993. Available at https://www.ohchr.or g/EN/ProfessionalInterest/Pages/ViolenceAgainstWomen.aspx (Accessed 21 June 2020).

United Nations. 1948. *Universal declaration of human rights.* Geneva: United Nations Organization.

United Nations. 1994. 'Declaration on the elimination of violence against women, New York', A/RES/48/104. https://www.ohchr.org/EN/ProfessionalInterest/Pages /ViolenceAgainstWomen.aspx.

United Nations Department of Public Information. 2001. Beijing Declaration and Platform for Action with the Beijing+ 5 Political Declaration and Outcome Document United Nations, New York, pp. 73.

United Nations Development Programme. 2013. Human Development Report. Available at http://hdr.undp.org/en/humandev/ (Accessed 21 June 2020).

United Nations Economic Commission for Latin America and the Caribbean ECLAC. 2011. Gender equality observatory for Latin America: Autonomy in decision-making. Available from https://oig.cepal.org/en/autonomies/autonomy-decision -making.

United Nations Office on Drugs and Crime, UNODC. 2014. Global Report on Trafficking in Persons: 2014. https://reliefweb.int/report/world/global-report-traffi cking-persons-2014.

UN Women. 2012. Facts and figures on peace and security. Available at http://www .unifem.org/gender_issues/women_war_peace/facts_figures.php.

UN Women. 2014. Women's leadership and Political Participation. Available from http://www.unwomen.org/en/what-we-d/leadersship-and-political-participation (Accessed 15 May 2019).

UN Women. 2015. Women in Politics 2015 Map. UN Women Headquarters.

UN Women. 2016. Facts and figures: Leadership and political participation. http: //www.unwomen.org/en/what-we-do/leadership-and-political-participation/facts -and-figures.

UN Women. 2017. Facts and figures: Leadership and political participation. http: //www.unwomen.org/en/what-we-do/leadership-and-political-participation/facts -and-figures.

UN Women. 2017. *Women in Politics 2017 Map*. United Nations Entity for Gender Equality and the Empowerment of Women. UN Women Headquarters.

UN Women Nigeria. 2014. Sociocultural determinants of voting patterns in Nigeria: Reference to women's participation and representation. UN Women, Nigeria.

Urua, E. E., Etim, F. E., Udofot, I. M., Udoh, I. I., Ikpeme, E., Udoudom, J. C. and Uduk, H. E. 2014. *Nigeria's centenary: 100 Years of Akwa Ibom women's imprint in national development*. Uyo, Nigeria: Centre for Gender Studies, University of Uyo.

Van Allen, J. 1972. 'Sitting on a man: Colonialism and the lost political institutions of Igbo women', *Canadian Journal of African Studies,* 6(2), pp. 165–182.

Van Allen, J. 1976. 'Aba Riots' or Igbo 'women's war'? Ideology, stratification, and the invisibility of women', in N. J. Hafkin and E. G. Bay (eds.), *Women in Africa: Studies in social and economic change*. Stanford: Stanford University Press.

Verba, S., Burns, N. and Schlozman K. L. 1997. 'Knowing and caring about politics: Gender and political engagement', *Journal of Politics,* 59(4), pp. 1051–1072.

Verba, S. and Nie, N. 1972. *Participation in America: Political democracy and social equality*. New York: Harper & Row.

Verba, S., Nie, N. and Kim, J. 1978. *Participation and political equality.* Cambridge: Cambridge University Press.

Verba, S., Schlozman, K. L., and Brady, H. E. 1995. *Voice and equality: Civic voluntarism in American politics.* Cambridge, MA; London, England: Harvard University Press.

Vernellia, R. 2003. 'Theories that appear in African literature of domestic violence in race, health, care and the law'. *Speaking truth to power.* Available at http://aca demic.udayton.edu/health/06world/Africa03a.htm (Accessed 21 June 2020).

Watts, C. and Zimmerman, C. 2002. 'Violence against women: Global scope and magnitude', *The Lancet* 359(9313), pp. 1232–1237.

Waylen, G. 1996. *Gender in third world politics.* Colorado: Lynne Rienner Publishers, Inc.

Weiss, R. I. 1997. *We want jobs: A history of affirmative action.* New York: Garland.

Welch, S. 1993. *The concept of political culture.* New York: St. Martin's.

Welch, S. 2013. *The theory of political culture.* Oxford: Oxford University Press.

West, C. and Zimmerman, D. H. 1987. 'Doing gender', *Gender & Society,* 1, pp. 125–151.

White, S. C. 1996. 'Depoliticising development: The uses and abuses of participation', *Development in Practice,* 6(1), pp. 6–15.

Whitneck, P. 2003. 'The order of merit', *Community College Week,* 15(19), pp. 4–6.

Whitworth, S. 1994. 'Feminist theories: From women to gender and world politics', in F. D'Aminco and P. Beckman (eds.), *Women, gender, and world politics.* Westport: Bergin and Garvey, pp. 75–77.

WHO, London School of Hygiene and Tropical Medicine and South African Medical Research Council. 2013. *Global and regional estimates of violence against women prevalence and health effects of intimate partner violence and non-partner sexual violence.* Available at https://reliefweb.int/report/world/global-and-regional-estim ates-violence-against-women-prevalence-and-health-effects (Accessed 2 June 2020).

Williams, C. 2007. 'Research methods', *Journal of Business & Economic Research,* 5(3), pp. 65–72.

Wilson, A. 1989. "Mary Wollstonecraft and the Search for the Radical Woman', *Genders* 6 (1989): 88–101.

Witaker, L. D. 1999. *Women, equality and feminist theory: A collection of readings* (3rd edn). Prentice Hall.

Women Advocates Research and Documentation Centre. 2014. *Report of gender audit of political parties in Lagos State.* Lagos: WARDC.

Women Aid Collective. 2014. Report of gender audit of political parties in Kaduna State, (October–November 2014) Kaduna, WACOL.

Worden, S. and Sudhakar, N. 2012. 'Learning from women's success in the 2010 Afghan Elections', *Special Report,* 309, United States Institute of Peace.

World Bank. 2011. *World Development Report 2012: Gender equality and development.* Washington, DC: World Bank Group, p. 152.

Worldometers. 2020. *Nigerian population.* Available at https://www.worldometers .info/ world-population/Nigeria-population/ (Accessed 15 June 2020).

Appendix I

Historical Timeline of International Events and Treaties Promoting Gender Equality

Year	Organisation and Actions
1945	Adopted UN Charter – the first international tool setting the principle of equality between man and woman
1946	Established Commission on Status of Women
1948	The Universal Declaration of Human Rights reflects discrimination against women (Article 2); International Labour Organisation (ILO) adopted the Night Work (Women) Convention
1949	UNGA adopted the Convention for the Suppression of the Traffic in Persons and the Exploitation of the Prostitution of Others. Calls for the punishment of those procuring others for prostitution.
1951	ILO adopted the Equal Remuneration for Men and Women Workers for Work of Equal Value
1952	Adopted the International Convention on the Political Rights of Women
1955	ILO issues a Convention on Maternity Protection
1957	The Convention on the Nationality of Married Women
1958	Discrimination (Employment and Occupation) Convention promotes equality of rights between men and women in the workplace.
1960	Convention against Discrimination in Education adopted by the General Conference of UNESCO paves way for equal educational opportunities for girls and women
1960	ILO Discrimination (Employment and Occupation) Convention took effect
1962	Convention on the Political Rights of Women obliged the country members to ensure voting rights for women and their representation in public organisations on equal basis with men
1963	The adopted Convention on Consent to Marriage, Minimum Age for Marriage and Registration of Marriages decrees that no marriage can occur without the consent of both parties
1964	Convention concerning Equality of Treatment of Nationals and Non-Nationals in Social Security took effect
1965	UN Recommendations on consent to marriage, minimum age for marriage and registration of marriages

(Continued)

Year	Organisation and Actions
1966	Adopted International Covenant on Civil and Political Rights that obliged the country members to ensure civil and political rights of everybody within their respective jurisdictions irrespective of race, sex and other circumstances, including the right to life, the prohibition of torture, the right to freedom and privacy, the right to freedom of religion, expression and conscience
1966	Adopted Optional Protocol to the International Covenant on Civil and Political Rights
1966	Adopted International Covenant on Economic, Social and Cultural Rights that spelt out working conditions, social security, adequate standards of living, physical and mental health, education, and employment
1967	UN General Assembly adopted the Declaration on the Elimination of All Forms of Discrimination against Women
1972	UN General Assembly proclaimed the year 1975 as the International Year of Women
1974	Declaration on the Protection of Women and Children in Emergency and Armed Conflict
1974	The Economic and Social Council (ESC) convenes a world conference on women's problems on the threshold of the International Year of Women
1975	UN General Assembly proclaims the decade of 1976–1985 as Women's Decade
1976	UNGA establishes UNIFEM (then named the United Nations Voluntary Fund for the UN Decade for Women) and INSTRAW (the UN International Research and Training Institute for the Advancement of Women)
1976	UN General Assembly approved a decision of ESC to establish the International Research and Training Institute for the Advancement of Women (UN-INSTRAW), the most important objective, which was to study how to monitor and evaluate the impacts of programmes and projects for woman involvement in development activities
1976	UN General Assembly creates the UN Voluntary Fund for the International Research and Training Institute for the Advancement of Women (transformed later into the UN Women's Fund for Development)
1979	UN General Assembly adopted Convention on the Elimination of All Forms of Discrimination against Women (CEDAW), a first international bill on women's rights and on abolishing of distinction, exclusion or restriction made on the basis of sex which has the effect or purpose of impairing or nullifying the human rights and fundamental freedoms in all fields
1980	The UN Second World Conference for Women held in Copenhagen. Action Programme adopted for latter half of the decade.
1980	UN-INSTRAW became an autonomous body within UN
1982	First meeting of the Committee on the Elimination of All Forms of Discrimination against Women
1983	ILO Convention concerning Equal Opportunities and Equal Treatment for Men and Women Workers: Workers with Family Responsibilities came into force

Year	Organisation and Actions
1984	The UN Voluntary Fund for the International Research and Training Institute for the Advancement of Women becomes an autonomous body within the framework of the UN Development Programme and was renamed the United Nations Development Fund for Women (UNIFEM)
1985	The Third World Conference for Women was held in Nairobi. The Strategy of the Future for the Advancement of Women was approved
1988	UN's Database on Women Indicators and Statistics acts as a coordinating framework for the collection of the world's statistics on women
1988	Adopted Convention on Employment Promotion and Protection against Unemployment (Convention 168)
1989	Adopted Convention on the Rights of the Child
1990	Adopted International Convention on the Protection of the Rights of All Migrant Workers and Members of their Families
1990	Adopted Protocol to ILO's Night Work (Women) Convention
1991	UN issued publication *Women of the World: Tendencies and Statistics*
1993	The UN World Conference on Human Rights held in Vienna, Austria. The UN General Assembly adopted the Declaration on the Elimination of Violence against Women. UN recommends standard rules for ensuring equal opportunities for the disabled
1994	Commission on Human Rights appointed a Special Rapporteur on the problem of violence against women for the collection of data and the development of recommendations for the elimination of violence and its consequences. UN International Conference on population and development held in Cairo
1995	The Fourth World Conference for Women held in Beijing, China adopted the Beijing Declaration and Action Platform
1995	Issued second publication *Women of the World: Tendencies and Statistics*
1996	Meeting of the UN Expert Group for the development of guidelines on gender mainstreaming in programmes and measures for human rights
1998	Adopted UN General Assembly's Resolution on measures for the prevention of crime and the criminal justice in order to eliminate violence against women
1999	Adopted Optional Protocol to the Convention on the Elimination of All Forms of Discrimination against Women. ILO adopted Convention of the worst forms of child labour
2000	UN Commission on Human Rights adopts the Resolution on Land Ownership – for the first time, the resolution on women's rights was adopted within an agenda of the UN Commission on Human Rights
2000	UN Security Council passes Resolution 1325 addressing not only the inordinate impact of war on women, but also the pivotal role women should and do play in conflict management, conflict resolution, and sustainable peace
2000	UN General Assembly's Resolution 55/2 approved the Millennium Declaration, which obliged the Governments to advance gender equity as an effective way for the eradication of poverty and feminine diseases
2000	Adopted Optional Protocol to the Convention on the Rights of the Child regarding child trafficking, child prostitution and child pornography

(Continued)

Year	Organisation and Actions
2000	Campaign Beijing+5 for the equality between men and women and the improvement of women's status
2000	Twenty-Third UN General Assembly Special Session held on gender equality
2002	Charter of the International Criminal Court came into effect that set violent use as weapon of war as an outrage upon humanity
2003	The Protocol to the African Charter on Human and Peoples' Rights on the Rights of Women in Africa, better known as the Maputo Protocol, which guarantees comprehensive rights to women in Africa, was adopted by the African Union in Maputo, Mozambique
2005	Having been ratified by the required fifteen-member nations of the African Union, the Maputo Protocol entered into force
2005	UN set the Basic Principles and Guidelines on the Right to Legal Protection and Damage Compensation for Victims of Gross Violation of International Rules in the Field of Human Rights and of Serious Violation of the International Humanitarian Right
2012	Landmark System-wide Action Plan (UN-SWAP) on gender equality and women empowerment adopted by United Nations Chief Executives Board for Coordination throughout the UN system – a set of common measures with which to measure progress in its gender-related work, including the mainstreaming of the gender perspective across all its operations
2015	Beijing + 20: Recommitting for women and girls. Aimed at renewing political will and commitment; revitalising public debates through social mobilisation and creating; strengthening evidence-based knowledge; enhancing resources to achieve gender equality and women empowerment

Sources: (1). The United Nations Gender Team Group in Nigeria (2013) Gender Equality Briefing Kit The UN System in Nigeria. http://www.ng.undp.org/content/dam/nigeria/docs/IclusiveGrwth/UNDP_NG_inclusiveGrwth_Gender-Briefing-Kit230513.pdf

(2). UN Women, beijing20-unwomen.org/~/media/field office Beijing plus/attachments/events/b20 new briefweb.pdf

Appendix II

Geopolitical Zones of Nigeria

NIGERIA GEO-POLITICAL ZONES

Appendix III

Population Projection and Sample Size Calculation

A. POPULATION PROJECTION

Since the population figure available from the National Population Commission is the 2006 census figure, a projection was done to 2015 for each study location using this formula.

$$\text{Log}\,(1+r) = \frac{\text{Log}\,P_2 / P_1}{N}$$

Where:

P_1 = Population of the based year (2006 population figure);

P_2 = Projected population for 2015;

N = Number of years (9 years);

r = Annual growth rate (at 3.5%).

B. SAMPLE SIZE CALCULATION

The required sample size is calculated using the formula below, although it can also be picked from the sample size table (as attached).

$$n = \frac{X^2 * N * P * (1-P)}{(ME^2 * (N-1)) + (X^2 * P * (1-P))}$$

Where:

n = sample size

X^2 = Chi – square for the specified confidence level at 1 degree of freedom

N = Population Size

P = population proportion (.50 in this table)

ME = desired Margin of Error (expressed as a proportion)

Source: **Research Advisors (2006)**

Appendix IV

Questionnaire

Dear Respondent,

The questionnaire is strictly meant to elicit and generate data for a PhD thesis on **'Geopolitical Analysis of W*omen's Participation in Nigeria Politics'*.** All information provided shall be treated with the utmost confidentiality. **Thanks**.

SECTION I: SOCIODEMOGRAPHIC CHARACTERISTICS (*PLEASE TICK OR FILL AS APPROPRIATE*).

1. State:_____ LGA:_____ Settlement:_____
2. Age Range (in Years): (a) 18–25 [ ] (b) 26–35 [ ] (c) 36–45 [ ] (d) 46–55 [ ] (e) 56–65 [ ] (f) Above 65 [ ]
3. Marital Status: (a) Married [ ] (b) Widowed [ ] (c) Divorced [ ] (d) Separated [ ] (e) Never Married [ ]
4. Religion: (a) Christianity [ ] (b) Islam [ ] (c) Traditional [ ] (d) Others:_____
5. Highest Level of Education: (a) Primary or Less [ ]
   (b) Secondary [ ]
   (c) Polytechnic/Colleges [ ]
   (d) University [ ]
   (e) Postgraduate [ ] (f)
   Others:_____

6. Annual Income (in Million N):
  (a) Below 1M [ ] (b) 1M–2M [ ]
  (c) 2M–3M [ ] (d) 3M–4M [ ]
  (e)Above 4M [ ]
7. Employment Status and Occupation:
  (a) Trading, Artisan or Farming [ ]
  (b) Civil Servant or Professional [ ]
  (c) Private or Corporate Sector [ ]
  (d) Not Working or Unemployed [ ]
8. Self-reported Social Class:
  (a) Upper [ ] (b) Middle [ ] (c)Lower [ ]
  (d)Others [ ] (e)Refuse to say [ ]

SECTION II: POLITICAL PARTICIPATION LEVEL

A. Party Participation

9. Do you have sympathy towards any political party?   Yes [ ] No [ ]
10. Are you a card carrying member of a political party?   Yes [ ] No [ ]
11. How often do you attend party meetings? Very often [ ]   Often [ ]   Seldom [ ]   Never [ ]
12. How often do you mobilise other women to attend party meetings? Very often [ ] often [ ] Seldom [ ] Never [ ]
13. Do you watch, listen or read about party politics in the media?   Yes [ ] No [ ]
14. If yes (in 13 above), choose the sources from which you gather information. (Tick as many as possible)
  (a) Radio/TV [ ] (b) Newspapers/Magazines [ ] (c) Friends [ ] (d) Internet or Social Media [ ] (e) Other [ ]

B. Election Participation

15. Did you register for voter's card?   Yes [ ] No [ ]
16. Do you have the permanent voter's card (PVC)?   Yes [ ] No [ ]
17. Do you intend to vote in the next election?   Yes [ ] No [ ]
18. At what level do you intend to vote? (a) Presidential [ ] (b) Senatorial [ ] (c) House of Representative [ ] (d) Governorship [ ] (e) State House of Assembly [ ]

19. Which of the following post have women in your locality contested for?
    (a) Councillorship [ ] (b) Local Government Chairperson [ ]
    (c) State House of Assembly [ ] (d) Governorship [ ]
    (e) House of Representative [ ] (f) Senate [ ] (g) Presidential [ ]

C. Other forms of Political Participation:

20. How often have you participated in the following political activities? Tick as appropriate

	Forms of Political participation	Very Often	Often	Seldom	Never
a.	Political Campaign				
b.	Electoral Campaign				
c.	Contacted government officials on policy issues				
d.	In a protest against government policy				
e.	Wearing a button, displaying bumper sticker in support of a candidate				

SECTION III: FACTORS AFFECTING WOMEN'S PARTICIPATION IN POLITICS

21. The following are some of the factors affecting women's participation in politics. Kindly read through and tick as appropriate the extent of your agreement with each of them.

    Responses: SA – Strongly Agree, A – Agree, U – Undecided, D – Disagree, SD – Strongly disagree

VARIABLES: Factors Affecting Women's Participation in Politics	Responses				
SOCIAL FACTORS	SA	A	U	D	SD
Lack the skills needed for politicking.					
Lack the confidence to stand for election					
Mass media minimise coverage of women's political activities					
Lack of media attention to women's contribution and potential					
Type of quota provisions does not encourage women					
Women have low self-esteem					
Lack of coordination on the part of women organisations and other NGOs					
There are already designated seats for women.					

(Continued)

I do not have adequate support to pursue my political ambition.
Inability to cope with time set for meetings
Expectation from friends and peers curtails me
Women's Multiple roles/domestic role hinder(s) my political ambition

CULTURAL FACTORS
Women are not encouraged to be active in public activities
In my community it is a taboo for a woman to contest for a political post
The prevailing values in our community hinder women from participating
Prevalence of the masculine model of political life serves as an impediment
Male domination in my community affects women's participation in politics
Women's are expected to take care of the home front
Women are marginalised on the basis of place of indigene

POLITICAL FACTORS
The use of gangsters in Nigeria's politics/ political violence
The use of thugs during political activities for example, campaigns
The practice of godfathers in Nigeria politics
Gender discrimination is visible in Nigeria politics
Perception of politics as a dirty game
Inability of some contestant to accept defeat

INSTITUTIONAL DESIGNS
Violation of party regulations
Rules of engagement not clear
At the primaries women are technically disenfranchised
Lack of women in referendum
Lack of provision for gender equality

ECONOMIC FACTORS
Lack of financial support
High cost of registration
Inability to access loans from financial institutions
Unemployment
Women groups lack adequate fund

RELIGIOUS FACTORS   *SA A U D SD*
My religion does not allow me take part in partisan politics
My religion does not encourage women representation in politics
Our religious leaders discourage women from participating in politics
Our religious doctrine discourages women from contesting
My religion has nominated a woman for political appointment

LEGAL FACTORS
The constitution does not recognise women's participation
Government policies are biased against women
Discriminatory laws/customary laws against women

SECTION IV: VIOLENCE AGAINST
WOMEN IN POLITICAL ACTIVITIES

EMOTIONAL VIOLENCE	*Ever Experienced*	*Never Experienced*
Has anyone ever said or done something to humiliate you in front of others?		
Has anyone ever threatened to hurt or harm you?		
Has anyone ever insulted you or made you feel bad about yourself?		
PHYSICAL VIOLENCE		
Has anyone ever pushed you, shaken you or thrown something that could hurt you?		
Has anyone ever slapped you?		
Has anyone ever twisted your arm or pulled your hair?		
Has anyone ever punched you with a fist or with something that could hurt you?		
Has anyone ever kicked you, dragged you or beat you?		
Has anyone ever tried to choke you or burn you on purpose?		
Has anyone ever threatened or attacked you with a knife, gun or any other weapon?		
SEXUAL VIOLENCE		
Has anyone ever physically forced you to have sexual intercourse with him even when you did not want to?		
Has anyone ever physically forced you to perform any other sexual acts you did not want to?		
Has anyone ever forced you with threats or in any other way?		

SECTION V: FACTORS ENHANCING
WOMEN'S PARTICIPATION IN POLITICS

22. The following are some of the factors that can enhance women's partici-
    pation in politics. Kindly read through and tick as appropriate the extent
    of your agreement with each of them.

    Responses: SA – Strongly Agree, A – Agree, U –Undecided, D – Dis-
    agree, SD – Strongly disagree

VARIABLES: Factors Enhancing Women's Participation in Politics	Responses				
SOCIAL FACTORS	SA	A	U	D	SD
Training should be given to women in the accept of politicking					
Socialise women to know the important roles they occupy					
Mass media should give adequate coverage to women's political activities					
Media attention to women's contribution and potential					
Quota provisions must encourage women on merit					
Older women in politics should encourage upcoming women					
Women organisations and other NGOs should serve as a spring board for women in politics					
Scheduled time for meeting should be gender-sensitive					
Friends and spouses should support women who are aspiring.					
Multiple roles/domestic role of women should be put into consideration					
CULTURAL FACTORS	SA	A	U	D	SD
Women should be encouraged to play active role in public activities					
The role played by women in history should be reiterated to encourage women					
The prevailing values in our community can be modified via socialisation processes to encourage women's participation					
Men should support women to participate in politics					
Married women should not be marginalised on the basis of place of indigene					
INSTITUTIONAL DESIGNS					
Political parties should have women-friendly policies					
Rules of engagement must be clear					
At the primaries women should not be technically disenfranchised					
Gender policy must be put to work at all levels					
ECONOMIC FACTORS					
Women must have financial support					
The cost of registration should be reduced to encourage women					
Women should be able to access loans from financial institutions to support their political ambitions					
Women groups should be able to raise fund for women willing to run for political offices					
RELIGIOUS FACTORS					
My religion should encourage women take part in partisan politics					
My religion should encourage women representation in politics					
Our religious leaders should encourage women to participate in politics					
Our religious doctrine can be modified to include the important role women can play in politics					

My religion can nominate a woman for political appointment
LEGAL FACTORS
The constitution should state clearly that women can be
  involved in politics
Government policies must be gender-friendly
Discriminatory laws/customary laws against women should be
  done away with
Ratified UN protocols and conventions enhancing women's
  participation in politics should be implemented
Adequate provision should be in place to punish those
  violators of such laws protecting women's interest in
  politics.

SECTION VI: ADDITIONAL COMMENTS ON WOMEN'S PARTICIPATION IN POLITICS

23. Are there other factors not mentioned above within your locality that impede your participation in politics?

_____

_____

24. What can be done to enhance the participation of women in politics?

_____

_____

25. Please, can you share any other comment on women's participation in politics that you have?

_____

Thank you for your audience and responses

Appendix V

Interview Guide

Interview Guide for the Study: *'Geopolitical Analysis of Women's Participation in Nigeria Politics (1999–2015)'*

CATEGORIES	QUESTIONS
Personal Data	• Age, political party affiliation, position in party or community, duration on position.
General Questions	• Knowledge of women's participation in politics and how women in your area participate in politics.
	• Perceptions in your localities about women politicians and women's participation in politics.
	• Factors that can facilitate or hinder women's political participation and representation.
	• Challenges and factors affecting women's participation and female politicians in your area.
	• Who participate more in politics between men and women in your area and community.
	• Major challenges confronting women's participation and representation in politics.
	• Effect of religion, culture, beliefs and traditions on female politicians in your area.
	• Roles played by traditional leaders in your area as regards women's participation in politics.
	• Positions women politicians occupy in your area and their contributions to the community.

(Continued)

CATEGORIES	QUESTIONS
Women Politician and Political Party Leaders	• Your success stories as a woman politician, challenges and personal experiences in politics. • Roles played by spouses, families, in-laws and friends in support or against women politicians. • Impacts of political parties and party structures on women's participation in politics in your area. • Conditions of women's political participation in your area and comparison with male politicians.
Community Women Leaders (Market or Other Associations)	• Some things the community leaders and local members are doing to address this challenge. • Your success stories as a woman leader, challenges and personal experiences in politics. • Conditions of women's political participation in your area and comparison with male politicians. • Your working relationship with political parties to ensure women's participation in politics. • Support to political parties and other stakeholders in enhancing gender mainstreaming in politics. • Extent you can say the government is committed to gender mainstreaming in politics. • Strategies that have worked and/or not worked in mobilising women's participation in politics.
Policy Makers (Legislatures and Ministry of Women Affairs)	• Roles played by spouses, families, in-laws and friends in support or against women politicians. • Roles ministry/legislature plays in addressing the challenges confronting women politicians. • Roles ministry/legislature plays in mobilising active political participation of women in this area. • Difficulties the Ministry/legislatures have encounters in mobilising women into politics. • Some of the success stories the Ministry/legislatures have had in the past. • Will you say that the government is committed to gender mainstreaming in politics in this area. • Strategies that have worked and/or not worked in mobilising women's participation in politics. • Mention some new developments/changes in women's political participation. • Conditions of women's political participation in your area and comparison with male politicians.

CATEGORIES	QUESTIONS
LGA Women or Ministry Staff	• Roles local government/legislatures play in addressing challenges confronting women politicians. • Difficulties that can be encountered in mobilising grassroots women into politics in your area. • Mention some new developments/changes in women's political participation and representation. • Strategies that have worked and/or not worked in mobilising women's participation in politics. • What is your view of the numbers of women's participation at the local, state and federal levels? • What are the emerging issues in women's participation in politics your area.
Women in CSOs, NGOs and Academics	• How your organisation is mobilising grassroots women for active involvement in politics. • How your organisation is addressing challenges confronting women's participation/representation. • Challenges confronting your work in the area of mobilising women for political participation. • Kind of supports your organisation provide for women politicians. • Success stories on your activities in mobilizing women into politics. • International instruments/conventions that guide your work in mainstreaming gender in politics. • Extent you can say that the National Gender Policy is implemented by the political parties. • The specific challenges in implementing the National Gender Policy in this country. • Your working relationship with political parties to ensure women's participation in politics. • Support to political parties and other stakeholders in enhancing gender mainstreaming in politics. • Extent you can say the government is committed to gender mainstreaming in politics. • Strategies that have worked and/or not worked in mobilizing women's participation in politics.
Recommendations	• How to encourage and improve women's participation in politics in your community/area/region.

Appendix VI

Distribution of Acts of Political Participation by the Respondents (Women)

	Political Activities		Anambra	Kaduna	Ondo	Total
s/n	Activities	Options	[Freq.(%)]	[Freq.(%)]	[Freq. (%)]	[Freq. (%)]
1	Sympathy for political party	Don't have sympathy	275 (69.6)	160 (40.2)	272 (65.9)	707 (175.7)
		Have sympathy	120 (30.4)	238 (59.8)	141 (34.1)	499 (124.3)
2	Card carrying member of a political party	Not card carrying member	296 (74.9)	191 (48.0)	344 (83.3)	831 (206.2)
		Card carrying member	99 (25.1)	207 (52.0)	69 (16.7)	375 (93.8)
3	How often do you attend political part meetings?	Very often	11 (2.8)	118 (29.6)	18 (4.4)	147 (36.8)
		Often	62 (15.7)	94 (23.6)	31 (7.5)	187 (46.8)
		Seldom	44 (11.1)	42 (10.5)	45 (10.9)	131 (32.5)
		Never	278 (70.4)	144 (36.2)	319 (77.2)	741 (183.8)
4	How often do you mobilise for party politics?	Very often	39 (9.9)	146 (36.7)	20 (4.8)	205 (51.1)
		Often	53 (13.4)	73 (18.3)	29 (7.0)	155 (38.7)
		Seldom	37 (9.4)	29 (7.3)	51 (12.4)	117 (29.1)
		Never	266 (67.3)	150 (37.7)	313 (75.8)	729 (180.8)
5	Voters card registration	Did not register	63 (16.0)	68 (17.1)	104 (25.2)	235 (58.3)
		Registered for voters card	332 (84.0)	330 (82.9)	309 (74.8)	971 (241.7)
	Having voter's card	Don't have PVC	94 (23.8)	83 (20.9)	137 (33.2)	314 (77.9)
		Have card (PVC)	301 (76.2)	315 (79.1)	276 (66.8)	892 (232.1)

(Continued)

s/n	Political Activities Activities	Options	Anambra [Freq.(%)]	Kaduna [Freq.(%)]	Ondo [Freq. (%)]	Total [Freq. (%)]
6	Voted in the last election	Did not vote	117 (29.6)	69 (17.3)	187 (45.3)	373 (92.2)
		Voted	278 (70.4)	329 (82.7)	54 (54.7)	661 (207.8)
7	Political campaign	Very often	63 (16)	126 (31.7)	19 (4.6)	208 (52.3)
		Often	31 (7.9)	95 (23.9)	36 (8.7)	162 (40.5)
		Seldom	44 (11.1)	42 (10.5)	66 (16.0)	152 (37.6)
		Never	257 (65.1)	135 (33.9)	292 (70.7)	684 (169.7)
8	Contacted government official	Very often	53 (13.4)	66 (16.6)	10 (2.4)	129 (32.4)
		Often	47 (11.9)	89 (22.4)	34 (8.2)	170 (42.5)
		Seldom	38 (9.6)	64 (16.1)	46 (11.1)	148 (36.8)
		Never	257 (65.1)	179 (45.0)	323 (78.2)	759 (188.3)
9	Protest against government	Very often	29 (7.3)	67 (16.8)	16 (3.9)	112 (28.0)
		Often	40 (10.1)	72 (18.1)	20 (4.8)	132 (33.0)
		Seldom	69 (17.5)	58 (14.6)	69 (16.7)	196 (48.8)
		Never	257 (65.1)	201 (50.5)	308 (74.6)	766 (190.2)
10	Wearing a campaign shirts, button or wrist bands	Very often	41 (10.4)	82 (20.6)	18 (4.4)	141 (35.4)
		Often	33 (8.3)	87 (21.9)	35 (8.5)	155 (38.7)
		Seldom	49 (12.4)	57 (14.3)	70 (17.0)	176 (43.7)
		Never	272 (68.9)	172 (43.2)	290 (70.2)	734 (182.3)
Total			**395 (100)**	**398 (100)**	**413 (100)**	**1206 (100)**

Source: Field Survey (2015).

Appendix VII
List of Respondents for In-Depth Interview

KADUNA

Elizabeth Abukas (Female Politician party – PDP) (K1)
Ruth Alkali (Politician) (K2)
Hauwa Yusuf (Kaduna State University) NGO and Woman Leader (K3)

ANAMBRA

C. Ego Uzoezie (Politician) (A1)
U. K. Anakiwe (Politician, Awka) (A2)
Rose (Director of Women Affairs – Policy Maker) (A3)
(NGO Awka) (A4)
Hon. (Mrs.) Promise C. Eseigwe–JP (APGA Agent-2015 general election/ Market leader) (A5)

ONDO

M. I. Edward (Acting Principal of School of Nursing) (O1)
Adekunbi Modupe Eshofomie (Permanent Secretary Ministry of Women Affairs – Policy marker) (O2)
Alhja Shittu (Ward 3 PDP – Women Leader) (O3)

Index

Page numbers in *italics* refer to figures/tables.

www.ingramcontent.com/pod-product-compliance
Lightning Source LLC
Chambersburg PA
CBHW050443280326
41932CB00013BA/2220

* 9 7 8 1 5 3 8 1 9 8 8 1 0 *